Political Psychology

G000075195

This book provides an introduction to political psychology through a focus on European politics and topics. It describes a style of doing political psychology in Europe that has developed out of dialogue with, as well as critique of, North American approaches. By emphasising the theoretical and methodological diversity of political psychology, the book is intended to contribute to a greater understanding of the strength and utility of the field.

- Opens up and extends the study of political psychology to a variety of socio-political contexts and manifestations of political behaviour.
- Clearly outlines the usefulness and promises of distinctive critical approaches in social and political psychology.
- Explicitly considers the role of language, communication, identity and social representations in the construction of political meanings.

Political Psychology will appeal to upper-level students and to scholars who seek to extend their knowledge of the complex relationships between psychology, politics and society.

CRISTIAN TILEAGĂ is a Senior Lecturer in Social Psychology and a member of the Discourse and Rhetoric Group at Loughborough University. His research centres on developing critical frameworks for researching social and political behaviour, and his research interests include the discursive analysis of political discourse, collective memory, critical psychology of racism and social representations of history.

Political Psychology

Critical Perspectives

Cristian Tileagă

CAMBRIDGE
UNIVERSITY PRESS

CAMBRIDGE
UNIVERSITY PRESS

University Printing House, Cambridge CB2 8BS, United Kingdom

Cambridge University Press is part of the University of Cambridge.

It furthers the University's mission by disseminating knowledge in the pursuit of
education, learning and research at the highest international levels of excellence.

www.cambridge.org
Information on this title: www.cambridge.org/9781107672529

First published 2013
First paperback edition 2015

A catalogue record for this publication is available from the British Library

Library of Congress Cataloguing in Publication data
Tileagă, Cristian, 1975–
Political psychology : critical perspectives / Cristian Tileagă.
    pages   cm
Includes bibliographical references and index.
ISBN 978-1-107-01768-9 (hardback) – ISBN 978-1-107-67252-9 (pbk.)
1. Political psychology.   2. Political psychology – Europe.   I. Title.
JA74.5.T55 2013
320.01′9–dc23   2013019970

ISBN 978-1-107-01768-9 Hardback
ISBN 978-1-107-67252-9 Paperback

For my parents

Contents

Figures

Acknowledgements

This book could not have happened without the support offered by my colleagues in the Discourse and Rhetoric Group and Department of Social Sciences at Loughborough University. I would especially like to thank Michael Billig, Jovan Byford, Susan Condor, Cristina Marinho, Sabina Mihelj and James Stanyer, who have offered me friendly encouragement and criticism on earlier drafts. Any mistakes that remain are mine.

Parts of Chapters 1 and 6 originally appeared in *Integrative Psychological and Behavioral Science*, *Memory Studies* and *British Journal of Social Psychology*. I am grateful to the publishers for permitting me to reuse excerpts in the present form.

I am indebted to Loughborough University for a period of six months study leave that allowed me to complete the manuscript. I would also like to thank Hetty Marx, Carrie Parkinson and Hayley Macdonald at Cambridge for their invaluable advice and support.

Lastly, I would like to thank my parents, Kendra, Corina, Tomas, Tony and Bela, for managing, in their very distinctive ways, to keep me on track.

Transcription notations

(.)	Micro-pause
(2.0)	Pause length in seconds
[overlap]	Overlapping speech
°	Encloses speech that is quieter than the surrounding talk
<u>yes</u>	Underlining indicates stress or emphasis in the speech
>faster<	Encloses speeded-up talk
<faster>	Encloses speech delivered at slower pace
(clears throat)	Comments from the transcriber

For a full list of transcription conventions, see Jefferson (2004).

Introduction: political psychology as an interpretive field

Psychology and politics

The American political scientist Charles E. Merriam described psychology as a 'kindred' science (Merriam, 1924). McGuire (1993) writes about the 'long affair' between psychology and political science underpinned by frequent transformation of topics, procedures and theories. What Merriam and McGuire have in common is that they understand the relationship between psychology and politics as the study of 'political behaviour'. A variety of 'definitions' of this relationship has been suggested. For example, Sears *et al.* (2003) see the relationship between psychology and politics as the 'application of what is known about human psychology to the study of politics' (p. 3). For others, it is about discerning how 'human cognition and emotion mediate the impact of the environment on political action' (Stein, 2002, p. 108). According to Lavine (2010), the relationship is 'defined by a *bidirectional* influence: just as the psyche influences political orientation, the polity leaves its mark on who we are' (p. xx, emphasis in original).

This book does not attempt to offer yet another definition. Instead, it tries to qualify the relationship between psychology and politics by proposing alternative approaches, different conceptual tools and a different vision of human psychology and political behaviour with roots in epistemological, theoretical and methodological presuppositions arising from the discursive (Billig, 1987; Harré and Gillett, 1994; Middleton and Edwards, 1990), narrative (Bruner, 1986; Polkinghorne, 1988) and sociocultural (Middleton and Brown, 2005; Valsiner, 2007; Wertsch, 2002) turns in psychology, the human and the social sciences, giving rise to what can be broadly termed an *interpretive* political psychology. An interpretive political psychology suggests that political psychologists can attain a deep level of understanding of political behaviour by researching different social and political orders – discursive, cultural and semiotic – in their own terms. When political psychologists research attitudes, racism, public opinion, political ideology, and so on,

1

they are, arguably, describing universalistic and particularistic presuppositions of *modern culture*. An interpretive political psychology likens the work of the political psychologist to that of the anthropologist who uncovers the various meaning-making layers through which society is organised and reproduces itself (Moscovici, 1972).

The book describes a style of doing political psychology in Europe that has developed out of dialogue with, as well as critique, of North American approaches. It has been argued that political psychology can be described as a 'problem-centred field', whose concerns arise from 'those social problems and puzzles that emerge throughout history and in specific locales' (Nesbitt-Larking and Kinnvall, 2012, p. 46). European social and political psychologists have a long tradition of exploring distinctively European political and social psychological issues such as fascism and bigotry, ideology and nationalism, social and political identity, values and political attitudes, collective action, mass and elite constructions and understandings of politics. To these one can add more recent concerns with the relationship between national and European identity, 'New Europe', political memory and identity, ethnic minority construction and ethnic identification, understanding social and political change in Western and Eastern Europe. It is hoped that the book will make a timely contribution and advance political psychology by putting European research perspectives firmly on its intellectual and empirical agenda.

There are many books on political psychology, but very few devote much attention to European approaches. For instance, the latest four-volume set on *Political Psychology*, edited by Howard Lavine (2010), makes only scant reference to European political concerns or European social psychological contributions. This conspicuous absence cannot be disregarded because it reproduces a skewed vision of what political psychology is and how it is actually practised around the world. This book is an attempt to redress the balance by fostering debate around relatively underrepresented perspectives in political psychology that can provide a renewed foundation or check for contemporary analyses of political behaviour. The aim is not to further divisions, but encourage perspectives particularly suited to the declared task of developing a genuinely international dialogue of traditions of research in political psychology around the world (Haste, 2012).

Interpretive political psychology

The inclusion of an interpretive dimension in political psychology has three major implications. First, it can expand political psychology's traditional focus on political behaviour, narrowly understood in an individualistic theoretical and methodological framework. Much of the theoretical and empirical content of contemporary political psychology is driven by the search for explanations of real-life events in the 'real' political world and scene. These explanations have as a basis the testing of abstract academic theories, the prediction and modelling of political behaviour rather than real-life events and practices, interpreted in their own terms, with academic theory or models merely as an *appui*. As Marková has recently argued, the discipline of social psychology has historically nurtured and enforced the use of 'methods of proof', opposed to 'methods of discovery' (2012, p. 113). This has led to social and political psychologists not being able to address directly in their work the tension between the requirements of scientific knowledge and the less easily definable and discernible features of political behaviour they are researching. As Serge Moscovici has aptly noted, the relationship between psychology and politics is necessary, functional and yet sometimes unpredictable and not at all obvious (Moscovici, 1989).

Second, it can foster a debate about the meaning of 'scientific knowledge' that crosses beyond the experimental or survey canon that dominates contemporary political psychology. As Sandra Jovchelovitch argues, 'within psychology... there is a strong tendency to consider lay knowledge and everyday understandings as obstacles, noise and errors to be removed: the superstitions, mythologies and false beliefs they carry should be replaced with the truth of expert or scientific knowledge' (2008, p. 437). It should be the task of political psychology to discover principles; not only universal, but also contingent, relative principles underlying the interpenetration of discursive, cultural and semiotic orders. One must broaden the sweep of social scientific enquiry, away from the nature of the thinking individual and belief systems to mass-mediated communication, social interaction, social practices and lay sources of knowledge. It is perhaps erroneous to think that simply using 'adequate methods is equivalent to scientific investigation' (Moscovici, 1972, p. 21). Political psychologists need to respond to explicit challenges of studying social and political behaviour and challenges set by their colleagues in other disciplines. Political psychology has started the dialogue with biology, genetics, neurosciences; yet, at the same time, it neglects its dialogue with linguistics, critical psychology, sociology, media studies, or philosophy. In order to enrich the depth and breadth of its conclusions and impact in the 'real' world it needs to draw upon some of their assumptions, questions and methods. As a genuinely interdisciplinary project political psychology should be able to provide the intellectual space in which concepts and theoretical traditions from different fields can cohabit.

Third, it can lead to a reconsideration of the image of the person and society implicit in contemporary scientific approaches and a re-examination of political psychology's conception of the relation between human nature, language and culture. As the chapters of this book show, public opinion, democratisation, personality, prejudice, collective memory, and many other notions with origins in social and political theory are concepts connected in myriad ways to concerns of culture, language and community. The increasingly fine technologies of polling, experimentation and neuro-imaging construct individuals that 'come to "fit" the demands of the research; they become, so to speak, persons that are by nature "researchable" from that perspective' (Osborne and Rose, 1999, p. 392). We tend to confine to strict experimental situations and cognitive modelling what is already diffused (in some form or other) in culture (cf. Moscovici, 1972). As Moscovici suggested, it is society's 'social theory' that we need to be able to discern, to describe, to analyse; social and political psychology is not practised in a 'social vacuum' (Tajfel, 1972).

Political psychologists seem to stop short of examining social and political life in depth and very rarely concern themselves with what Allport called 'the concrete person'. Political psychological analyses should not only be derived from general laws and psychological concepts but rather from lives (as actually lived) and social practices (as actually performed). One ought to start not only with the question of how reality is intelligible to us, as researchers, but how reality is intelligible to social actors who experience it as such. As political psychologists we should consider seriously idiographic aspects of social existence, and treat people and politics as products of social activities and social practices.

The relationship between psychology and politics stands in need of explanation; it does not explain anything in itself. What we make of it is constituted, and limited, by our techniques of measuring it, our narratives, our discourses, our representations, our identities, our collective memories. Following Moscovici, this book argues that political psychology has remained for too long the prisoner of a 'pragmatic culture' that evades the contingent, relative, particularistic aspects of social and political experience.

There is a further point to be made, and this pertains to European political psychology. Only by becoming an interpretive discipline can European political psychology develop itself as a worthwhile enterprise. The themes of its research and the contents of its theories do not need to be borrowed from across the Atlantic; they must reflect the issues of its own social and political organisation. In 1972, Moscovici identified the 'advantage' of American social psychology as being not necessarily one of methodological or theoretical advance but more an issue of taking 'for its theme of research and for the contents of its theories the issues of *its own society* ... and making them an object of scientific enquiry' (1972, p. 19, emphasis in original; see also Moscovici and Marková, 2006 for a history of the development of social psychology in Europe).

Contemporary European political psychology must heed Moscovici's message; it must turn towards its own social and political realities, devise its own axioms, hypotheses and questions, from which it can derive its own 'scientific consequences' (Moscovici, 1972, p. 19).

Political behaviour as social practice

It is conventionally assumed that the task of the political psychologist is to account for the variety of manifestations and complexity of political behaviour. The political psychologist is generally interested in problems and solutions to these problems that are valid in their own right for everyone, at any time and at any place. A consequence of this is that political behaviour is mostly conceived of as the result of universal, habitual and automatic processes rather than as a product of human social practices. Another consequence of this is that actual behaviour is given less and less attention (Baumeister *et al.*, 2007; Potter, 2012).

Political psychologists devise more and more complex technical vocabularies used to describe political behaviour. The contemporary political psychology of political behaviour is founded on the epistemological structure of 'justified belief' against a reality 'out there' which expects description and explanation. The route to knowledge is *positive*, and more than often based on normative models of social and political reality. Yet, what makes political psychology distinctive is that it deals with what Hannah Arendt has called the 'realm of human affairs' (Arendt, 1958). Politics (and political behaviour) is not a dimension outside this realm of human affairs; it is only, sometimes, mistakenly treated as such. Some political psychologists treat political behaviour as a substantive entity (that can be measured and aggregated, and whose distribution can be accounted for in statistical form); others have treated it as a concept or idea, a sensitising concept that guides rather than prescribes the steps taken by their enquiries, anything other than fixed, stable, inevitable or 'real'.

There would be no talk of public opinion, values, prejudice, collective memory, political rhetoric, social and collective identities, and so on outside the social practices of people and outside 'the psychological social contract' witnessed in the 'collaboratively constructed and collectively upheld versions of social reality that come to dominate society' (Moghaddam, 2008, p. 882). Political psychologists tend to restrict themselves to describing what the social and political world means to them, neglecting, in the process, what it means to the social actors that participate in and create that world.

Overview of the book

The field of political psychology is a continually expanding one. The book offers a selective, yet coherent, presentation of a diverse field. Inevitably, only a segment of relevant literature has been included.

Each of the chapters of this book argues that political behaviour must be looked at as an issue in its own right. This includes exploring the idea that political behaviour should be treated more as an evolving and transforming field of social activities and social practices, charting its symbolic, communicative, social interactive manifestations, made and unmade in social relations between people. Chapters also discuss the value of analysing the range of social judgements, political commitments and positions, issues of stake and accountability, made relevant by social and political actors in talk or texts. Political meanings and communications are 'far more volatile than is commonly supposed' (Edelman, 2001, p. 82). Increasingly, it is the subjective, contingent meanings that people attach to political behaviour that can predict or determine its political consequences.

The first two chapters of this book focus on public opinion and human values against the background of understanding social change and democratisation processes. The first chapter focuses on public opinion, dilemmas of ideology and the rhetorical complexity of attitudes in the context of researching nostalgia for communism and appreciating the democratic competence of individuals. Chapter 2 focuses on universalistic and aggregate models of human values and extends the argument from the first chapter to the democratic competence of nations and the spreading of democratic values. The two chapters urge political psychologists to resist the temptation to purge political behaviour of dilemmas, ambiguities and apparent contradictions.

Chapter 3 proposes a discussion of the political psychology of intolerance by suggesting an alternative conception of prejudice as social accomplishment and discursive study of delegitimisation and dehumanisation of ethnic minority groups. Chapter 4 introduces the reader to the study of social representations as building blocks of understanding community life and meaning-making. The chapter asserts that social and political reality 'has no smooth and direct passage to knowledge' (Jovchelovitch, 2007, p. 99); rather, it is *mediated* by social representations as cultural resources and foundations of 'thinking' societies.

Chapter 5 contends that the key task of political psychology is to analyse the social nature of identities and group practices. It argues that identities are not merely *activated* but rather *elicited* and *moulded* by the social context in which they become relevant. The chapter constructs an argument against the commonly held idea that 'singular identities [can] reliably predict behaviour, attitudes and values' (Wetherell, 2009b, p. 10). Chapter 6 discusses the issue of collective memory and its link to and influence on political narratives. It proposes a sociocultural approach to researching collective memory that can help political psychologists to turn it into a proper object of political psychological concern. The chapter argues that political psychologists need to study memory as a social and cultural product, and remembering/forgetting as social and cultural practices.

Chapter 7 extends the notion of political behaviour to the pragmatics of discourse and communication, and the mutual relationship between discourse and politics. The chapter argues that discursive actions are socially constitutive of social conditions, social and political 'realities' and discursive practices of various kinds reproduce visions of people, society and politics. Chapter 8 continues the discussion in Chapter 7 by arguing that political discourse needs to be studied as a social activity. Both chapters argue that the key aim of political psychology is to further the systematic study of politics in *action*, the study of people's practices and social interaction. Both chapters argue for a reorientation of political psychology to researching how politics is *done* in everyday and elite language practices, and identifying the 'rhetorical conditions' under which politics is actually performed. Social and political 'reality' or 'context' cannot be said to exist without social interactions and communications between people.

Chapter 9 introduces a discursive approach to political communication and mass-mediated politics. The chapter argues that political communications should be considered as carefully produced discourse, an *interactive* and *social interactional* process of political meaning making. A focus on language and communication processes can give political psychologists a more comprehensive foundation from which to address the complexity and the continually transforming nature of political communications. The chapter shows how political psychologists can learn from conceptions of political behaviour in media, communication and discourse studies.

The Epilogue argues that political psychology can only move profitably forward if it does not continue to ignore its past and its rich heritage from around the world. The field of political psychology has the potential to contribute to understanding and tackling social problems in the real world. Fulfilling its potential will require not only devising state-of-the-art methodological innovations or insisting on theoretical borrowings from neighbouring disciplines of psychology. It will require, primarily, extending its (many) definition(s) of political behaviour to include language, culture, social representations, communication and alternative approaches which are no less 'scientific' than the experimental or survey canon. It will require reconsidering the image of the person implicit in contemporary scientific approaches and theoretical imports. It will require re-examining its conception of the relation between individual psychology ('human nature') and collective performances ('culture'). Only by exploring, developing and pursuing systematically an interpretive outlook, can political psychology become a genuine social and political anthropology of modern culture.

1 Public opinion and the rhetorical complexity of attitudes

The collective will and the 'ideal' democratic citizen

'We, the people, feel and know that we have become more significant than ever before, with the narrowing of the barrier that separates "us" and our range of experiences from our elected representatives and their range of experiences.' This is what social psychologist, Hadley Cantril, in his 1942 paper, 'Public Opinion in Flux', was writing about the importance of 'good morale' in American democracy, especially 'national morale' associated with the war effort. What Cantril acknowledged in 1942 (and he was not the only one) is what politicians, 'spin doctors', and so on take for granted today: the fundament of democracy lies in the 'faith in the judgment of the common man'. Cantril was writing about the person, the 'citizen' who 'given sufficient facts and motivated to pay attention to those facts ... will reach a decision based on his [her] own self-interest as a member of a democratic community' (1942, p. 151). When writing about 'we, the people' Cantril points to the direction of political democratic accountability (from citizens to their elected representatives) and thus brings into the foreground one of the most fundamental political hopes – that the will and reason of 'the people' ought to prevail. Cantril's words express faith in the self-governing, autonomous and omnicompetent citizen (Dalton, 2008) – the 'ideal' democratic citizen.

This chapter shows how political psychologists' concern with the 'collective will' is paralleled by a concern with, search for and description of the democratic citizen. The first part of the chapter maps the various meanings and expressions of this collective will condensed into the notion of 'public opinion'. The chapter then goes on to describe the main assumptions behind researching and understanding the democratic competence of citizens, especially those related to political knowledge and political sophistication.

The remainder of the chapter is dedicated to exploring the idea that public opinion is one of most debated expressions of democratic politics. It focuses on the rhetorical complexity of attitudes and paradoxes of opinion that arise in the course of attempts to reconcile with the communist past in Eastern Europe. In doing so, it challenges the notion that people carry in their heads fully formed or preformed attitudes. The chapter argues that it is important to show how social actors are appraising social/political realities and how attitudes and political experiences possess a highly visible rhetorical complexity. These concerns are developed further in later chapters of this book, especially Chapter 6 (with reference to collective memory and political narratives), Chapter 7 (with reference to the role of language in politics) and Chapter 8 (with reference to the complexity of political rhetoric). The chapter ends by arguing that political psychology scholarship should be more about what citizens themselves expect of democracy and perhaps less about what democracy expects of citizens.

The ideological cleavages of societies create their own models, images of 'ideal' democratic citizens – what Lakoff (2002) has called 'model citizens'. In the United States, for instance, national politics engenders its own categories of moral politics and moral action (the 'ideal' conservative citizen is diametrically opposed to the 'ideal' liberal citizen).[1] Political psychology offers the best examples of a search for the 'ideal' democratic citizen, where the stability of preferences and world views (Ansolabehere et al., 2008; Converse, 1964) goes together with the belief that democratic experience can be maximised by accommodating individual differences (Mondak and Hibbing, 2012; Stenner, 2005). In their search for the 'ideal' democratic citizen, political psychologists build and rely on 'convenient fictions' (Riesman, 1954), and they build models of social and political behaviour that emphasise rationality over irrationality, responsibility over irresponsibility, citizenship over other means and ways of belonging and acting in society. It has been argued that this search for and description of the collective will and 'ideal' democratic citizen is one of the foundational 'mystical fallacies of democracy', an unattainable, 'false ideal' (Lippmann, [1927] 2009).

Political knowledge and the democratic competence of citizens

The study of democratic *competence* of citizens and *involvement* in politics starts with the classic observation that the ordinary citizen *fails* to

---

[1] As Lakoff argues 'conservative and liberal categories for moral action create for each moral system a notion of a model citizen – an ideal prototype – a citizen who best exemplifies forms of moral action' (2002, p. 169).

develop an overall point of view about politics (cf. Converse, 1964).[2] It has been argued, and rightly so, that political information is the 'currency' of citizenship and democracy (cf. Delli Carpini and Keeter, 1996). The economical metaphor used by Delli Carpini and Keeter testifies to a common propensity of political psychologists – responding to and describing the enlightened, liberal, 'ideal' of the 'well-informed citizen'.

There is no apparent disagreement in political psychology over the idea that political information is unequally distributed, and that unequal distribution leads to inequalities in political information. This stems from another basic assumption: that some people know very little about politics, whereas others know quite a lot. According to Converse, political information 'varies in natural electorates from very close to zero up to enormous heights' (Converse, 2009, p. 157). Political sophistication is given by the degree of 'absorption of contextual information' that is then organised into a meaningful belief system with firm connections between all its constituent parts. Most members of the mass public do not show or work with meaningfully organised belief systems. Concrete, rather than abstract conceptualisations, capture ordinary citizens' attention. The 'truly involved citizen' (described in terms of high conceptual organisation) needs to be distinguished from the vast majority who can barely navigate the political landscape or make sense of complex political information (described in terms of the muddled, narrow, low conceptual organisation).[3]

Contemporary political psychology nuances, and at the same time confirms, some of Converse's original insights. It is now taken for

---

[2] In 1940 Gallup and Rae were expressing similar sentiments: 'the public contains many people who have never been fitted by education for the task of citizenship. Others have found their economic life so insecure that they readily fall victim to false panaceas. They are so engrossed in the daily struggle to make ends meet that they have neither the time nor the opportunity to think coherently about the nation's problems' (1940, pp. 286–7). Before that, Lippmann was also making a similar point: 'the citizen gives but a little of his time to public affairs, has but a casual interest in facts and but a poor appetite for theory' (Lippmann, [1927] 2009, pp. 14–15).

[3] If Converse was sceptical about individual capacity (capacities) of organising political information in meaningful, consistent belief systems, contemporary political psychologists' hope rests with the superiority of collective judgement and choice. The contemporary image is that of active publics and mediated politics (see Chapter 9 for an extensive account). With the increased and increasing public participation in new social media, the concerns of media with the visibility and instant availability of electoral opinion (see, e.g., the 'Worm' experiment on British television in the UK general elections of 2010), the recent forays into measurement of the 'Twittersphere', static publics are replaced with new, active, interactive and interacting publics. The contemporary public is, according to Castells, 'a mixture of political consumers and reactive audience' (2011, p. 163).

granted that there is a huge variation in interest, political attention and political knowledge of mass publics. Accounting for this huge variation can pose several problems. Some political psychologists suggest that political psychologists should stop asking if citizens 'meet the ideal expectations of democratic theorists' and start instead observing 'that people are regularly making political choices and ask how these choices are actually made' (Dalton and Klingemann, 2009, p. 6; see also Mutz, 2009). What Dalton and Klingemann refer to are the procedures that individuals use to navigate and make sense of the political landscape: information shortcuts, political heuristics, and so forth. Converse argued that the information intake of the individual is limited, on the one hand, by the quantity of formal and informal organisation and flow of political communication, and on the other hand, by the individual's motivation to attend to existing flows of political communications (cf. Converse, 1962). That being the case, he argued, individuals need to use judgemental 'yardsticks' (such as the liberal–conservative continuum in the USA, or the left–right spectrum in Europe) in order to be able to 'tame' the diversity of the political landscape (Converse, 2006b; Lau and Redlawsk, 2006; Taber, 2003; Taber and Lodge, 2006). Individual points of view, and more general political information itself, may survive, be enforced or disappear depending on whether they are part of various political communication networks (Huckfeldt, 2009; Huckfeldt et al., 2002, 2004).[4]

The meanings of public opinion

As Mutz argued, 'most political psychologists *wish* citizens had perfect information, and think the political process would be far better off if citizens could at least better approximate this goal' (2009, p. 95, emphasis in original). This is paralleled by a common belief and aspiration among contemporary students of political behaviour: that the collective will and democratic competence of citizens can be enlisted, drawn upon, aggregated and averaged *as* the expression of a public or publics under the semblance of 'public opinion'.

With the development of the polling industry, 'public opinion' has become the source and principle of authority in democratic societies (Edelman, 2001; Schütz, 1976). From the perspective of the public opinion poll, 'public opinion' is 'accepted and treated as though it were

---

[4] The effects of predispositions (Lakoff, 2002) and weight and salience of political information are usually balanced by deliberative engagement with societal and political debates (Becker and Scheufele, 2011) and issue participation (Becker et al., 2010).

an objective reality to be discovered by polling or otherwise' (Edelman, 2001, p. 53).[5]

'Opinion is to the modern public what the soul is to the body, and the study of one leads us naturally to the other' (Tarde, [1969] 2010, p. 297). This is how Tarde opened his 1898 essay *Opinion and Conversation*. In the 1940s Gallup and Rae were considering public opinion to be the 'pulse of democracy', as the title of their 1940 book suggests. For Converse, in the 1980s, public opinion is 'what opinion polls try to measure' or 'what they measure with modest error' (Converse, 1987, S14). The contemporary meaning of public opinion, as Herbst puts it, overlaps with the 'aggregation of anonymously expressed opinions' (1995, p. 44).

Political psychologists have been mostly concerned with the 'foundations', or the organising principles, of opinions. In order to understand why citizens choose to support one policy over the other, and why they declare themselves, say, in favour of gay marriage, one needs to understand the principles underlying public opinion: ideological orientations (e.g. liberalism vs. conservatism, left vs. right), traits (e.g. ethnocentrism), or values (e.g. self-expression). For example, writing about the ethnocentric foundations of public opinion, Kinder and Kam (2009) argue that Americans are 'more or less ethnocentric' and that ethnocentrism influences the way in which Americans think about their society and politics, and the issues debated in the public sphere. Identifying the principle(s) that organise public opinion confers structure, coherence and stability to opinions.

In political science, one of the most popular models of public opinion is proposed by John Zaller. Public opinion is understood 'as a response to the relative intensity and stability of opposing flows of liberal and conservative communications' (Zaller, [1992] 2005, pp. 185–6). People's attention to politics will determine whether and how they receive (new) information, whereas their ideological predispositions will determine whether information is accepted. According to him those ideas that are highly salient and available shape the attitudes expressed by respondents. The process that Zaller describes is a reasoned and rational process of selection, helped by cognitive heuristics such as availability.

Zaller describes the (technical) *apparatus* of opinion formation and expression but does not satisfactorily account for how citizens (voters)

---

[5] For excellent accounts of the history and meaning of public opinion see Herbst (1998) and more recently, Herbst (2012). Berinsky (2012) provides a very useful collection of recent texts on new directions in public opinion research, covering a range of perspectives including survey research, political ideology, personality, campaigns and public policy.

align (to use Lippmann's term) themselves for or against something or someone. Following Lippmann it might be more reasonable to assume that citizens (voters) are not solely involved in a process of cognitive selection (or 'sampling', to use Zaller's term). Lippmann argues that 'what the public does is not to express its opinions but to align itself for or against a proposal' ([1927] 2009, p. 51).[6] Lippmann's argument leads to a radical conclusion: the public is a mere 'phantom', an abstraction.[7]

Lippmann's position resonates with that of Blumer ([1948] 1969) and Bourdieu (1979). In *Public Opinion and Public Opinion Polling*, Blumer (1948, p. 543) argued resolutely that 'public opinion gets its form from the social framework in which it moves, and from the social processes in play in that framework.' Blumer writes of a failure of public opinion polling to 'catch' opinions as they are structured and as they function in society. Bourdieu (1979) is more radical. For him 'public opinion' simply does not exist. It is a social and political 'fiction'; an especially powerful one that politicians, the state, interest groups, and so on can use to their own advantage. For Bourdieu polling, and overreliance on polling, creates an 'artificial' political environment, where the political issues of the pollsters are not really 'issues', and, moreover, they are not those of the 'average' citizen or voter.

For Blumer and Bourdieu, referring to 'public opinion' is misleading, as the 'real', actual, pragmatic dimensions of the public sphere are thus obscured. Yet, the very activity of politics, public debate, political marketing, and so on seems inconceivable without (or outside) the framework given by phrases such as the 'public', the 'people' or 'public opinion'. Rhetorical references to 'unobservable' people are at the centre of political appeals and rallying cries around values, morality and national policies. Nixon's famous reference to the 'great silent majority' in his most successful speech about the Vietnam War is such an example. Its exhortation 'Let us be united for peace' is a rallying cry for support that seems to rely on an unseen, imagined community. As Edelman argued, 'for anyone looking for a reason to support the President and the war, the silent majority serves its purpose even if it does not exist' (1977, p. 30). Political rhetoric all around the world is replete with statements that refer to 'unobservable' people (the 'public', the 'majority', the 'people'). For politicians, potentially problematic and

---

[6] For instance, for Lippmann 'a vote is a promise of support' (p. 46). As a consequence, 'the public does not select the candidate … it aligns itself for and against somebody who has offered himself, has made a promise' (p. 47).

[7] In Lippmann's words, 'the public is not … a fixed body of individuals. It is merely those persons who are interested in an affair and can affect it only by supporting or opposing the actors' (p. 67).

equivocal references to the 'people', the 'majority' or the 'public' offer opportunities to build political platforms and to justify accountability for political actions. For mass publics they are triggers that structure responses to anxieties and fears, or hope and expectations.[8]

Public opinion can also be thought of in terms of its functions. Noelle-Neumann (1993) distinguishes between a manifest and latent function of public opinion. The manifest function is associated with conceiving of public opinion as linked to the rational process of opinion creation and decision-making in democratic polities. The latent function is associated to conceiving public opinion as an instrument of 'social control', whose function is to 'promote social integration and to ensure that there is a sufficient level of consensus on which actions and decisions may be based' (Noelle-Neuman, 1993, p. 220). For others, public opinion can be understood as both a dependent as well as an independent variable (cf. van der Eijk and Franklin, 2009), and evolving longitudinally over time. As a dependent variable it can be studied in relation to the influence of opinion leaders, reference groups, media framing, issue identification and party identification. As an independent variable it can be studied for its influence on policy makers and policy making. Whether treated as independent or dependent variable, public opinion is portrayed as something that can be operationalised and measured.[9]

Other researchers urge us to consider public opinion as a 'created', 'manufactured' or 'engineered' phenomenon. According to Osborne and Rose (1999), the social sciences (its methods, techniques, theoretical assumptions) have played a very significant role in the creation of what they call 'opinioned persons' and an 'opinionated society' (see also Riesman, 1954 for an earlier, yet similar argument). As Osborne and Rose argue, 'the phenomenon of opinion is an artefact of the technical procedures that are designed to capture it' (1999, p. 382; see also Bauer and Gaskell, 2008). Technologies of polling tend to obscure the fact that 'people *learn* to have opinions; they become "opinioned" – or perhaps, even, "opinionated" – persons' (1999, p. 392, emphasis in original) in and through interactions and conversations with others, in processes of primary and secondary socialisation, and as part of social practices of different cultures. There is increasing demand and pressure on individuals to be 'opinionated'. Atkinson and Silverman (1997) contend that

---

[8] For more details on these concerns and for a paradigm of researching political rhetoric and political discourse as a complex form of social activity, see Chapters 7 and 8.

[9] According to this view, one can simply inspect poll trends – for instance, the reactions to the terrorist attacks of 11 September 2001 (Huddy *et al.*, 2002) or support for the women's movement (Huddy *et al.*, 2000) – in order to get a sense of what people think about pressing societal issues.

we live in an 'interview society', which strategically 'invents', 'creates' and 'produces' an opinionated self.[10]

Paradoxes of opinion: attitudes and rhetorical complexity

The image of the democratic citizen arising from early concerns with the stability of democratic systems and civic capacity of democratic citizens (e.g. Berelson, 1952; Converse, 1964) and contemporary concerns with the structural complexity of political ideology (e.g. Jost *et al.*, 2009) is that of the citizen who is capable of understanding and 'navigating' the ideological landscape of political issues and allegiances, exhibiting consistency in beliefs and political behaviour.

As argued previously, the democratic 'ideal' is that citizens base their political behaviour on 'informed' choice, on weighing their preferences towards public issues. This idea is linked to the core assumption of any public opinion research, that citizens possess reasonably well-formed attitudes on major political issues and that surveys can be used to 'harvest' these attitudes (Zaller and Feldman, 1992).

Understanding this point depends, of course, on how we treat 'attitudes' and what counts as political experience. For example, Bartels (2003) writes: 'if "attitudes" are taken to mean logically consistent summary evaluations of any conceivable political object ... then ... even splendidly well informed, attentive citizens will routinely flunk the test' (p. 63). Another cogent description comes from Gallup and Rae's classic account of public opinion polling:

a man may not be able to decipher a Congressional appropriation bill, but he can tell whether or not he approves of the objects for which it is to be passed; a man may not be able to understand the technological causes of his unemployment, but he knows what it means to be out of work, and his experience will contribute to the solution of the general problem. (1940, p. 288)

Contemporary political psychologists may perceive Gallup as an idealist, although the techniques that he and his colleagues have devised are now used to combat idealism, and argue against a political psychology based on the study of everyday political meanings and experiences. Nevertheless, it can be argued that Gallup was very much aware that

---

[10] The technologies of the poll lay out the premises for a distinction between a dignified, enlightened public opinion (that engendered and supported by the polls themselves) and a potentially disqualifiable, non-enlightened public opinion (that which is not supported or represented in or by polls). In the words of Bourdieu (2012), public opinion is predominantly the opinion of those who are *worthy* of having an opinion.

when gathering opinions the pollster is also gathering a good deal of precious information, which can be used to locate those opinions in a meaningful social context.[11]

As Lane (1962) argued 'an opinion, belief, or attitude is best understood in the context of other opinions, beliefs, and attitudes, for they illuminate its meaning, mark its boundaries, modify and qualify its force' (pp. 9–10). Riesman also urged social scientists to move towards the study of 'grounds of opinion', and of a social and political world 'where every question has many sides and many perspectives in which it may be viewed, each tinged with varying degrees of meaning and affect' (1954, p. 494).

Riesman and Lane suggest that attitudes and political experiences possess a highly visible social and rhetorical complexity.[12] The idea that people carry in their heads fully formed or preformed attitudes or 'a mix of only partially consistent ideas and considerations' (Zaller and Feldman, 1992, p. 579) is arguably less important than showing how social actors themselves engage with ideology and how their attitudes display rhetorical complexity (Billig, 1996, 1991; Condor, 2010; Gamson, 1992; Lane, 1962).

Answering the question of what attracts people to different ideological positions cannot proceed without understanding how social actors display rhetorical complexity in the expression of their attitudes. For instance, even political views that can be described as 'strong' (Billig, 1991) or 'extreme' (Tileagă, 2005) can be seen as flexible rhetorical accomplishments. Speakers and writers orient their statements to the social and rhetorical context in which they are talking or writing. Commonly shared values and beliefs can be mobilised variably and flexibly, and are part and parcel of the contemporary common sense of democracies. Societal discourse (especially talk on sensitive issues) is suffused with ideological dilemmas; for instance, the denial of prejudice, where prejudice is both denied and perpetuated (Billig, 1985; van Dijk, 1987) or arguing against affirmative action, where the *topoi* of tolerance intermingle with those of intolerance (Augoustinos *et al.*, 2005).

It is perhaps more profitable (and more plausible) to think of attitudes as rhetorical positions in matters of controversy (Billig, 1996), products

[11] Ironically, Gallup's argument is appreciated more by political psychologists interested in the discursive, social and cultural determinants of opinion formation and expression than by public opinion pollsters interested in the quantification of opinions.

[12] Their insights parallel those of social psychologists interested in the study of language and social action in social psychology (cf. Potter and Wetherell, 1987; Wetherell and Potter, 1992; and Chapter 7 for a detailed description of such a preoccupation).

of socio-communicative encounters and collective practices, rather than pre-existing features of people which are expressed on request in opinion polls (Condor and Gibson, 2007; Myers, 1998; Puchta and Potter, 2004) (turn also to Chapters 7 and 8 for a detailed discussion of some of the implications of this position, especially as applied to researching political discourse).

As Billig *et al.* (1988) have shown, common sense or ideology is not unitary but is *dilemmatic*, in that it contains antagonistic, contrary themes. Without such contrary themes there could be no attitudes, no values; there could be no argument.

Dilemmas of ideology: nostalgia for communism

On most policy and political issues people will offer straightforward, non-contradictory answers, but on others paradoxes abound. The phenomenon of 'nostalgia for socialism/communism' (Ekman and Linde, 2005; Todorova and Gille, 2010; Velikonja, 2009; Willinger, 2007)[13] is such an example. One of the most striking observations around coming to terms with the communist past (and its legacy) in Eastern Europe is related to the persistence of what is, for some, a 'nostalgic', backward-looking, anti-democratic mindset. As Pridham has argued, 'the legacy that usually proves most difficult to handle is not so much institutional as attitudinal' (2000, p. 49).

Various public opinion polls/surveys in Eastern Europe reflect the 'attitudinal legacy' to which Pridham refers. Instead of a relatively straightforward national agreement on the official moral evaluation of the collective memory of communism (enemy of human rights, illegitimate, criminal) (see, e.g., Tismăneanu's (2008) account of the condemnation of communism in Romania and Chapter 6 for approaches to the collective memory of communism), what one notices is a striking and intriguing contemporary phenomenon: positive public perceptions of the communist period.

Positive public perceptions of communism are usually seen as 'paradoxical', 'bewildering', 'mind-boggling', 'bizarre' or 'ambivalent'. For some researchers these perceptions can be explained by a 'trauma of collective memory' (Sztompka, 2004, p. 183). For others, nostalgia for communism reflects and expresses a 'retrospective utopia ... a wish and a hope for the safe world, fair society, true friendships, mutual solidarity, and well-being in general' (Velikonja, 2009, pp. 547–8).

---

[13] For theoretical appraisals of the concept of nostalgia see Lowenthal (1989), Pickering and Keightley (2006) and Radstone (2010).

Velikonja (2009) offers some examples of various public surveys conducted in different countries in Eastern Europe that show 'nostalgic' stances towards the recent communist/socialist past. In 1999, 50% of Slovakians considered the former socialist regime to be 'better than current democracy'. In the same year, in Russia, it was found that 85% of Russians regret communism's and the Soviet Union's demise. In 2004 the figure fell to 74%. In 2002, 56% of Poles were telling opinion pollsters that life 'was better before'. In 1995 and 2003, 88% and, respectively, 86% of Slovenians considered life in the former Yugoslavia, as 'good' and 'very good'. More recently (2009) 72% of Hungarians, 62% of Bulgarians and Ukrainians, 60% of Romanians, 45% of Russians, 42% of Lithuanians and Slovaks, 39% of Czechs and 35% of Poles declared they were worse off than during communism.

Recent Romanian polls commissioned by the *Institute for the Investigation of Communist Crimes and the Memory of Romanian Exile* and *Romanian Institute for Evaluation and Strategy* have identified striking paradoxes of opinion. Although 50% believe that 'it was better before' December 1989, 41% do consider that the communist regime was 'criminal'. Although more than half of Romanians consider that communism was a repressive regime, only 13% of them consider they have 'suffered' under communism. Although more than half of Romanians consider that access to the communist Secret Police files is unimportant, a vast majority think that those who have collaborated with the Secret Police should not occupy public posts.

Within the context of public positive perceptions of communism, public opinion is turned into a *social problem*, one that requires explanation: How is it that people can regret the communist regime? How can people just ignore its criminal and oppressive legacy? In the Romanian context, 'nostalgia' for communism and the range of contradictory opinions are considered (and explained) as 'escape from freedom' (Tismăneanu, 2010a), a 'latent complaint' in relation to 'present everyday frustrations' and 'identity crises' (Tismăneanu, 2010b). For others, nostalgia for communism and paradoxical opinions are seen as originating *in* and explained *by* a lack of elite management of social memory and a lack of information and individual insight, failings of memory and deep confusion in ideas, values and perspectives:

the population lacks a sophisticated understanding of 'suffering' during the communist regime. One needs to explain, in order to make one's own, the criminal nature of dictatorship ... Perceiving yourself as a victim of a totalitarian regime entails a full understanding of the inner workings of the regime ... there is a danger of creating a selective memory of communism, based primarily on personal experience and which disregards the repressive nature of the regime. (Iacob, 2010)

What is interesting to note is that these explanations place ambiguities, contradictions and paradoxes under the 'control' of a normative conception of society, politics and morality (and a normative representation of the recent past).[14] Yet these explanations point not only to a normative conception of society, politics and morality, but also to a conception of the person: empty-headed or muddled-headed, confused, lacking in civic and democratic capacity, providing an uncertain, unreliable, often misleading (and potentially immoral) account of what is, 'in actual fact', the 'reality' of communism. These explanations do not seem to take into account the sense in which 'opinions regarding controversial issues are always ambiguous ... they are often inconsistent or mutually contradictory ... they are typically so volatile and subject to change with new cues' (Edelman, 2001, p. 55). Explanations paper over the multiplicity of social frameworks of memory (Halbwachs, [1952] 1992), multiple realities, memories and meanings attached to communism as 'lived ideology'. Such explanations fail to accommodate the idea that ideology comprises contrary themes (Billig *et al.*, 1988). More generally, these interpretations seem to downplay the idea that not all members of society take the same segment/slice of the social and political world as 'fixed' beyond question. This can obscure the multiplicity of 'grounds of opinion' and the variety of identity constellations and networks of interpretation (Bucur, 2009; Gallinat, 2009).

These interpretations are given more in the spirit of Converse's ideas: that some people cannot form meaningful political beliefs, and that most people are 'innocent' (not to say 'ignorant') about political and ideological issues, that they fail to 'see' or 'make' connections where they need to and fail to form meaningful ideological conceptualisations. It is the role of elites, the role of education, to inculcate ordinary people/ citizens with desirable values and virtues. The public is 'gullible', 'suggestible', 'easily manipulated', and does not possess the capacity of understanding the complexity of political life. This has implications for the study of public opinion, political knowledge and political choice. To say that knowledge or information on politics (in this case, communism) is unequally distributed in society is perhaps true. It is usually argued that citizens act in a universe of uncertainty, where 'full information' is lacking. But what counts as 'full information': who decides that? against what? In order to overcome this quandary Dalton distinguishes between rational choices and reasonable ('good enough') choices. As he suggests, 'pretty good choices – not perfect choices – are

---

[14] See Tileagă (2009a) for an extended discussion of this in the context of social representations of communism.

the foundation of democracy' (2008, p. 27). People's positive public perceptions of communism are pretty good guesses, not perfect guesses; arguably, they present only apparent paradoxes and reflect a variety of experiences.

Attitudes towards the recent past (as well as political information) are not given or pre-existing and then harvested with the help of opinion polls, but rather *circulating* and *circulated* by active social actors at various levels of social organisation through the use of narratives, written records and material artefacts (Wertsch, 2007). Although the results of opinion polls can be *explained* in psychological, sociological and political terms, the heart and nature of these seemingly paradoxical standpoints are left untouched. Difficulties arise for opinion pollsters and commentators from wanting to attain 'objective and verifiable knowledge of a subjective meaning structure' (Schütz, 1973, p. 36). The existence of contradictory, ambiguous and paradoxical standpoints towards communism does not point necessarily to a lack of knowledge or insight, a lack of democratic capacity or competence, or low conceptual organisation, but rather to an essential characteristic of how commonsense functions and is reproduced by social actors in society (Billig, 1996; Wetherell and Potter, 1986). It points to the *argumentative* character of social life, where holding opinions is fundamentally an unfinished process of argumentation and debate (Billig, 1996). Lay standpoints and meanings attached to the recent communist past are far from orderly, homogeneous and predictable. Researchers need to look beyond explaining the results of public opinion polls to analysing the past and present social and argumentative context of forming opinions and viewpoints around communism as a socially constituted phenomenon that acquires very different meanings and interpretations for different people.

Modelling diversity: public opinion as practice

This chapter has described the main assumptions behind researching and understanding public opinion and the rhetorical complexity of attitudes towards the recent past (nostalgia for communism). This chapter has focused predominantly on the democratic competence of citizens. The next chapter (Chapter 2) extends this argument to the democratic competence of nations and the spreading of democratic values. This chapter has argued that attitudes possess a highly visible rhetorical complexity. Researching attitudes as rhetorical accomplishments is a much-needed distinctive and original complement to existing approaches that claim that people carry in their heads fully formed or preformed attitudes. It has the potential to move the political psychology of public opinion from an almost exclusive focus on information processing towards the study of how and why opinions matter to people.

It can be rightly argued that the 'new' challenge of a political psychology of mass beliefs and mass publics is to model 'diversity'; that is, to offer a systematic account of the diversity of viewpoints, positions, perspectives and frameworks that make up national and cross-national public spheres. Until now the challenge has been met by an increased sophistication of measurement techniques; yet puzzles remain. As researchers devise ever-more intricate methods of measuring citizens' opinions, these do not automatically lead to a more complex understanding of clusters of opinions, attitudes and ideology. One of the consequences of this is that political psychologists refer more to 'averaged' individuals/citizens than to actual individuals. In doing so, they privilege 'the national over the local, the aggregate over the individual, the average over the unique' (Igo, 2007, p. 282).[15] In this context, it is all the more important to understand and research public opinion as the foundation of the 'ideal' democratic polity but also as practice.

Understanding public opinion as practice entails making reference to not just the measurement of 'mass subjectivity' and mass publics, but also, and perhaps more importantly, to the *making* of mass subjectivity and mass publics. As this chapter has shown, mass publics and mass subjectivity can also be thought of as a product of social science methods and empirical procedures prevalent at a particular time in society. Survey methods carve out of the national and cross-national fabric the 'typical' citizen or the 'average' voter. In their search for the 'ideal' democratic citizen, political psychologists have shaped an academic and political culture with the 'averaged' individual at its centre. Political psychologists are too readily looking for that elusive 'variable' (or cluster of variables) that would predict an individual's or, for that matter, a public's political behaviour. In doing so, they segment social and political life to suit their objectivist empirical purposes, rather than investigating how social and political life segments itself along subjectivist, relative, contingent outlines. They arguably neglect the idea that what we refer to as 'public opinion' is also contingent on the historical, political, institutional and technological contexts with which social actors interact, and that allow us to talk of 'public opinion' in the first place.

It is usually a normative vision of democracy, politics and morality that informs the way in which political psychologists approach and

---

[15] On opinion quantification and democratic processes see also Herbst (1995).

study the notion of public opinion and its relation to political behaviour. Political psychologists are more inclined to test prescriptive models of how public opinion *ought* to manifest itself, rather than how it *actually* manifests itself. The focus should be more on how people *actually* make sense of themselves and their politics, and not on how they *ought to* (cf. Lakoff, 2002). Moreover, when political psychologists express optimistic or pessimistic forecasts about the 'quality' of public opinion, democratic or civic capacity, they also, implicitly, express value judgements on categories of people that are 'fit' for democracy. One has to remember that the 'ideal' of the democratic citizen does not include everyone; in most post-industrial societies it excludes minorities, immigrants, and so on.

Conventionally, contradictions, inconsistencies, ambivalence and dilemmas of common sense are viewed as evidence of the irrationality of common sense. In contrast, it can be argued that the contrary aspects of (cultural) common sense represent the very precondition for rational deliberation, within and between members of a particular community. The dilemmatic character of common sense means that political attitudes and arguments are often expressed in hedged, qualified terms ('on the one hand … on the other hand') and can be conceived of as rhetorical unfinished business in matters of controversy. One must not abandon the idea that democratic government can be the direct expression of the will of the people. One just needs to study the relationship differently. Political psychology research should be more about what citizens themselves expect of democracy and less about what democracy expects of citizens. There can be no public opinion without publics, no publics without communication and without the different representations of society and personhood that these publics construct and perpetuate (see Chapter 4 on the link between beliefs, social representations and communication), and without the discursive strategies employed by social and political actors to make sense of themselves and political reality (see Chapters 7 and 8 on discourse and political rhetoric). One needs to move from the 'averaged' individual (the by-product of surveys) to the 'dilemmatic' individual (the individual whose sense-making of themselves and their politics is an unfinished process of argumentation and debate), a move from information processing to discourse and communication.

2 Mass subjectivity, values and democracy promotion

Mass subjectivity and the democratic competence of nations

As argued in Chapter 1, citizens and publics inhabit 'a political environment where they are continually encouraged by various actors to vocalize their views' (Stanyer, 2007, p. 157). Some of the 'actors' to which Stanyer refers are academic psychologists, experts in public opinion polling who are interested in the aggregate description and distribution of the various dimensions of social and political behaviour: attitudes, motives, preferences, wishes, value orientations, and so on. Value orientations are perhaps the most important to understanding issues around political attitudes, social and political change, and political participation (Inglehart, 2009).

This chapter sketches the various attempts at describing the universal psychological structure of human values and the implications of such attempts for understanding democracy promotion and democratisation. It explores the tension between aggregate and universalistic models and contingent, contextual, particularistic manifestations of political behaviour. By focusing on the issue of questioning democracy promotion, this chapter shows how value orientations cannot be satisfactorily conceptualised outside an inter-subjective framework and ordinary ways of reasoning about values. The promotion of 'formal democracy' cannot work outside the framework of mass values offered by the existing socio-political context. The chapter ends by arguing that values should be treated as ideologically and culturally situated argumentative resources, and that researchers should emphasise not only their universalistic, but also their particularistic features, especially the fragmentary, multiple and unfinished nature of value searches, value expressions and value orientations.

Social and political action, and evaluation and judgement of social policies, are supported or opposed on the basis of being understood to reproduce cherished values and impeding the reproduction of pernicious ones. The promotion of democracy and democratic values is, for some, the most cherished humanistic ideal. This chapter explores the limits of the idea according to which the driving force behind understanding the democratic process is the robust *aggregation* of personal and political preferences, wishes, values, and so on, the large-scale study of mass subjectivity. The contemporary political psychology of human values is a direct expression of this trend (Inglehart and Welzel, 2005). The image of society arising from these concerns is that of the polity capable of expressing democratic values, whose functioning is underpinned by a clear set of mass (democratic) value orientations.

Chapter 1 has argued that there is a widespread tendency to consider that people are too unpredictable, too inconsistent, to grasp the ideological complexities of political life. It is the role of elites, experts and, in some cases, the state, to inculcate individuals, groups and communities with the desired outlook, values and value orientations. The case of democratisation is a case in point. The conventional view is that democracy promotion enlightens citizens and brings with it a different value cluster that, in turn, facilitates and promotes more democracy. According to Inglehart (2003) support for democracy is intimately linked to value orientations such as tolerance of out-groups, interpersonal trust, political participation and sense of subjective well-being. Aggregate value measurements of such value orientations are said to accurately describe democratic political orientations and beliefs of very diverse communities and their citizens. Yet, as this chapter will show, the realities of democratisation are very complex and demand complex interpretative frameworks, and may not fit neatly the predicted (universal) association between aggregated collective values, political culture and democratic outlook. Some mass publics may fail to display the normative pattern of 'democracy'.

This chapter argues that the issue of mass subjectivity should not be reduced to aggregate measures of attitudinal syndromes, but rather extended to and studied as a product of socio-communicative encounters. If it is true that values can be defined as generalised standards, criteria people use to select and justify actions, evaluate themselves and others, then values should be studied more as ideologically and culturally situated argumentative resources: *ways of talking* about people, society, democracy, and so on, and less as features of statistical, predictive models, cutting across social and political contexts and life experiences.

The universal psychological structure of human values

Alongside voting, trust, social activism and social membership, social values are some of the most familiar measures of civic (democratic) health. Values and value orientations are particularly relevant descriptors of the politics (and political organisation) of societies. For instance, commentators describe contemporary US politics as a mixture of three value orientations (i.e. individualism, egalitarianism and post-materialism), whereas European politics tends to be described mostly in terms of communitarianism. Most values are 'omnibus symbols'; that is, they incorporate under a specific 'label' other different social and value orientations and assumptions. American 'individualism' incorporates assumptions and orientations to equal individual rights, equal opportunities, small government, laissez-faire politics and so on (cf. Lukes, 1973) and virtues (hard work, sacrifice). European 'communitarianism' incorporates assumptions and orientations to the welfare state and state-led policies.

If one considers the history of research on human values one can notice a shift from unidimensional to multidimensional value models (for early theoretical underpinnings and historical roots of research on values see Tsirogianni and Gaskell, 2011). Perhaps the most influential, early attempt to understand the societal dynamic of social values is that offered by Rokeach (1968). This is constructed around the notion of values as *guiding principles in people's lives*.[1] For Rokeach, values are likened to the self-concept or personality and are anchored in the interdependent relation between 'the desired' and 'the desirable'. Rokeach postulated the existence of a very close relationship between values, attitudes and behaviour, while drawing attention to both overt, as well as latent, manifestations of values.

Moving up from the individual level to the domain of political ideology, Rokeach (1973) proposes that one could obtain a more sophisticated understanding of political ideologies if these were conceptualised using a two-value dimensions model: 'equality' (equal opportunity for all, comradeship) and 'freedom' (free choice, independence). According to Rokeach's view different ratios (high vs. low) of equality and freedom can be used to describe the appeal and nature of different ideological systems and political orientations: capitalism (low equality, high freedom), socialism (high equality and freedom), communism (high equality, low freedom), fascism (low equality and freedom). What described

---

[1] Rokeach distinguishes between values as goals (what he calls 'terminal' values) and values as modes of conduct (what he calls 'instrumental' values).

the different political orientations was not the competition between equality and freedom, but rather the priority, stability and preponderance of one value over the other over time.[2]

The perspective espoused by Rokeach is complemented and enriched by contemporary approaches that concentrate on trade-offs among *competing* values, crucial to understanding political attitudes and behaviour. Contemporary research on social values marks a shift from ranking and priority of values to the identification of 'value domains' and understanding the structural representation of 'core' human values. For instance, Schwartz's value theory (e.g. Roccas *et al.*, 2010; Schwartz, 1992, 2006, 2009; Schwartz and Bardi, 2001) argues that values are 'cognitive, social representations of basic motivational goals that serve as guiding principles in people's lives' (Roccas *et al.*, 2010, p. 394). Up to a point, Schwartz's definition is similar to that offered by Rokeach, the difference lies in treating values as binary 'motivational profiles'. It is not the loading of values (high vs. low) that counts but rather their compatibilities and conflicts which, according to Schwartz (1992), can be reduced to two broad motivational, goal-orientated 'domains': on the one hand, motivations guided by respect for tradition, concern for personal and national security, and propensity for conformity, and on the other hand, motivations to seek and get social rewards, control and prestige as opposed to social justice and fairness.

As Schwartz (1992) contends, these dimensions are relatively independent, although in some societies they can crop up together and show a relative degree of association. Motivational goals underlie both personal and cultural values. Schwartz's typology of values organises them in ten types and, in theory, allows for infinite variations and diversity in individual values. Schwartz's ten values form a motivational 'circumplex' (see Figure 2.1) based on a pattern of compatibility and conflict. The proximity of two values on the circle is the basis on which one can infer the similarity of their underlying motivations; the more distant apart, the bigger the 'motivational' difference. This leads to the creation of several motivational binaries. For instance, one can notice how *openness to change* (consisting of stimulation and self-direction) is opposed to *conservation* (security, tradition and conformity), whereas *self-transcendence* (universalism, benevolence) is opposed to *self-enhancement* (power, achievement, hedonism).

[2] Rokeach's assumption is shared by contemporary researchers. The central assumption of most research is that value priorities are generally constant over time and are key elements in the structure of political knowledge, the organisation of political attitudes and behaviour (Feldman, 2003).

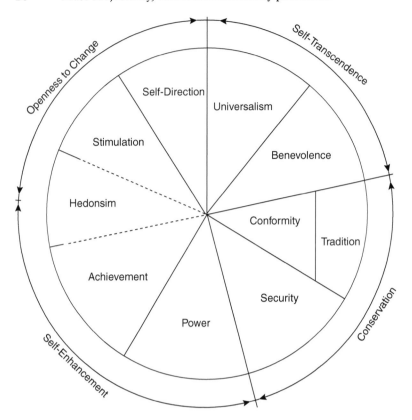

Figure 2.1 Schwartz's circumplex model of values

The motivational/value structure posited by Schwartz opens the way for the study of the link between values and political behaviour. For instance, Schwartz *et al.* (2010) propose a causal model of basic personal values, which influence core political values, which, in turn, influence political behaviour.[3] Considering voting behaviour, Schwartz and colleagues argue that 'people's values rather than their social locations [age, education, class] are now more critical determinants of political choice' (2010, p. 446). For instance, what underlies respect for core political values such as law and order is the motivational opposition

---

[3] There are similarities between Schwartz's value theory and work stemming from Hofstede's findings on individualistic and collectivist societies (Hofstede, 2001), especially work that tries to link traits to dimensions of culture (Hofstede and McCrae, 2004).

between the cluster security–conformity–tradition and the cluster self-direction–hedonism–stimulation.

Research work that tries to link values, traits and political choice also shows the primacy of values as critical guides to political behaviour. For instance, in a study of the Italian election of 2001, Caprara *et al.* (2006) show how 'values subsume traits in predicting political orientation' (p. 24). Caprara has found that security values tended to be associated more with voting for the centre-right, whereas self-direction values tended to be associated more with voting for the centre-left. The conclusion of Caprara's study is that values rather than personality traits account for 'substantial variance' in predicting future voting and changes in political choices.

What Schwartz's theory describes are 'universals' in content, structure and relationships of values. The ultimate aim is to describe the 'universal psychological structure of human values' (cf. Schwartz and Bilsky, 1987). Schwartz's search for 'universals' resonates with that of other researchers who are predisposed to study the universality of psychological orientations, especially those towards modernity and modernisation, and as they relate to the 'human development sequence' (e.g. Inglehart, 2009; Inglehart and Welzel, 2005; Welzel, 2009). In empirical terms, this involves researching aggregate mass subjectivity dimensions of modernisation. The key insight is that modernisation brings along and engenders an open-minded orientation, reflects 'democratic character', 'personality strength' and self-fulfilment (e.g. Inglehart and Welzel, 2005; Welzel, 2009).

The vast research programmes of the World Values Survey and the European Values Survey[4] (not to mention the other 'value barometers' around the world) present the most sophisticated and multidimensional picture of human values. One of the most important insights coming out of the World Values Survey is that consequences of modernisation can be witnessed in a marked, noticeable shift from survival (a syndrome of mass attitudes built around materialist and physiological needs and motives) to self-expression or emancipative values (a syndrome of mass attitudes with an emphasis on freedom, tolerance of diversity and participation) (Inglehart and Welzel, 2005). The shift from survival to self-expression values is the driver behind the emergence of new political issues on the political arena and the main motivator of new political movements.

---

[4] For details see www.worldvaluessurvey.org/ (last accessed July 2012), a comprehensive resource of theoretical and empirical material on the different 'waves' of the World Values Survey. For the European Values Survey, see www.europeanvaluesstudy.eu/ (last accessed July 2012).

Inglehart and Welzel (2005) have shown the existence of a shift towards post-materialistic values among the publics of nine Western societies over the period 1970–2000.[5] What Inglehart and Welzel term 'post-materialism' subsumes distinct orientations – liberal, ecological, idealistic orientations, according to Welzel (2009), better termed as 'liberty aspirations'. Post-materialist values or liberty aspirations are central to what Inglehart and Welzel (2005) call 'self-expression values' – a syndrome of emancipative values comprising the following: (a) esteem of human freedom; (b) esteem of political self-expression; (c) esteem of nonconformity; (d) esteem of other people; and (e) high life satisfaction.

Self-expression values are crucial to understanding the dynamics of liberal, constitutional or electoral democracies, political action and choice. These values correlate strongly with democratic orientations and institutions. Moreover, they are key motivators to seeking (and gaining) the range of civil and political rights that describe liberal democracy. The correlation between 'genuine' democracy and self-expression values is consistently very high. The distribution of self-expression values and open-minded orientations (Welzel, 2009) in a society can explain and predict the 'extent to which liberal democracy is actually practiced' (Inglehart and Welzel, 2005, p. 154).[6] Socioeconomic development leads to higher levels of self-expression values, which, in turn, lead to higher levels of democracy (Inglehart, 2003).

The crux of Inglehart and Welzel's approach is that people's orientations are shaped by socioeconomic forces and that low-order (materialist, physiological) values are inevitably replaced/displaced by higher order (postmaterialist, psychological self-actualisation) values (Inglehart, 1977, 1990, 2009; see also Inglehart and Abramson, 1999). Self-expression/emancipative values make publics more assertive and defiant of authority. For instance, emancipative values can have an 'elevator', or 'amplifier', effect on (non-violent) protest (Welzel and Deutsch, 2011). They also exert 'healthy pressures to keep elites honest, accountable and responsive to what people want' (p. 203).

One can notice a close relationship between the study of human values, mass subjectivity and the study of 'public' or 'publics'. It was the French sociologist Gabriel Tarde who declared, in contrast to LeBon's

---

[5] They also find large value orientation differences between older and younger birth cohorts that, according to them, seems to reflect 'a process of intergenerational value change' (p. 228).

[6] Inglehart and Welzel go as far as to suggest, 'rising self-expression values strongly increase the probability that a society will become democratic (if it not yet is) or will remain democratic (if it already is)' (p. 157).

emphasis on crowds, that his era was the era 'of the public or of publics' ([1969] 2010, p. 281).[7] When commenting on the society's division into publics, Tarde wrote about 'differences in states of mind' (p. 284) or the influence of people's 'goals or their faith' (p. 288); contemporary political psychologists write of individual differences in 'political attention', 'value circles' and shifts in value orientations.[8] Whereas Tarde was trying to understand and describe a social phenomenon, how 'currents of opinion' take shape when people are not meeting each other, considering what is the 'bond' between these people, political psychologists presume from the onset the existence of a bond and are more interested in averaging the opinions of large samples of individuals.

It is the 'statistical sense organ' of polling and aggregation that constitutes 'the link that connects the person with the collective' (Noelle-Neumann, 1993, p. 115). For political psychologists, it is the aggregate, quantitative, *public expression* of motives, preferences, wishes, value orientations, and so forth that testifies to the existence of a social bond. In their search for quantified and quantifiable data, political psychologists (and especially survey researchers) infer and describe the content and distribution of political behaviour and national values using representative cross-sections of a national community (cf. Rose, 2009). Aggregate measures make relevant and thematise certain value orientations. Once aggregated, these value orientations function culturally and politically as a metalanguage that provides support for and justifies the existence of a mass 'subject' that purportedly shares those value orientations. Aggregate value measures also tell us about the universal desirability of identified patterns. Value orientations, in the aggregate, present a structure/organisation that can be said to correspond to the universal psychological structuration of human values and nature of political organisation in a particular sociocultural context.

Questioning democracy promotion: a breakdown of value priorities?

As stated previously, value orientations are said to be reflective of what 'national publics' think; they are the values of a national mass subject not of separate individuals. Individual subjectivities are aggregated

---

[7] For both Tarde and contemporary political psychologists 'the public ... is the social group of the future' (p. 281).

[8] On the other side of the Atlantic, the American pragmatist philosopher John Dewey was writing about the differences between 'older', 'homogenous', static publics and 'newer forces' that 'have created mobile and fluctuating associational forms' (Dewey, [1927] 1954, pp. 139–40).

and turned into a faceless mass subjectivity. A preoccupation with the democratic competence of nation-states relies on the assumption of the existence of a national mass subjectivity that can be uncovered using rightly calibrated techniques, yet, at the same time, overlooks the extraordinary diversity that characterises national mass publics.

One of the central tenets of Inglehart and Welzel's value theory is the statement that a major driver in promoting democracy is increased levels of self-expression of values. Democracy itself is re-specified – democracy is 'more than just a political regime. It is a way of life anchored in an emancipatory world-view' (Welzel, 2009, p. 203). But this vision of 'democracy' does not seem to be displayed by all national publics and nations. Sheer exposure to, or promotion of, self-expression values, and sheer experience with democratic institutions does not unavoidably lead to acceptance and legitimacy of democracy (Inglehart, 2003). Latin America and some post-communist states are the most cogent examples.[9] For instance, according to Inglehart and Welzel, Bulgaria, Romania and India are cases of high levels of formal democracy, which are not matched by high levels of self-expression values. In such cases, high levels of formal democracy translate in actual low levels of effective democracy. No surprise here, as according to Inglehart and Welzel, relative weakness of self-expression values predicts actual deficits in democracy.

The notion of intergenerational value change is closely related to understanding social and political changes and the impact of socioeconomic conditions. As Inglehart argues, 'intergenerational value change will occur if younger generations grow up under different conditions from those that shaped earlier generations – so that the values of the entire society will gradually change through intergenerational replacement' (2009, p. 225). Inglehart writes about the 'values of the entire society', treats values as homogeneous standards that shape political behaviour and assumes they are shared uncontroversially, evenly and uniformly distributed in society. Writing about the 'values of the entire society' also downplays the identity projects and representations associated with different social groupings and communities within a given society. Social representations theorists have demonstrated that there are no values without different social representations of social issues and social objects. Issues as different as psychoanalysis or the genetically modified tomato 'are anchored and elaborated in relation to the varying projects of different societal groups or milieus' (Bauer and

---

[9] It is argued that 'since their dramatic move toward democracy ... people of most of these societies have *not* become more trusting, more tolerant, happier, or more post-materialist' (Inglehart and Welzel, 2005, p. 159, emphasis in original).

Gaskell, 2008, p. 349) (see Chapter 4 for a detailed outline of social representations theory).

The most common explanation for low levels of self-expression values is that the broad cultural heritage of a society does leave a mark on commonly shared values and this endures despite social and political change (Inglehart and Baker, 2000).[10] Other explanations focus on what Sztompka (2004) has called traumatogenic social change, characterised by sudden, comprehensive, rapid, radical, unexpected and shocking change. The metaphor of 'cultural trauma' (Sztompka, 2004) is one of the several proposals about the 'reality' and 'effects' of rapid and extreme social change.[11] Symptoms of cultural trauma are the collapse of trust, a pessimistic picture of the future and nostalgic images of the past (cf. Sztompka, 2004).[12]

Yet the cultural heritage of society, coupled or not with rapid social change and 'trauma' in itself, cannot account for the diversity and ambiguities of individual positioning. What counts is the importance and meaning individuals and groups attach to change rather than absolute value positions or orientations (Jervis, 2004).

In order to understand the original appeal of communism (but also its post-fall appeal; see Chapter 1 for various interpretations of nostalgia for communism), one may perhaps need to entertain the idea that behind 'formal' value orientations runs a 'second discourse', a second value orientation. Satter (2012, p. 97) captures this idea brilliantly when he writes of the failure of Western commentators to understand the appeal of communism: 'Westerners often assumed that Soviet citizens suffered from their lack of freedom and yearned for the collapse of the Communist regime. This perception is not accurate. It was born of contact with a minority of Soviet citizens who held democratic values,

---

[10] Welzel (2009), Inglehart (2009) and Shin (2009) provide useful outlines of more recent empirical issues on post-materialist, self-expression and other values linked to democratisation processes.

[11] It is argued that 'traumatizing situations or events occur as side-effects of major social change ... traumatizing events or situations may produce dislocations in the routine, accustomed ways of acting or thinking, change the life-world of the people in often dramatic ways, reshape their patterns of acting and thinking' (Sztompka, 2000, p. 456). Instances of traumatising situations are unemployment, poverty, or corruption among the political elite.

[12] Marková (2004) shows the quandary of trust in East European states that entailed a move from social situations where trust was intermingled with fear, to post-communist social situations where trust was intermingled with risk. Marková demonstrates how these two positions are not mutually contradictory tropes but rather complementary resources in the individual, group and national struggle to come to terms with the legacy of the former regime and the legitimacy of the new democratic system.

and of the assumption that Soviet citizens could not be but appalled by the regime's crimes.'

The realities of 'democratisation' across very different socio-political contexts are very complex and demand complex interpretative frameworks. For instance, identifying the 'real' causes of social and political change can lead researchers to explain the same phenomenon in very different ways. The recent debate on the Eastern European 'colored revolutions' is an example of that. Way (2008)'s suggestion that the 'real' causes of 'colored revolutions' lie with the degree of state and party capacity as well as the strength or weakness of links to the West has been met with alternative explanations in terms of inter-related waves of protest matching democratisation attempts elsewhere in the world (Beissinger, 2009), the popularity of authoritarian and post-authoritarian incumbents (Dimitrov, 2009) or the role of political actors who enacted and developed a new model of change (Bunce and Wolchik, 2009).

Democratisation is characterised by value orientations that reflect both progressive and conservative forces. Kaltwasser (2012) shows how populism can be both a 'democratic corrective' (in terms of inclusiveness and social justice) as well as a 'democratic threat' (with regard to public contestation). Dzihic and Segert (2012) illustrate the limits of post-Yugoslav democratisation by pointing to the existence of a peculiar form of 'limited electoral democracy', which can be described as a 'stable hybrid form comprising democratic and authoritarian elements' (p. 249). Dzihic and Segert argue that as more and more countries are included in comparative analyses of democracy promotion and consolidation, it is less clear what the comparison means for those polities themselves. Stan (2012) analyses recent Romanian parliamentary debates on lustration and shows the multiplicity of moral and value positions on a continuum from 'witch-hunt' to 'moral rebirth'. According to Stan, evaluative meanings attached to the Romanian continual process of democratisation range from moral cleansing (and a break with the past), providing retributive justice for victims of communism to punishing individuals portrayed as being against European values, or impractical and unconstitutional.

Furthermore, Korosteleva (2003) proposes a radical argument by suggesting there may be a variety of forms of democracy, just as there are different states and different cultures. She uses the example of Belarus to show how one can conceptualise and identify different types of democracy that are, sometimes, better descriptions of very specific socio-political contexts. When researching Belarus she describes it as a very peculiar form of democracy, which includes elements of authoritarian democracy with more prominent aspects of a 'demagogical' democracy (see also Korosteleva, 2012 for Belarus's response to the 'colored revolutions').[13] When discussing the application of the external governance framework to the European Neighbourhood Policy (ENP) in less motivated states, such as Belarus, Korosteleva (2009) points to the limits of 'hierarchical'/vertical European Union (EU) governance as opposed to building horizontal networks of cooperation and the virtual absence of a rhetoric of joint partnership that undermines the implementation of the strategy. Other studies show that although there is a continued weakness of civil society in Eastern Europe (Wallace *et al.*, 2012) and lack of civic engagement (Mondak and Gearing, 2003), there are nonetheless no significant differences between countries who have joined the EU and those who have not.

What research shows is that there are limits to democratic (European and world) norm promotion. Universal value orientations, such as self-expression or emancipative values, might not be the sole, or primary, orientations that people will choose or use in their assessment of democracy. One cannot understand these limits (or barriers) if one does not step outside a framework that considers democracy promotion as a 'duty' to be dealt with through policies of intervention or vertical/hierarchical imposition, and if one does not take seriously into account the different pathways to cultural democratisation (Shin, 2009).[14] It should not come as a surprise that increasingly citizens of the world's nation-states are merely paying lip service to democracy and attempts at democracy promotion (Inglehart, 2003). As Shin and Wells argue, 'large majorities favor democracy *as a regime*' and yet 'still have not fully embraced the set of norms and processes that constitute the structure of the democratic system' (2005, p. 99, emphasis in original).[15] Inglehart

---

[13] Korosteleva's argument resonates with that of research on hybrid regimes (Levitsky and Way, 2010; see also Levitsky and Way, 2002) where political (democratic) regimes are described as a mixture of formal democratic institutions (inclusive of free and fair elections) and informal institutions and arrangements that work against those.

[14] As Shin (2009) argues one should perhaps draw a distinction between democracy-in-principle and actual practical support for democracy. One could argue that the distinction between democracy as 'ideal political system' and democracy as a 'political system-in-practice' is not operative solely for political scientists, but also for ordinary social and political actors. Survey-based studies show that 'democracy as an ideal political system has achieved overwhelming mass approval throughout the world' (Shin, 2009, p. 270), yet the East Asia and New European Barometers seem to indicate that 'although the citizens generally support democracy, they do not want to live in a complete or nearly complete democracy' (2009, p. 271).

[15] Perhaps the presence of 'lingering affinity for authoritarianism' in emerging democracies (see Shin and Wells, 2005, for East Asia) is perhaps more a problem of considering 'authoritarianism' as the (perfect) opposite of 'democracy', rather than an actual anti-democratic orientation.

and Welzel are correct when they write that there is an 'evolutionary logic' behind understanding cultural change, that is 'driving people to adopt those values that fit given existential conditions' (2005, p. 38). The only problem is that the complex reality of existential conditions in some countries of the world shows us that those values are not always emancipative values.[16]

Plurality and context in value orientations

As argued previously, what lies at the core of the contemporary political psychology of values are the assumptions of stability and primacy of values, and the almost miraculous belief in a causal link between value orientations and political behaviour. However, a wealth of research shows that the assumptions of causality, stability and primacy are problematic, and that one can identify a set of contingent, multiple, contextually bound links between values and value orientations and political behaviour. For instance, researchers have shown the ability of people to hold multiple value orientations linked to different social and cultural identities. Stelzl and Seligman (2009) have investigated the link between value systems and mixed cultural identities with a group of Asian Canadians. They found that when participants responded as Canadians (when their identity as Canadians was made salient) they tended to emphasise value orientations such as universalism, self-direction, hedonism and stimulation; whereas when they responded as Asians they were more likely to emphasise conformity and tradition. In one of their studies on the identification of recent Russian immigrants to Israel, Roccas et al. (2010) found a link between personal value priorities and national identification. They observed a correlation between the pressure immigrants felt to assimilate and different value orientations. This relationship was moderated by the context of social identification: with the country of residence (Israel) or with the country of origin (Russia). When people identified more with Israel they were more likely to endorse conservation values and showed less openness to change values. What these two studies show is that when the context of social identification changes, different value orientations may be affirmed or asserted (for similar research that focuses on the context of social identification, see Chapter 5).

According to Tsirogianni and Gaskell (2011) contemporary value theory relies strongly on the ability to prescribe and predict value linkages based on theoretical models, which undermines the plausibility of

---

[16] On successes and failures of democratisation, see also D'Anieri (2006).

individuals endorsing conflicting, contradictory values. This current tendency of contemporary value theory downplays the multiplicity of positions and roles that take centre-stage in analyses of social identity (see, e.g., research by Crisp and colleagues on multiple categorisation in Chapter 5). What research finds over and over again (and what political reality is showing us) is that individuals do adhere to oppositional values.

An interesting example is offered by the 'value balance model' (Braithwaite, 2009a, b) where most people are perceived as having balanced value orientations, which include seemingly opposing value orientations (see also Braithwaite, 1994). Citizens of a polity are said to possess different value balances (both sharing and self-protective values; security and harmony values) and it is the task of the visionary politician to 'weave different strengths into the national fabric from citizens with value balance of different kinds' (Braithwaite, 2009a, p. 95). According to Braithwaite, one can distinguish between 'dualists' (people who take stances that show compassion and responsibility to others, are potentially 'bridge builders' and engage constructively with democratic contestation) and 'relativists' (people who are suspicious of committing to value positions and continually look for contextual factors to guide their political behaviour).

Moreover, as research on the psychology of morality has shown, people are ready to be flexible with their values and even abandon important ones if they need to. People do not work at all times with absolute and 'sacred' standards of morality, but rather strategically fashion and transform the very character of moral boundaries around what is 'thinkable, alternately punitively rigid and forgivingly flexible' (Tetlock, 2003, p. 320). Most often people strike compromises between moral ideals and strict standards and pragmatic pressures; they can use contextually appropriate versions of morality to justify their own actions and those of others (Tileagă, 2012). The prevailing conception of value orientations cannot satisfactorily account for this. Values are confined within the symbolic space of nation-states and national publics. There is an assumption of national uniformity in value orientations (or, indeed, value shifts). This reproduces an essentialist notion of national culture and values, which does not incorporate nor does it explain issues of intra-variety, multiple contexts, multiple influences and 'the complexity and situational variability of the individual subject' (McSweeney, 2002, p. 113). It is perhaps more profitable to consider value orientations as extending on a continuum, along a plurality of divergent or mutually supporting dialogical positions (Marková, 2000) across different life spheres and life worlds.

From aggregation to language games

A great deal of research suggests that an exclusive focus on the 'markedly quantitative character of ... hopes and fears' (Tarde, [1969] 2010, p. 201) may fail to capture significant aspects of value orientations, and ignores the heterogeneity of citizens' understandings of political issues and public affairs. It has been shown that social and political actors adopt ideological and value identifications/orientations by drawing on symbolic resources such as metaphors, commonplaces, or the vocabulary of 'virtue words' (McGee, 1980, p. 6), such as 'community', 'change' or 'choice' (Edelman, 2001) (see Chapters 7 and 8 for some examples of the role of a vocabulary of 'values' in political rhetoric).

Different value orientations and vocabularies of 'values' may impose different meanings on the left–right (or liberal–conservative) continuum (White, 2011a, b). This suggests that the study of human values cannot be reduced to aggregate value 'measures', which are said to represent accurately the political orientations and beliefs of communities and their citizens. The political psychology of human value orientations tends to be more about what democracy, as a normative politico-moral framework, expects of citizens, and less about what citizens themselves expect of democracy and how the normative framework of democracy is actually interpreted by individuals through various ideological self-placements and social positioning. As I have shown in Chapter 1, if expressing opinions can be understood as a process of *alignment* (for or against a person, act, discourse), in the same way, values can be understood as alignments for or against social relations and social arrangements, and discourses circulating in society.

In the contemporary world, value orientations are as much the product of methods of investigation constantly refined by researchers, as they are the product of individual positioning. In an increasingly global world, there is a sense of assurance (reassurance) given by the fact that the values of New Yorkers are actually shared to a large extent by the inhabitants of Benin.[17] Schwartz, Inglehart and colleagues have effectively produced a new kind of phenomenon, a new 'sphere of reality' (Osborne and Rose, 1999, p. 386). There is, of course, no doubt that values and value orientations 'exist' (in the same way as

---

[17] Some authors have argued that we have been witnessing the relatively successful 'export' of survey research methodologies around the world, without paying too much attention to the consequences of such a move (Heath *et al.*, 2005). The only problem is that the globalisation of survey research methodologies has led to the 'dominance of a particular intellectual framework and set of assumptions that may not be quite appropriate outside their homes' (Heath *et al.*, 2005, p. 298).

personality traits are said to 'exist'), they can be robustly measured, they are important for all sorts of social and political action. The only problem is that their existence is derived and determined by employing certain research technologies of measurement that stand over and above individual social positions. The existence of questionnaire items that purport to measure survival or self-expressive value orientations, individualism, collectivism, trust, and so on, promotes the idea that clusters of values exist, they can be 'objectively' measured and that they are organised and manifest themselves in a way predicted by the conceptual and empirical scaffolding of researchers.

It can be argued that the distinctions (e.g. between survival vs. emancipative values) with which researchers work are the product of what a technology of measurement and aggregation produces out of a fragmented, multi-modal, dilemmatic, individual position towards relevant social objects (including the self). It is perhaps too easily forgotten that the term 'value' itself is an 'evocative concept' (as much as 'public opinion' is) – and by using it (and qualifying it drawing upon various psychological attributes) political elites, as well as academics, can categorise beliefs in a way that postulates and promotes a world view, interest, and so on that is theirs but not necessarily that of lay actors.

Values are understood to be reflective of what 'publics' think, they belong to a 'public' (to nations) rather than to individuals. The European and World Values Surveys not only measure mass subjectivity – they engender and shape it. Value surveys can tell us a lot about the distribution or spread of value orientations in a given society or cross-nationally, but less about the question of where do value orientations come from. An emphasis on modernisation, aggregation and universal structure misses their crucial local origin – the specific common sense of a community, which includes (but is not limited to) the discursive history of specific ways of talking about society, morality, social change, and so forth. There can be no theory of values without an acknowledgement of whatever can obstruct, limit, distort, and so on the formation and reproduction of values in society (e.g. Billig, 1998 and Tileagă, 2012 have shown the dynamic, discursive and rhetorical character of values). As Tönnies has argued, opinions can be sometimes conceived of as the 'common property' of the political public (cf. Hardt and Splichal, 2000). Values can too be understood as the common standards, shared-in-common property of individuals and political communities.

As I have shown, according to Inglehart, self-expression or emancipative values are the true sovereign values of post-materialist societies;

they reflect the open and collective will of 'the people', of 'citizens' of democracies, a global 'spirit' and drive for democracy. Opinion polls are exercises of calibration as well as prediction of aggregate mass values. Opinion polls are accompanied by a lot of assumptions around how the polls 'should' behave or the results they 'should' yield.[18] What frequently occurs in the reception of values surveys is the reification of 'values' in the data. Researchers, and receiving public alike, are 'sucked into this confusion of phenomenon, concept and measurement' (Bauer and Gaskell, 2008, p. 349). More is known about the quantitative and statistical distribution of values than about their qualitative heights or depths.

When one positions oneself on a scale that is part of the European or World Value Survey is that to be taken as a *report* about a state of mind? (Cf. Wittgenstein, 1953.) Are values a reflection of a persistent, stable, conscious awareness of something that is outside the person? These issues are not decidable in abstract, but by exploring how values, as ordinary language concepts, are actually oriented to, pointed to and used in socio-communicative situations. There is a comprehensive, adequate ordinary vocabulary of values, a wealth of lay public language games around persons, individuality, morality, politics and social relationships that social actors actively use. If one analyses values using predetermined, abstract, statistical models, one is bound to miss the myriad language games in which vocabularies of values (including those of researchers themselves), become relevant. People routinely and unproblematically use the language of self-expression, tradition, survival, and so on, as they use what Jeff Coulter (2001) has called the 'language of the macro level' (e.g. the 'army', the 'bank', the 'economy'). It is this common-sense language that operates as a 'scheme of interpretation and expression' (cf. Schütz, 1973). Values should be studied more as ideologically and culturally situated argumentative resources: *ways of talking* about people, society and democracy, and less as *predictions* based on statistical models, or emergent *properties* of aggregation across contexts and life experiences.

The social organisation of values constructs various argumentative and social positions that are otherwise obscured by the aggregation of individual responses. Aggregation-based accounts and concerns with taxonomies of values tend to downplay or ignore the extraordinary

---

[18] For instance, in their 2005 book Inglehart and Welzel spend an entire chapter on a predictive analysis of the results of the new wave of surveys based on previous findings. What this shows is that the model 'works', is highly predictive. What it also shows is that what you know predicts more of what you already know.

diversity that characterises modern mass expression of values (Kinder, 2006). Human values are described as macrosocial and 'objective' variables with predictive power, variables that influence individual dispositions, orientations, political actions, political attitudes, and so on. There is an entrenched belief that, unless aggregated, human values are unobservable hidden sources of social action lodged in people's heads. The contemporary political psychology of values defines them broadly as symbolic, omnibus dimensions that describe political behaviour across a multitude of different socio-political contexts. But social and political reality is likely more complex than academic (or political) commentary; the discourse and the paradigms of political psychologists should reflect that. The vocabularies of values are open-textured language games. Thus, the point is to present not only a distribution of values, but also things that are harder to see or intuit, less accessible situations, frameworks of meaning, feelings and circumstances which underlie values and their expression, and how values are diffused in time and social space.

Whose values? Universalism and particularism in the structure of human values

The political psychology of human values starts from the premise that it is vital to measure the standards and criteria that people use in their interpretations of themselves, others, or social and political action. As this chapter has shown, political psychologists are striving to find matches between survey data and political culture, between patterns in the data and democratic outlook, between aggregated value orientations and collective values. Yet complex socio-political realities point to an ontological hiatus between aggregate and universal academic models and contingent, contextual, individual or group manifestations of political behaviour. Value surveys put forward a vision of politics and society divided into and spread across circumplex or orthogonal dimensions and as determined by relations of probabilistic association. The usefulness of a distinction between value orientations on the basis of universal structure is itself a matter of value judgement and value orientation. It is debatable and requires as much discussion as the specific values or value orientations that it contains or reflects.

This chapter has argued that values should be treated as argumentative resources that inform the evaluative logic of individual or group descriptions and judgements. We know that each society devises and upholds its own cultural methods in their use and 'trading off' of values. Values in general refer back to relations between individuals and not to statistical aggregates or 'statistical citizens' (Igo, 2007). As some of the research reviewed in this chapter has shown, values and value orientations are social and political resources conventionally tied to group and community membership, social relationships, personal experience, knowledge in the public sphere, power relations and wider political action. It is this normative tying-up that social actors themselves make relevant in the course of confronting, understanding and interpreting different aspects of their societies' past, present and future.

The most pressing issue arising from research on human values, the link between self-expression values and democracy promotion, is one that requires further unpacking. There is a question that is, routinely, not asked: whose values are 'we' promoting? Moreover, a direct relation between value orientations and democracy is posited; whereas in fact the 'reality' of democracy and democratic political behaviour is much more complex. It is the fragmentary, multiple and unfinished nature of value searches and value orientations that political psychologists should emphasise more. J. S. Mill contended that (each) society required 'different opinions' and 'different experiments of living' (2008 edition, p. 30). Political psychology should strive to explore more the 'different experiments of living' that different social and political realities and organisations engender, as well those experiments of living that people themselves support, defeat, create, and so on. In doing so, political psychologists can discover explicit but also latent ideological themes, can discern better the structure of political behaviour and thought both in its premises, as well as in its application to real life.

et al.'s (1950)'s 'authoritarian personality' to the clusters of attitudes facilitated by social learning of Altemeyer (1981, 1996), and the more recent model of the interaction between authoritarian predisposition and threat of Stenner (2005), social and political psychologists have tried to establish a clear link between authoritarianism and prejudice by demonstrating the existence and pervasiveness of a predisposition to intolerance (Duckitt, 2003). This has arisen out of the awareness of the danger that Adorno's 'authoritarian type of man' would replace Allport's 'democratic person'. Although the Authoritarian Personality study has come under intense criticism (see Brown, 1995; Martin, 2001; Roiser and Willig, 2002), it has also been described as 'the single most important contribution to the psychology of fascism' and as 'a major landmark in the history of psychology' (Billig, 1978, p. 36). It still gathers quite a sizeable intellectual and empirical support (see Winter, 2006 for a defence of the appropriateness of the continual development of 'authoritarianism' research).

The authoritarian mindset

'Some people never live comfortably in a modern liberal democracy.' This is how a contemporary social psychologist opens her book on what she terms the 'authoritarian dynamic' (Stenner, 2005). This is a similar point to the one that Adorno *et al.* (1950 [1982]) were making in *The Authoritarian Personality*. Under the influence of the Freudian psychodynamic tradition, prejudice was seen as intrapsychically determined. For instance, one of the concerns of the seminal 'authoritarian personality' study was to document how personality dynamics and unresolved inner conflicts determined the extent to which stereotypes were used to discriminate self from out-groups (by making such groups homogeneous and negative). Within the context of the 'authoritarian personality', stereotypes were considered major pathologies of social cognition: they were rigidly held as protection against ambivalence and ambiguity, were considered fundamentally incorrect and derogatory generalisations about groups of people.

As Billig (1978) suggests, with writers such as Adorno *et al.* ([1950] 1982) and precursors such as Fromm (1942), 'ideas directly derived from psychoanalytic theory found their way into the traditions of empirical social psychology' (p. 31).[2] Adorno and colleagues were

---

[2] Imbued with influences from Marxist social theory, Freudian and neo-Freudian psychoanalysis, the 'authoritarian personality' analyses of racism have attempted to link prejudice and socialisation practices. Adorno *et al.*'s (1950) authoritarian personality' includes elements from both perspectives with an emphasis on the broader ideological and characterological patterns that would explain anti-Semitism.

interested in mapping the psychological basis of what they came to describe as 'authoritarian' forms of political ideology. Starting with the rather simple question of why do competing political ideologies have such differing degree of appeal for different individuals (Adorno *et al.*, 1950, p. 2ff.), they were interested in charting individual differences in ideological affiliation. The main assumption behind this was that there is an intricate relation between the content of an ideology and psychodynamic factors of personality structure. For Adorno *et al.*, political and social attitudes of an individual cluster together and are the expression of 'deep lying trends in personality' (Adorno *et al.*, 1950, p. 1). Adorno and colleagues were interested in what (type of personality) rendered people *susceptible* to racist or fascist ideas. They were interested to describe the 'authoritarian' personality of the *potential* fascist. The 'authoritarian personality' was seen as a complex syndrome of behaviours, attitudes and dispositions consisting of nine dimensions, including an overly rigid cognitive style, which does not easily accommodate ambivalence and ambiguity, conventionalism, authoritarian submission and aggression, stereotypy and destructiveness (cf. Adorno *et al.*, [1950] 1982).

The rationale of Adorno *et al.* was that it should be possible to measure prejudice by describing the fascist (authoritarian) personality without precise reference to a particular ethnic group – the hope was that they could offer a *general* theory of prejudice. Adorno *et al.*'s exegesis turned the F-scale into *the* measure of 'authoritarianism' (for critiques see Billig, 1978, 1985; Heaven, 2001; Stenner, 2005). However, some other researchers (e.g. Siegman, 1961) concluded that, although the basic theory of Adorno *et al.* was confirmed, not all prejudices were related to the authoritarian personality. Research conducted by Pettigrew (1958) in South Africa and the southern USA has offered evidence that in some cultures the pressure to conform to racist views is so powerful that it has a significant effect on personal views. Authoritarianism alone is not sufficient to account for the differences in prejudice and the levels of support for racial discrimination.

Research has also revealed a range of methodological and theoretical flaws in Adorno *et al.*'s research (Brown, 1965; Christie and Jahoda, 1954; Rokeach, 1956; see also Altemeyer, 1981 and Billig, 1978). Problems were identified with the design and validation of the F-scale and mainly the reported correlations with variables such as intelligence, social class or level of education, which, when investigated closely, suggest alternative explanations for the genesis of authoritarianism. Altemeyer (1981) has levelled important criticism related to the F scale. He argues that the nine components said to comprise authoritarianism are too vague and he offers evidence in support of the idea that successive factor analytic studies have failed to uncover the nine dimensions, which are said to form the core of 'authoritarianism'. A more important criticism of Adorno *et al.*'s research was that it dealt with only a variant of authoritarianism, namely right-wing authoritarianism. The argument that people with other political views are also authoritarian and hence also prejudiced was developed and turned into a systematic psychological theory by Rokeach (1956, 1960).[3]

Altemeyer (1981, 1996) has revived the interest in authoritarianism and concerns with its measurement. He proposes the notion of 'right-wing authoritarianism' (RWA), which comprises three dimensions: authoritarian submission to authority, authoritarian aggression and conventionalism (adherence to social conventions). Altemeyer (1981, 1996) moves authoritarianism from a psychodynamic to a social learning perspective. The RWA scale, Altemeyer's creation, was not, technically, a personality scale. As Reynolds and Turner (2001) argue, the RWA scale could be seen 'as a measure of widespread societal values and ideologies rather than an assessment of an individual's personality' (p. 177; see also Billig, 1976). Altemeyer himself was cautious about whether RWA was a personality scale at all. Notwithstanding the quite significant links between RWA and prejudice in a variety of settings and with diverse samples from different cultures, laboratory research has demonstrated that RWA only predicts prejudice under particular conditions (for a recent account see Cohrs and Stelzl, 2010).[4]

Other researchers have argued that the salience of personal and social identity was also important in understanding prejudice (cf. Reynolds and Turner, 2001; see also Haslam and Wilson, 2000; Verkuyten and Hagendoorn, 1998). Too close a focus on personality can lead to the underestimation of the 'power and importance of the immediate social

---

[3] The syndrome of intolerance was labelled the 'closed mind' or dogmatic personality. At the other end of the continuum, Rokeach talked about the 'open mind' or the non-prejudiced person (Rokeach, 1960). Another attempt to link personality to prejudice was made by Eysenck (1954). In a similar fashion to Rokeach, Eysenck argued that people's propensity towards intolerance was independent of their endorsement of left- or right-wing ideology. This tendency was called 'tough-mindedness' as opposed to 'tender-mindedness' and was associated with the personality trait of extraversion (and, later, psychoticism). Controversially, Eysenck went as far as to suggest that people's attitudes, including their level of prejudice, could be genetically determined.

[4] In an attempt to extend Altemeyer's unidimensional model, Duckitt *et al.* (2010) propose a tripartite approach to right-wing authoritarianism: the Authoritarianism-Conservatism-Traditionalism model of RWA based on the covariation of three traits: authoritarian submission, authoritarian aggression and conventionalism. For Duckitt and colleagues, authoritarianism, conservatism and traditionalism are three distinct, yet related, 'ideological attitude constructs'.

situation in shaping people's attitudes' (Brown, 1995, p. 31; see also Augoustinos and Reynolds, 2001). This criticism is linked with the unaccounted for influence of other people's attitudes, the norms of the group and intergroup relations. Situational and societal norms, intergroup contact, the relations with the others, and the historical specificity of prejudice can prove to have a more critical influence than any personality disposition (e.g. Duckitt, 1988; Pettigrew, 1958). It was suggested that authoritarianism may actually be an effect of sociocultural and historical conditions rather than deriving from particular inner dispositions or child-rearing patterns.[5]

Contemporary approaches to 'authoritarianism' retain the essence of Adorno's seminal argument: social and political psychologists can predict a range of (anti-democratic) attitudes, world views and opinions only by assuming the existence of some *common*, relatively enduring predisposition to intolerance (of difference). The notion of 'authoritarianism' refers to people whose political (and everyday) behaviour is influenced by 'deep-seated predispositions', which are associated with moderate or extreme anti-democratic stances. For instance, in a cross-national survey of attitudes of college and university students towards authority, democracy and educational policy choices, Farnen and Meloen (2000) show that higher authoritarianism levels tend to be associated with low scores on democratic attitudes and internationalism, and higher ones on nationalism and militarism, and support for monocultural, rather than multicultural, educational policy options.

For some authors, the authoritarian mindset is not characteristic to any particular society or era; it is a universal phenomenon (Stenner, 2005). Stenner offers a 'dynamic' model of authoritarianism that claims to overcome the difficulties of Adorno's and Altemeyer's models. Stenner (2005) proposes a simpler model based on two descriptive variables and their interaction: authoritarian predisposition and conditions of threat. The interaction between the two variables is tested in various domains of intolerance – racial, political and moral intolerance, and explored through in-depth interviews with 'authoritarian' and 'libertarian' participants. Stenner *universalises* the antecedents and consequences of authoritarian predispositions. According to her we

need not resort to particularistic accounts … the peculiar propensities or traditions of different peoples and cultures, or simmering ethnic tensions kept in

---

[5] Another limitation of any personality account is its inability to explain the uniformity of prejudiced attitudes across whole groups of people and its difficulty in explaining how it is that prejudice can become virtually consensual in certain societies (e.g. the former apartheid society in South Africa) and why certain groups rather than others are more likely to become the target of (historical) prejudice.

check by charismatic leaders. The Serbs are intolerant of the Croats for the same reasons (i.e., from the same sources) that the Croats are intolerant of the Serbs, which are the same reasons the Germans are intolerant of those seeking refuge from this genocidal conflict, that the Czechs are intolerant of the Roma and the French of North African immigrants, and that all are intolerant of dissidents, deviants, and criminals. (Stenner, 2005, p. 115)

The quotation encapsulates Stenner's position. Stenner points to a common source and a universal process that applies across groups and across socio-political contexts. One very interesting aspect of Stenner's dynamic model of authoritarianism is given by the in-depth interviews which she conducted with what she described as 'extremely authoritarian' and 'extremely libertarian' participants. By manipulating the race of interviewers and type of interviewer ('primary' and 'partner'), Stenner wanted to see whether authoritarian predisposition could predict actual behaviour towards different others. The interviews (conducted by two interviewing partners) consisted of a general discussion of American society, including a dialogue on issues such as race, minority rights, government, education, and so on.

Stenner showed, for instance, how, when contacted by a White interviewer 'authoritarians' were more willing to be interviewed than when contacted by an African American interviewer. In contrast, no 'libertarian' has expressed any reluctance when contacted by an African American interviewer. When the interviewing partner was African American 'authoritarians' were more inclined than 'libertarians' to 'display more hostility' – this was based on the impressions and ratings of the interviewers from the interview. Both 'primary' and 'partner' interviewers judged 'authoritarians' 'a good deal less intelligent than libertarians' (Stenner, 2005, p. 213). 'Authoritarians' were also described generally as less interested in the discussion and as 'less appealing as a person' than 'libertarians'. This seemed more to be the case for African American 'primary' and 'partner' interviewers. 'Authoritarians' were perceived as 'more guarded, dishonest, and evasive than libertarians' around an African American 'partner' interviewer. 'Authoritarians' 'seemed uncomfortable talking about race' (2005, p. 227) in the presence of an African American person.[6] Libertarians' open-mindedness was noted by both White and African American interviewers; they were also generally perceived as happier, active and gregarious people.

---

[6] 'Authoritarians' were perceived as intimidating, tough, and male-oriented in their discourse. When the interviewer was African American 'authoritarians' were described as 'bitter' and 'unfriendly', even 'psychologically/emotionally disturbed'.

Stenner reduces the 'characteriological' descriptions of her interviewers to 'traits', relatively stable characteristics of a person. She comes up with a range of attributes, inner 'essences' that describe 'authoritarians', on the one hand, and 'libertarians', on the other. 'Authoritarians' and 'libertarians' are two clearly distinguished 'characters' that shape everything, from inter-individual behaviour to societal responses to social problems. An analysis of the actual content of these interviews revealed a manifest difference between 'authoritarians' and 'libertarians'. Generally, 'authoritarians' exhibited 'substantially greater racial animosity, prejudice and discrimination than libertarians' (2005, p. 240). For instance, when discussing issues of race, 'authoritarians' were more likely to point out that African Americans had largely themselves to blame for the unequal position in society. 'Libertarians' were more inclined to argue for the necessity of more extensive contact between African Americans and Whites, and they did not perceive race relations as 'getting worse'.

Stenner is adamant that her theory 'is entirely general and the phenomenon persists cross-culturally, with little modification other than the designation of "us" and "them" and (to a lesser extent) of what counts as right and wrong' (2005, p. 9). When writing about 'authoritarians' and 'libertarians', Stenner writes implicitly about what she calls the 'paradox of American democracy'. Although it claims generality, across contexts, her argument is very much located in a very peculiar social and political organisation, that of the USA. The image that Stenner conveys is also that of unchanging authoritarianism. She goes as far to suggest, quite disturbingly, that 'authoritarians' cannot be expected to change, as they are predisposed to exhibit such traits and behaviours (cf. Winter, 2006). Stenner's view is close to that of other researchers that suggest a link between personality traits and underlying genetic factors (Verhulst et al., 2012).

Whether in its psychodynamic interpretation or contemporary interactive models, one of the principal difficulties of 'personality' research is mounting a serious challenge to societal prejudices, and the consequences of authoritarianism: racism and intolerance. Personality-based accounts need to be complemented with perspectives that emphasise the diverse social positions, discourses, motivations, reasons, and so on that social actors produce, use and enact in social and political life. For instance, research has shown that questions such as what motivates people to join right-wing parties, or what factors are related to the popularity of right-wing extremism, can be answered with less emphasis on 'authoritarian' personalities and more on individual reasons and motivations, biographies and sociocultural contexts. It is not enough to say that democracy is threatened by authoritarian predispositions. One also needs to understand the manifestation and display of everyday prejudices, tolerant or intolerant stances, and their various personal, social and ideological consequences.

Social psychological aspects of extremism and right-wing activism

The 'authoritarian' personality is not the exact opposite of the 'democratic' personality. Contemporary analyses of extremism and right-wing activism support this conclusion and paint a complex picture of intolerance. The various social and political discussions around what draws people to the extreme – what 'radicalises' them – seem to move slowly away from an understanding in terms of personality structures and predisposition to intolerance, to social identification and the role of self-categorisation (Perreault and Bourhis, 1999; Reynolds *et al.* 2007; Verkuyten and Hagendoorn, 1998).

Verkuyten and Hagendoorn (1998) explored the level of prejudice towards Turkish people living in the Netherlands. They manipulated participants' identification by making salient either personal identity (as individuals) or their national identity (as members of the national group, Dutch). Authoritarianism correlated significantly with prejudice in the personal-identity condition, but not in the national-identity condition. What Verkuyten and Hagendoorn show is that the salience of identity (personal vs. social/national) matters, and mediates the expression of prejudice. Thus the antecedents of prejudice may be related to authoritarian predisposition in some circumstances, but not in others; what matters is the participants' contextually salient self-categorisation (see also Chapter 5 for other examples that emphasise the role and importance of the context of self-categorisation). In a minimal group setting, Perreault and Bourhis (1999) aimed to explore the role and effect of intrapersonal variables on in-group identification and discrimination. Authoritarianism (alongside ethnocentrism and personal need for structure) was included in the analysis as possible predictors of in-group identification and out-group discrimination. Minimal groups were then created by random allocation or personal choice. Perreault and Bourhis found that ethnocentrism (but not authoritarianism) was positively correlated with in-group identification, and discrimination of out-groups. In the same vein, using the minimal group paradigm, Reynolds *et al.* (2007) conducted a series of experiments to see whether personality can explain in-group identification and discrimination. They found no evidence of significant relationships between traditional personality measures and either in-group identification or discrimination.

The rise and appeal of right-wing politics in Europe is a puzzling phenomenon. Focusing solely on the authoritarian and ethnocentric mindset, one is restricting the scope of critical explorations.[7] Some researchers claim that extremism can be understood with reference to the process of uncertainty reduction. It is generally believed that 'right-wing political ideologies are better suited than left-wing liberal ideologies to reducing uncertainty' (Hogg and Blaylock, 2012). In a study trying to link uncertainty and threat, Doosje *et al.* (in press) examine the radicalisation process among Dutch Muslim youth. They found that four social psychological variables are most likely to predict 'radicalisation': personal uncertainty, perceived injustice, perceived group threat and a feeling of being socially disconnected.

There is a tendency (both within the academic community and in the public sphere) to paint extremism as the absolute political evil. In the most common view, extremism 'means going beyond the limits of the normative procedures which define the democratic political process' (Klandermans and Mayer, 2006, p. 4). Yet, what is ignored is that both extremism and moderation have different meanings for different people; they acquire meaning in social contexts. An example is offered by Hopkins and Kahani-Hopkins (2009), who explore social actors' own meanings associated with 'extremism' and '"moderation'. They analyse Muslim community speeches and show the diversity of self- and social identity constructions, and constructions of 'extremism'. They show how self- and social identity constructions are linked to collective action projects which, in turn, bring to the fore, make salient, different sociocultural benchmarks against which 'deviant ... versions of identity may be judged and extremism identified' (p. 111). The Muslim speakers that Hopkins and Kahani-Hopkins analyse mobilise different constructions of 'extremism' (e.g. as antithetical to Islam) that support politicised identity projects and drive political arguments against essentialist constructions of Muslim identity (see Chapter 5 for a detailed discussion of collective and politicised identity). Hopkins and Kahani-Hopkins show that extremism and moderation cannot be approached in *abstract*, but rather as part of social activities and accounts of which they are part, and as serving specific social functions.

---

[7] See Billig (1985) for an early critique of the social psychology of extremism and moderation, and Backes (2009) for a conceptual history of political extremism. On the extreme right in Europe see Backes and Moreau (2011).

Although political psychology has made significant advances in understanding the more formal aspects of extremism (its link with authoritarianism, ethnocentrism, socioeconomic status), we know less of how individuals themselves account for (their) extremism, radicalism and moderation. Pioneering studies have aimed to redress the balance. Take, for instance, the thorny issue of how people decide to become paramilitaries in Northern Ireland. In interviews with individuals who had used violence to pursue political goals during the conflict in Northern Ireland, Ferguson and colleagues (Ferguson *et al.*, 2008) show how joining the paramilitary involves a process of rational decision-making as opposed to being an irrational response provoked by a deep-seated predisposition to violence or the 'environment'. Ferguson *et al.* show individuals actively deciding to seek membership of an armed group after witnessing a critical incident. Moreover, Ferguson and colleagues show that there are psychological costs attached to perpetrating acts of violence (Ferguson *et al.*, 2010) and that people are very much aware of these costs. Violence (and in this case, radicalism) is linked with and anchored within individual and group identity projects. In the same vein, Burgess *et al.* (2007) have conducted interviews with former IRA members and peaceful civil rights organisations. They show a complex image of how individuals experience daily life in a community where potential for future violence lurks under the surface. Burgess and colleagues show how people use the vocabulary of 'sectarianism' to account for their daily experiences. They note a tension, an expressed 'fear of the other', in accounts of former IRA members. They also show how the termination of involvement with paramilitary groups is associated with both pride, but also guilt.

In their ground-breaking study on the lives of extreme-right activists in Europe, Klandermans and Mayer (2006) treat right-wing extremism as a social movement. They held 150 in-depth interviews with active participants in right-wing organisations in the Netherlands, Belgium, France, Italy and Germany. The authors contend that right-wing extremists have a different 'profile' compared to voters or general sympathisers of right-wing parties. Klandermans and Mayer do not paint extremism as the absolute political evil. Authors argue against describing too hastily extremism in terms of an attitudinal cluster comprising authoritarianism, social isolation, lack of education, and economic insecurity. In contrast, Klandermans and Mayer start from the idea that participation to right-wing organisations or movements 'is as equally rational as in any other movement or organization' (p. 7). They show how not all right-wing organisations are the same; they show that there are different 'motives' and 'motivations' that drive participation and political action. For instance, in Italy, the issue of historical 'continuity' and family socialisation are the leitmotifs of fascist identity. France presents a completely different pattern; it is more heterogeneous, with 'the longest and most diversified tradition to build on' (p. 13). In Belgium, Flemish nationalism is a much more potent motive than xenophobia, whereas German activists construct their identities around nationalism as a collective identity.

The picture painted by Klandermans and Mayer is at odds with authoritarian personality accounts. This is not to say that prejudices are less daunting, just that the *source* of these prejudices is to be found somewhere else. Even when right-wing extremists are found to be authoritarian and ethnocentric, these are features less of personality, and more of biography, history and personal and organisational context. Intra-individual explanations do not account fully for the diversity of political behaviours, especially those around extremism, activism, participation, and so on. It is crucial to appreciate that individuals have agency: they can act on themselves and others; they can position themselves and others; and they can play an active role in drawing the boundaries of their ideological self-positioning.

Prejudice as social accomplishment

As the previous section has shown, legitimations of the status quo and extremist and right-wing ideologies do not always reproduce themselves through the inflexibility of the authoritarian mindset. Discourse analytic studies of racism complement this observation by showing how racist legitimations of social formations and unequal power relations can be both liberal and authoritarian in form (see Billig, 1991; Condor, 2006; van Dijk, 1984; Wetherell and Potter, 1992). Racist discourse is flexible and not the upshot of relatively enduring structures of an authoritarian or dogmatic personality. Prejudice presents rhetorical and ideological aspects (Billig, 1985, 2012).

As argued earlier, Stenner's argument relies on the idea that some fellow citizens are 'imperfect democratic citizens' (2005, p. 1). There is a wide array of stances considered to be damaging to liberal democracy, and these can be described by turning to personality. We need to understand not only inner 'fundamental' predispositions that may lie 'behind' such stances, but also the social circumstances and social practices in which these stances are enacted, are played up, how they are collaboratively, discursively and socially accomplished.

Everyday racism can play a pivotal role in the reproduction of prejudice and intolerance. In her analysis of the everyday language of White racism, Hill (2008) shows that language and culture are the main constituents of a range of presuppositions, forms of expression and practices of everyday racism. Commonsensical meanings we attach to race and racism, to language and the way in which we use language are said to be an integral part of how racism operates and perpetuates itself in society. Hill refers to the role of shared cultural understanding and human interaction, the implicatures, presuppositions, 'invitations and clues, the silences, the inferences that the literal content of a text or an utterance invites' (2008, p. 33). She shows, for instance, how racist metaphors and parodic imitations of Spanish, Arab and Latino accents in American everyday discourse are difficult to challenge (some of them are not even perceived as 'racist') because of their embeddedness in engrained ritualised discursive habits and social practices, and folk theories of race and racism. The examples of Native American, African American English and US Spanish linguistic 'appropriations' (most of them implicitly mocking the language and character of people) are offered as illustrations of 'invisible', yet pernicious, White racism. According to Hill, these are covert forms of racism that do not seem to require explanation as they are part and parcel of American English linguistic practice.

It is not only the language of ethnic minorities that is being mocked, but also their character and way of being. In everyday discourse, ethnic minorities are 'abnormalised' (Verkuyten, 2001) and reduced to group 'essences'. Extreme right-wing ideology is perhaps one of the most productive environments for the expression of prejudiced, 'essentialist' thinking about those designated as Others. Holtz and Wagner (2009) analyse postings on an extreme right-wing Internet discussion board and show a differential racist discourse directed at 'preferred' target groups: Jews and Africans/Blacks. In traditional conspiratory style, Jews are perceived as 'super-human' agents of control and world domination. 'Blacks' are perceived as endangering the 'purity' of the German race.

Holtz and Wagner argue that prejudiced discourses 'essentialise' the specific groups, giving them immutable, unchanging group-specific attributes. It is implied that 'essentialism' can have only negative, oppressive effects. In a very ingenious study, Verkuyten (2003) shows how essentialist talk can have both oppressive and progressive effects. In group discussions about Dutch society, ethnic Dutch and ethnic minority members flexibly define and use essentialist notions about ethnic groups. Verkuyten argues that essentialism is not necessarily oppressive, but rather 'a flexible conversational resource which is variously defined and deployed, depending on the interactional task at hand'

(p. 374). Verkuyten shows that both majority group members and ethnic minorities can use 'essentialist' talk, but they put it to different uses. For example, cultural 'de-essentialism' can work as a useful strategy for ethnic minorities to challenge and resist negative majority group representations and category descriptions (Leudar and Nekvapil, 2000).

In an excellent discussion of public discourses on asylum and asylum seekers (letters written to British national newspapers by members of the public), Lynn and Lea (2003) show how asylum seekers are written about in such a way as to justify a different, non-humanitarian treatment. Lynn and Lea note the extensive use of extreme case formulations and rhetorical questions to argue for treating asylum seeking as a 'problem'. The moral issue of integrity (of both asylum seekers and the state) was linked to a differentiation between 'bogus' and 'genuine' asylum seekers. A (pre)disposition discourse is used to legitimise racist discourse; its function is to essentialise the characteristics of social groups, to 'differentiate' between self and other, in-group and outgroup. Asylum seekers were constructed as being predisposed to 'succumb to a greedy, duplicitous and inherently criminal nature' (p. 447). Lynn and Lea note how 'disposition' is not so much an enduring structure, but rather a discursive construction and accomplishment. Using specific terms and references to an inner (pre)disposition to act or behave in a particular way, Lynn and Lea show how letter writers construct a special 'character' for people perceived as not entitled to live in British society.

In the same vein, focusing on discourses of immigration in the Netherlands, Verkuyten (2005) shows that social actors have a tendency to use familiar tropes, culturally available ways of talking about choice, entitlement and multiculturalism, to distinguish between categories of immigrants: 'real' vs. 'economic' refugees, 'fortune seekers', 'migrant labourers'. He also shows how both positive and negative social judgements on multiculturalism are shaped by the way categories of immigrants are 'defined' on the basis of certain 'dispositions' to behave in a particular way.

Prejudice denial in dialogue is one of the most pervasive moves in the management of prejudice in talk (Condor et al., 2006; van Dijk, 1992). When one studies prejudice using methodologies that rely on social encounters (e.g. semi-structured or open-ended interviews, focus groups) one should treat these encounters as social interactions in their own right. This has implications for researching the expression, denial and mitigation of prejudice in social dialogue. For instance, in multiparty conversations (interviews or focus groups) participants themselves may 'police' the expression or suppression of prejudiced talk (see

Condor *et al.*, 2006). Most of these social encounters can be treated as dialogic encounters where prejudiced talk is securely embedded in the 'delicate choreography of everyday sociability' (Condor, 2006, p. 15).

In a series of studies (Condor, 2006; Condor *et al.*, 2006), Condor and colleagues show how one can conceive of prejudiced talk as a collaborative accomplishment.[8] They show how hearably problematic (xenophobic) comments are 'defended' or disclaimed not only by their producers but also by the other participants to the conversation. Potential and actual charges of prejudice are dealt with dialogically, as conversational partners may attempt to 'deflect' accusations of prejudice. This is achieved through pronominal shifts (from 'I' to 'we' or from 'you' to 'we'), corrections and repairs, or through working rhetorically against the idea that the conversational partner is the kind of person who is prejudiced, and whose behaviour is a product of their 'disposition'. Participants' potentially prejudiced accounts are contingent on other interlocutors reinforcing, minimising or nuancing their positions, or sometimes giving them a suitable conversational opening, or allowing them to take and/or retain the floor. What Condor shows is that prejudiced discourse is *occasioned* in social interaction.[9] The responsibility for public expressions of ethnic and racial dislike does not lie in people's personalities. Public expression of prejudice does not represent the continuously monitored expression of inner cognitions, feelings, attitudes, and so on. Rather public prejudice is collaborative and strategic social action.

Moral exclusion and bigotry: delegitimisation and dehumanisation

As argued earlier, Stenner uses in-depth interviews with 'extremely authoritarian' and 'extremely libertarian' subjects to 'put a face' on her theory, to complement experimental results. She is claiming that by focusing on 'traits' one is able to clearly discriminate between the attitudes of 'authoritarian' and 'libertarian' subjects. Although in some contexts the distinction can be sustained, the case of extreme prejudice and moral exclusion presents an interesting example for reframing such a conclusion.

---

[8] For an overview on research on prejudice as an emergent product of social interaction, see Condor and Figgou (2012).

[9] See also Stokoe and Edwards (2007) on how potential accusations of prejudice in police and neighbour mediation interviews are occasioned and managed in social interaction.

There have been recent calls for a move 'beyond prejudice' (Dixon and Levine, 2012), beyond the traditional distinction between 'old' and 'new' racism (Pehrson and Leach, 2012). This move entails primarily taking into account the existence of different types of prejudice and the idea that not all prejudices (and for that matter, all target groups) are the same. Words are not just words. Words 'wound' (Matsuda et al., 1993), and they have ideological consequences for the construction of people as beyond the civilised moral order.

The moral exclusionary discourse directed at Romany or Gypsy people in Europe is a case in point. For instance, Tileagă (2005, 2006, 2007) shows how, when it comes to the Roma, both supporters of right-wing policies and those opposing these express extremely prejudiced comments. He identifies a 'consensus' around a moral exclusionary discourse against the Roma in Europe (a discourse that is different from prejudiced discourse on other minorities) that denies them humanity, places them outside the boundary where moral values, rules and considerations of fairness apply (cf. Opotow, 1990).

There is a well-established link between prejudice, delegitimisation and dehumanisation, from Tajfel's earlier studies (e.g. Tajfel, 1969) to more recent social psychological analyses (e.g. Bastian and Haslam, 2011; Haslam and Loughnan, 2012; Leyens et al., 2003; Moscovici and Pérez, 2005). For instance, Tajfel used the term 'depersonalisation' to refer to a 'milder' form of dehumanisation of out-groups (Tajfel, 1981a) without elaborating on the possible continuum between depersonalisation and dehumanisation. Depersonalisation has been mostly restricted to the depersonalisation of the self (e.g. in self-categorisation theory) and understood as a 'cognitive process that somehow lies behind language' (Billig, 2002, p.184). What social and political psychologists do not sometimes explicitly state is that it is 'primarily and sometimes exclusively by moral discourse that we separate from and exclude others' (Graumann, 1998, p. 47). One needs to investigate how particular ways of speaking might depersonalise (and sometimes, dehumanise) the 'other'; and how depersonalisation and dehumanisation are actually accomplished in interaction and in talk about 'others'. What experimental social psychologists call 'humanness' is not only a 'fundamental dimension of social perception' (Haslam and Loughnan, 2012, p. 91), but also a discursive accomplishment. There is no one dimension of humanity that can be operationalised, but rather analysts need to account for 'the continuum between prejudice and bigotry or between depersonalisation and dehumanisation' (cf. Billig, 2002, p. 183). Rather than conceiving, for example, concerns with delegitimisation and dehumanisation as reflections of what people carry inside their heads, people can be shown to flexibly work up, formulate the nature of actions, events, their and other people's accountability through ways of talking that depersonalise, delegitimise and dehumanise a particular group.

As Tileagă (2005, 2007) has shown, dehumanisation constitutes an extreme form of depersonalisation, a process that takes place in and through language, a matter of a contextual and discursive 'application' of a moral, as opposed to an intra-psychic, order. In his analyses of semi-structured interviews with middle-class Romanian professionals, discussing generally 'controversial' issues regarding prejudice and prejudice-related issues in the Romanian society, Tileagă showed that prejudiced and discriminatory discourse against the Romanies not only comes from political extremists, but also from across the whole Romanian civic and political spectrum. Both participants 'supporting' extremist politics and those 'opposing' it describe the Romanies as out-of-place, transgressing civilised conduct, as abject, as repulsive (or as inviting repulsion) (see Tileagă, 2006 for an example). These descriptions act as symbolic resources for reproducing their delegitimisation, their depersonalisation (and ultimately their dehumanisation). The behaviour and 'way of being' of Romanies is being problematised by pointing to 'extreme' cases and exceptional behaviour. They are presented as transgressing moral (and spatial) boundaries, and as a consequence are typically classified as 'matter out of place'. They are seen as violating social and moral conventions, placing them beyond what is *deemed* acceptable.

With extraordinary frequency, Romanies are presented as a 'problem' without a 'solution'. Evidence is also presented that rational solutions to the 'problem' have not worked. The implicit message is that there is no rational solution to deal with 'them'. Being cast as the 'problem' that calls for a solution, the Romanies are not regarded anymore as moral subjects, they are denied an autonomous moral standing in the world. For some people, they are the 'scum of society', for others they are not only dirty, they are literally 'dirt'. Various metaphors of residue (dirt, scum, etc.) are used as metaphors for residual people. To categorise Romanies as residual, as abject, means ignoring their visible human qualities and to allude to a conclusion with eliminationist connotations. Tileagă demonstrates how extreme prejudiced discourse is carefully managed: potentially eliminationist premises are there, are explicit, but not the conclusion. The conclusion is something that cannot be stated directly. Immoral and socially forbidden desires lurk under the surface of ideologies of moral exclusion.

When one is considering delegitimisation, depersonalisation and dehumanisation as discursive practices, one might also want to take into account that the dialogue between the interviewer and the interviewee might create its own unsaid matters. As Billig (1999) put it, dialogue provides the resources for a process of 'social repression' in relation to a specific category of people, that 'we', the settled, the civilised, and so on categorise as out-of-place, as abject, as horrible and deplorable, and try to place beyond reasonable bounds and moral 'being' in the world.

Extreme prejudice can be seen as an interactional accomplishment, rather than the expression of an inner racist predisposition. One needs to take into account the social context (in this case, the social research interview) in which attitudes (racist or otherwise) are expressed. One can also extend the analysis beyond the boundaries of the activities involved in interview-talk (Condor, 2006; Wetherell, 1998, 2003), placing them within discursive history, the social, political and ideological context. Accounts analysed by Tileagă (2007) are not intrinsically depersonalising, delegitimising or dehumanising. For example, in some circumstances, Romanies were not directly denied humanity, but they were nevertheless presented as the 'wrong sort' of human beings (Rorty, 1989) and in the 'wrong place'. As they were being cast as abject, as matter 'out-of-place', Romanies are not portrayed as sharing the same moral 'community' as other groups (Romanians, Hungarians and other ethnic minority groups). Discourses of extreme prejudice and difference are marked by an absence: Romanies have no homeland like other nations. As such, extreme prejudice contains or implies the 'differentiating power' of the absence of a national space.

Extending the scope of the political psychology of intolerance

This chapter has argued that in order to understand the nature of intolerance, prejudice and racism, one needs to pay close attention to what people say, to how prejudice or intolerance may be, on some occasions, a collaborative discursive accomplishment or an issue of delegitimising and dehumanising descriptions of people. One of Allport's (1954) hopes was that the person could be, ultimately, 'liberated' from under the sway of ethnic or political prejudice. Hope is, after all, the essence of liberalism.

Some political psychologists may think that Allport would have envied the contemporary multilevel and predictive techniques of contemporary social and political psychologists. That we will never know. But what we do know (or at least can infer from Allport's writings) is that for Allport studying the 'nature of prejudice' involved primarily the study, in its own right, of the sociocultural context in which prejudiced attitudes develop, are produced and reproduced. It is this context that the contemporary multilevel and predictive techniques of contemporary social and political psychologists neglect.

This chapter has argued that the specific psychological features of intolerance and moral exclusion cannot be reduced to inner mental predispositions or basic personality dispositions. One cannot understand fully the manifestations of extremism, the appeal and manifestations of right-wing extremism in Western Europe or extreme moral exclusionary discourse against the Romanies in Eastern Europe if one studies intolerance as a predisposition and authoritarian mindset. Intolerance needs to be taken seriously and studied in its own right, as something that is actively displayed, interpreted, defended, and so on in and as part of various social activities. A comprehensive political psychology of intolerance would include concerns with generality and universalism balanced, complemented by attention to culture, language, social interaction, and the actual ways in which intolerance is enacted and accomplished in social practices.

Research on the 'authoritarian mindset' tends to focus on a social type, a particular *type of person*, who, as Stenner argues, 'cannot treat with natural ease or generosity those who are not his own kindred or kind' (2005, p. 1). Yet what this approach neglects is that every society continually produces a stock of prejudices, common-sense experiences and knowledge that ordinary people use to operate distinctions between 'us' and 'them'. This stock of prejudices cannot be simply inferred from 'personality' or the internal organisation of mental processes. One should consider instead where are they located; where is their 'home'. Their 'home' is the ordinary organisation of social and language practices. Tolerance and intolerance are not just the appendage of the open-minded diametrically opposed to the closed-minded person, but rather dialogical *topoi* that span the entire political and ideological spectrum, from left to right, from liberalism to conservatism.

4   Social representations of political affairs and beliefs

From belief systems to social representations

There is an explicit consensus in political psychology that the functioning of a political community is linked to the kinds and variety of beliefs that social actors (elite and mass publics) develop in relation to politically relevant objects, or ideologies, and how these beliefs are organised in relation to others. As Doise and Staerklé argue, 'democratic functioning of a political community is characterised by antagonistic positioning towards socially relevant topics' (2002, p. 153). This chapter outlines some of the issues that arise from attempts to describe the social organisation of beliefs, with an emphasis on the links between communication, identity and community, and lay constructions of political categories.

In doing so, this chapter presents the main tenets of social representations theory as a theory of social communication and social knowledge. Serge Moscovici's notion of 'social representation' is one of the concepts that has been instrumental in the crystallisation of the idea of society as a 'thinking' and 'knowledge system'. The chapter ends with a discussion of the original contribution of social representations theory to explaining the heterogeneity and diversity of social and political knowledge, the tensions, changes and transformations of modern social and political life.

When one turns to the scientific study of beliefs, one is faced with the question: how can we think about beliefs in a way that can explain the antagonistic positioning towards socially relevant topics?

Philip Converse was one of the first researchers to be interested in systematically describing the organisation of what he called 'belief systems'. Converse's *The Nature of Belief Systems in Mass Publics* (1964) is the paper that, arguably, has most influenced the way in which political psychology has developed as a discipline in the last fifty years. It has influenced work on public opinion and political ideology, but

its original focus has been a practical one: evaluating th'
itical competence of ordinary citizens.

According to Converse, a belief system is defined
ation of ideas and attitudes in which the elements ar'
by some form of constraint or functional interdepen'
2006a, p. 3). Belief systems are made up of 'idea-eleme...
in a property we shall call *centrality*, according to the role that u..
play in the belief system as a whole' (Converse, 2006a, pp. 4–5). The
multiple idea-elements of a belief system are 'socially diffused ... they
tend to be diffused in "packages," which consumers come to see as
"natural" wholes, for they are presented in such terms ("If you believe
this, then you will also believe that, for it follows in such-and-such
ways")' (2006a, pp. 8–9).

He writes about the 'well informed person' and the 'truly involved
citizen', one who absorbs contextual information to disentangle the
connections between different areas of policy and political behaviour.[1]
What is known and what is not known, what is part and not a part of a
system of beliefs is given by the flow of information that is made available, at any one time, to the person. Starting from the assumption that
'information about politics is as inequitably distributed as wealth in
the mass public' (Converse, 1962, p. 582), he proceeded to hypothesise
that the organisation of more specific attitudes into wide-ranging belief
systems will be less present as one moves 'from the most sophisticated
few toward the "grass roots"' (p. 30). Converse's political geography is
that of the 'mountain range' or 'jumbled cluster of pyramids', that show
a 'sharp delineation and differentiation in beliefs from elite apex to elite
apex but with the mass bases of the pyramids overlapping in such pro-
fusion that it would be impossible to decide where one pyramid ended
and another began' (p. 66).

Converse's approach reflects a deeply engrained tendency among
political psychologists to search, identify and describe clearly definable,
differentiated patterns of political thinking and political behaviour
(that can be easily measured, compared and contrasted, for instance)
within the cognitive functioning of the individual and leaving aside
ambiguous, less defined and differentiated, patterns, the result of

---

[1] The 'well informed person' and the 'truly involved citizen' are opposed to the 'common citizen' who can never dream of achieving the same level of political sophistication. As Converse argues, certain 'rather concrete issues' may capture his or her
attention and 'lead to some politically relevant opinion formation', yet 'this engagement of attention remains narrow ... the common citizen fails to develop more global
points of view about politics' (p. 54).

cial processes.[2] The zone of the 'elite apex' expresses a (deep) concern with order, predictability, exact measurement, of political thinking and political behaviour; the 'base' is relegated to error, confusion, bias, ambivalence.

In his quest for generality, and a fair 'map' of the distribution of political knowledge and political involvement, Converse's vision does not leave much space for the notion that political knowledge (cultural and social knowledge) is relative to its context of production, and needs to be *represented, constructed* and *transmitted* in order to function as (shared) knowledge. Converse's vision can be fruitfully complemented by social psychological approaches that share similar concerns with the organisation and distribution of social and political knowledge. Converse's notion of belief systems can be extended and related to Serge Moscovici's notion of 'social representations' (SRs), understood as shared knowledge structures about issues debated in society that orient individual, group and community positioning when judging relevant aspects of those social issues.[3]

Political world as 'thinking' and 'knowledge' system

On numerous occasions, European social psychologists have argued and demonstrated the social nature of thinking and importance of thinking in social and political life. Society is seen as thinking *with* itself and, more importantly, as *thinking itself.* Serge Moscovici refers to this phenomenon as 'thinking society' (Moscovici, 1961, 1984). Thinking is not solely an internal property of human beings, but a constitutive dimension of society. Treating thinking and communication as antinomic and dialogical (e.g. Billig, 1996; Marková, 2006; Moscovici, 1984) European social psychologists have been successful in showing how the social functioning of a political and historical community is characterised by an ongoing argumentative and dialogical positioning towards socially relevant social objects and social meanings. People think when they are arguing with others or with themselves. Social thinking is a 'shared effort', where topics of the day, social relations and social knowledge are brought under close relational scrutiny.

[2] Kuklinski and Peyton (2009), Converse (2009), and Dalton and Klingemann (2009) provide useful outlines and critiques of classic and more recent empirical work on mass belief systems.

[3] There is, nonetheless, a crucial difference of vision between the two. Whereas Converse treats political thinking, society and political world as an order, and system, of *beliefs* (that is, *products* of thinking), Moscovici treats society and political world as 'thinking' and 'knowledge' orders, systems. Whereas for Converse cognition and information are conceived as pre-given phenomena, for Moscovici social actors jointly construct their cognitions, and, in doing so, they establish social relations.

The metaphor of the 'thinking society' introduces a shift of perspective from individually structured ideologies and belief systems to social beliefs, 'atomised opinions' (Billig, 2008) and commonsense knowledge. It introduces a shift of perspective on the study of common sense in its own right, the study of the less differentiated zone of the mass bases of Converse's pyramids overlapping at the bottom. In doing so, it places social thinking at the core of a new vision of communication processes (Billig, 1987; Moscovici, 1961; Rommetveit, 1968). Moscovici's notion of the 'thinking society' is a move against the idea that 'the majority of society merely reproduced and imitates the thoughts of its elites, its avant-gardes and nothing more' (Moscovici, 1988, p. 224). The notion of the thinking society points to the variety of ways of producing, communicating, disseminating and contesting knowledge in society. It institutes a move from 'thought about the world to thought in the world' (1988, p. 230). The relation between elites and mass publics is only one of a myriad of ways in which social knowledge is managed in society.

As Moscovici has argued, 'our public life is teeming with outbursts of illusions, syncretic ideologies and arborescent beliefs' (1988, p. 244). Social knowledge is not concentrated, or distributed only 'at the top', but rather constitutes and is constituted by an interrelated system of social relations, practices, institutions, communities. It extends along a continuum from the scientific facts of scientists, the specific political knowledge of political elites to how other (meaning-making) communities produce their (own) knowledge and representations.

Moscovici does not take the 'thinking society' for granted. He is urging us to inquire into the nature of a thinking society, and to explore the epistemological, theoretical and methodological implications of treating society as a thinking system. The 'thinking society' is the setting where SRs, as constituents of common sense, are formed, asserted, circulate and are circulated, contested and where they acquire a certain autonomy in the process. What the notion of 'thinking society' also implies is a move from *processing* information to *creating* and *constructing* social meanings. Social cognition and thinking is traditionally studied in terms of bias, reasoning errors, and so on. Natural, everyday thinking is seen to reflect naive perspectives, illusory correlations, stereotypes, error, confusion and bias; it is simply seen as irrational. There is a serious disregard for natural thinking as a phenomenon worth studying in its own right. Ivana Marková (2008, p. 477) expresses the importance and constitutive nature of natural thinking for social life:

Natural thinking is the thinking of daily life to which all humans are adapted. It is the thinking that uses knowledge shared by social groups; it focuses on human interactions and relations and therefore it takes diverse forms. Due to social circumstances it forces humans to take up their own positions and defend them; it is the thinking that judges, evaluates, criticises and makes proposals for action. Natural thinking uses knowledge and beliefs generated by established cultural and historical experiences and it makes inferences and deduction on the basis of these.

In what sort of 'universes' do we operate as human beings? According to Moscovici one can distinguish between consensual and reified universes. Moscovici (1981) identifies science with reified knowledge and everyday life with consensual knowledge.[4] In a consensual universe the communicative function of thought allows 'a continuous flow of deliberations between persons whose opinions and moods are always in flux' (Moscovici, 1988, p. 233). Everyday conversations, the focus groups set up by politicians, communicative genres of semi-institutional and institutional settings reproduce a consensual universe. This is a universe that functions on trust, trust in the information that is being circulated and people who circulate it. In contrast, in the reified universe there is structure and validated consistency of social knowledge (especially that of people, events, etc.). Information is organised into a 'unified' representational framework. Conventional rules of producing and circulating information are 'trusted'. What arises out of reified universes must conform to agreed, conventional ways, prescribed procedures and categories of knowledge.[5]

Social representations: a theory of social communication and social knowledge

Over the last fifty years, mostly in Europe, social representations theory (henceforth SRT) has developed as a theory of social communication processes, social knowledge and social change (Jovchelovitch, 2007; Marková, 2000). SRT is a constructionist approach that starts with and from the 'relation between individual cognition, "social" cognition (e.g. socially shared knowledge, ideology, beliefs, etc.) and an object of social knowledge' (Marková, 2000, pp. 433–4). From

---

[4] As Bauer and Gaskell (1999) have shown this distinction is far from unproblematic, as 'science and everyday life are spheres of knowledge production; reification and consensual processes play a part in both spheres' (p. 167).

[5] Take, for example, the existing distinctions between natural and traditional organic medicine. The former expresses the workings of a consensual universe, opinions, beliefs, commonsense views of the body's capabilities, while the latter that of a reified universe, with both feet firmly grounded in medical science.

such a perspective, 'representation' is not a mirror or reflection of a social object, but rather a 'process of reconstruction and creation. It involves both reconstruction of socially (culturally, historically) shared knowledge and its creation and innovation in the individual's activity' (2000, pp. 433–4).

SRT moves beyond two kinds of static epistemologies by proposing a dynamic and dialogical one: individualistic epistemologies, where what is at stake is the relation between the knower (in terms of internal representations of phenomena) and the object of knowledge; and a second, collectivist, concerned with the relation between collective representations, as societal 'facts', and the object of knowledge. Although Moscovici's early ideas have been inspired by Durkheim's notion of 'collective representations', contemporary SRT works with assumptions based on the study of common sense in its own right and triadic relations in theory of knowledge (Ego–alter–object) (cf. also Marková, 2000). Moscovici has advocated a move from 'representations as a means of recognising things to representation as means of constructing reality'. The study of the debates, disagreements, dialogues of social and political life, and the exploration of the increasing fragmentation of knowledge and of the knowing 'subject' require a new epistemological, theoretical and empirical apparatus. At the core of this apparatus is the notion of SRs.

The history and the transformations of the concept of 'social representations' are too complex to be encapsulated in a single definition. According to Moscovici, SRT is aimed at uncovering the intimate links that 'unite human psychology with contemporary social and cultural questions' (Moscovici, 1998, p. 241). Moscovici's phraseology is not unlike some other definitions that political psychologists use to study the mechanisms that 'unite' psychology and political questions and processes. But Moscovici does not stop at the relationship. In describing this relationship, do we critique or simply reproduce the existing scientific, social and political order? Moscovici's question is a profound one; one that still requires not only an answer, but rather careful reflection: 'We must ask what is the aim of the scientific community. Is it to support or to criticise the social order? Is it to consolidate it or transform it?' (Moscovici, 1972, p. 23).

SRT has aimed to reflect some specific and agreed upon social functions of representations linked to social practices and discourses: the 'constitution of social reality and social orders; operator of political and social transformations; symbolic mediation sustaining social identity and the social bond; and modelling of sensibilities and practices in mass culture' (Jodelet, 2008, p. 415). SRT has been used in the study of a range of social phenomena: the reception of psychoanalysis in 1950s France (Moscovici, 1961, 2008), public understanding of science (Bauer and Gaskell, 1999), common-sense interpretations of health and illness (Herzlich, 1973; Jodelet, [1989] 1991; Joffe, 2002), risk (Joffe, 2003), knowledge and public spheres (Jovchelovitch, 2007), modern biotechnology (Bauer and Gaskell, 2008), social identities and social representations of gender (Duveen, 2001), community and racialised representations (Howarth, 2006), human rights (Doise and Staerklé, 2002; Doise et al., 1993; Doise et al., 1999).

SRs have been seen, over time, as 'relational and dynamic organisations of common(-sense) knowledge and language' (Marková, 2000, p. 430). For Moscovici, SRs are collectively elaborated explanations of unfamiliar and complex phenomena that transform them into a familiar and simple form (Moscovici, 1988) and they 'concern the contents of everyday thinking and the stock of ideas that gives coherence to our religious beliefs, political ideas and the connections we create as spontaneously as we breathe' (1988, p. 214). For Bauer and Gaskell (1999) they are 'a space in-between, a medium linking objects, subjects and activities' (p. 167).[6]

In the context of SRT, the notion of 'representation' has a twofold orientation: individual and socio-cultural. Yet this does not mean that SRs are simply cognitive phenomena (a bit like schemas or scripts), but rather that SRs have a reality- and practice-constitutive role to play. As SR researchers have shown, 'representations pervade particular social practices in establishing and defending identities against the threat of "the other"' (Howarth, 2006, p. 73). Jodelet's ([1989] 1991) analysis of perceptions of and reactions to 'madness' in a French community, and Joffe's (2002) analysis of risk and social representations around AIDS show how marginalisation and exclusion are outcomes of social practices underpinned by social representations of the Other (the 'mad', the 'AIDS sufferer'). Jodelet's study shows how the social representation of madness as contagion regulates social practices: eating, washing and bodily contact. A more radical position states that SRs do not merely influence social action and social practices, but rather they are

---

[6] Moscovici has been critiqued on several occasions for the looseness or lack of definition for SRs (see, inter alia, Jahoda, 1988; Potter and Edwards, 1999). For Moscovici (1988) the issue of how to define SRs is intimately linked with what is the theory of social representations. SRT is 'both an approach, a way of looking at social phenomena, and a system describing and explaining them' (p. 213). That is, it includes both a view of society, of communication and everyday thinking and an attempt to describe and explain its mechanisms (ethical, social, political, etc.).

constructive and constitutive of social practices, used as orientation tools for acting *in* the world and *on* the world (Howarth, 2006).[7]

Communication, identity and community

How are the manifold meanings of social life condensed in images we call SRs? In order to understand this process one needs to start with a conception of social life organised as argumentative dialogue with self and others and the centrality of communication and social relations (Billig, 1996; Gillespie *et al.*, 2008; Howarth, 2010; Jovchelovitch, 2008, 2010). Social and political reality must be constructed and communicated. Language pervades social life, is the medium in and through which social relations, social meanings and social representations take shape. Communicative encounters, strategies and communicative genres 'are mutually interdependent with social thinking. They are formed through social thinking and they themselves transform social thinking' (Marková, 2000, p. 451).

Central to SRT is 'how different communicative genres produce different representational systems' (Jovchelovitch, 2007, p. 46). That was Moscovici's (1961, 2008) seminal goal in *La Psychanalyse: son image et son public*. He had attempted to show how psychoanalysis was perceived by different social groups/social milieux (Catholics, communists) and its reception in the newspapers of the liberal-urban middle class in 1950s France. Moscovici's key insight was that, in order to be understood, psychoanalysis needed to be turned from something unfamiliar into something familiar. Moscovici referred to anchoring and objectification as the two cognitive processes through which the 'taming' of psychoanalysis was achieved. For instance, the abstract and strange idea and image of the 'psychoanalyst' was reduced to the ordinary categories and images of the priest and doctor, which acted as anchors. Through the use of metaphors and other linguistic features psychoanalysis was objectified; that is, it was transformed from a set of abstract concepts (libido, repression) into concrete experiences.

In the process of representation, common sense has absorbed the meanings of the 'abstract science' and made them its own. Moscovici has shown that communication processes such as diffusion, propagation and propaganda were crucial to the very different receptions of

---

[7] According to Moscovici 'all behaviour appears at the same time as a given and a product of our way of representing it' (1988, p. 214). This idea should not surprise one as contradictory. It is, rather, the actual basis on which social actors construct their relation to themselves, society, and others.

psychoanalysis. *Diffusion* was described as a communicative strategy where the views and meanings of the audience are the ones that matter (this was the case in the mass circulation of newspapers that represented the views of the urban middle class). The aim was merely to inform and the outcome was a sympathetic image of psychoanalysis from a social milieu acquainted with new developments in science. *Propagation* was the communicative strategy used predominantly by the Catholic Church whose aim was to disseminate its own world view and to counter any world views that might challenge the dominance of its own belief system. The task of propagation was that of assimilating alternative knowledge systems. Psychoanalysis was re-presented in terms of religious beliefs and religious images that did not go against the accepted dogma of the Church. *Propaganda*, the communicative strategy adopted by the communist social milieu, was putting forward a world view that dismissed psychoanalysis as a legitimate rival belief system. Through the use of stock phrases, slogans, and so on, psychoanalysis was tagged as 'American, imperialist science' and alien to French values.[8]

SRs originate in communication processes and, at the same time, are communicated in text and talk. They can be used as a means of communicating, as well as topics of conversation, debate, and so on (Gillespie, 2008). For instance, studies of representations of minority groups have shown how predominantly negative representations are being used as a means of communicating as well as topics of discussion, debate, argument.

Racism and extreme prejudice can be understood as 'representational systems' where dominance and unequal power relations are enacted through various constructions of people, dispositions, practices, and so on (Howarth, 2006; Tileagă, 2005). The main 'representational' purpose, and ideological effect, of racism is segregation, moral exclusion, depersonalisation, and in extreme cases, dehumanisation of the other (Tileagă, 2007). As Moscovici (2011) argues, 'a minority's clearest distinguishing feature is the figurative kernel of its representation' (p. 454). In the case of Gypsies/Roma people, one of the largest minority group

---

[8] According to Bauer and Gaskell (1999), propaganda, the typical communicative genre of the communists, generated negative *stereotypes* of psychoanalysis. The aim was to exclude it from the communist milieu and discourse. Propagation, within the Catholic milieu, was aimed at the 'control of the reception of psychoanalytic ideas by shaping *attitudes* rather than stereotypes' (pp. 164–5, emphasis in original). Diffusion, the typical communicative practice of the urban milieu, generated *opinions*. 'Stereotypes', 'attitudes' and 'opinions' are all part of the social representation of psychoanalysis, a consequence of communicative strategies.

in Europe, the 'figurative kernel', that is, the core of their image for others, is articulated around the nomadic/sedentary *thema* (Moscovici, 2011). The nomadic/sedentary *thema* acts as a frame that organises the social representation of Roma people, and the everyday thinking about who the Roma are, how they behave, and so on. The nomadic/sedentary *thema* is both the 'core nucleus' of a negative social representation, as well as useful heuristic, a guiding tool for navigating the social geography of intergroup relations. The nomadic/sedentary dimension condenses a wealth of social knowledge about the Roma. In everyday thinking the basic theme of nomadic versus sedentary is associated with other social meanings: cleanliness versus dirtiness, way of being in the world, (pre)disposition to act in particular ways, and so on.

All these elements work together, shape a very specific and negative social representation of the Roma, and they appear together in discourse about the Roma (Moscovici and Pérez, 1997, 2005; Tileagă, 2005). The role of this representation is to distort and obscure the real lives and the challenges that it brings for the Roma. Its role is to further the dominance of majority groups over the Roma. When representations fulfil these functions, they 'become ideology' (Jovchelovitch, 2007, p. 114). Racism as a representational system presents power inequalities as 'natural', and works to obscure the actual 'reality' of racism and its consequences.

Caroline Howarth's (2004, 2006) work on racialised representations and differences enacted in relation to issues of school exclusion shows how young Black pupils in British schools can construct their own representations of what the school considers to be 'troublesome' behaviour, especially that stemming from the racial categorisation 'black'. They can both *mention* these representations in descriptions, or actively *use* these particular representations to resist attempts by the school to exclude them. They can tell the researcher, their teachers, or their parents at home that it is particular 'racialised representations' of what they are and what they are (sometimes) expected to do, that guide the way they are treated at school.

Howarth points to a certain political awareness of young Black pupils. They show awareness of the existence and role of racialised representations as institutional and symbolic tools for the school. It is this awareness of political processes at school that allows them to *recognise*, *understand* and *cope* with the consequences of their actions and those of others. Howarth's point is a cogent one. Social (racialised) representations are discursive and symbolic tools in the hands of both school and young black pupils. They are not 'quiet things' (Howarth, 2006), but rather political means through which one can resist, or reject, a set of institutionalised practices that can lead to different images of the self, unfair treatment, or worst of all, temporary or permanent exclusion. Racialised representations mediate the *recognition* of the social and political context (in this case that of school exclusion), they facilitate a deeper understanding of the context as a 'knowledge system', that includes issues of self-identity and self-presentation, how the process of exclusion works and how it can affect the people involved.

Social representations are *live* communicative issues for social actors, institutions and communities. They mediate and engender social identities and community concerns.

Jodelet's ([1989] 1991) seminal study on the social representation of madness in the small French rural community of Ainay-le-Château shows how belonging and knowing are two sides of the same coin; one cannot understand one without the other. She has documented some of the issues that arise when a community is faced with a programme of 'social inclusion' of mentally ill people in the community. In doing so, she has shown how health and illness are a system of interpretation, and the importance of a general interpretative framework that constitutes our socially acquired cultural knowledge and the practices of communities (Joffe, 2002). In order for the community to accept 'difference', the 'unfamiliar' (mental illness) requires explanation and needs to be turned into something 'familiar'. Jodelet has shown how a social representation of madness that contained ideas about contamination, hygiene and illness, and otherness, complex lay theories of origins of insanity, and representations of different elements within the person (brain, body, nerves) informs the way the community behaves (includes or excludes) towards the mentally ill.

In her study of social representations of a deprived London community, Howarth shows how different representations of self and community (e.g. those representations that portray people from the area as criminal, deviant and threatening vs. those representations that portray them in more positive terms; those representations that originate from 'outside' the community vs. self-representations of self and community) may compete and develop in an argumentative space (Howarth, 2006; see also Howarth, 2002). The issues that Howarth grappled with are expressed plainly by Jovchelovitch, when she argues, 'before we can even think of possessing knowledge we actually belong: belonging, not knowing, is where we all start from' (2007, p. 48).

Thanks to Jodelet's and Howarth's insights it is now firmly agreed that representations do not exist outside 'a project, or pragmatic context, of a social group within which the representation makes sense' (Bauer and Gaskell, 1999, p. 168). A focus on communication and identity points to the flexibility of social knowledge and its links with social identity and social interaction. A range of social and political behaviours informed by various dynamics (cooperation vs. conflict, symmetrical vs. asymmetrical relationships of power) can lead to the formation of different types of social and political knowledge, and can affirm a variety of social identities (see also Chapter 5).

Researching political knowledge in everyday life

How can people understand things about which they do not have first-hand experience and things or phenomena that are abstract, strange and unfamiliar to them? They do so by forming social representations for everyday use. Metaphors, theories and symbolic meanings attached to the latest developments in science, the brain, the economy and the computer 'are integrated into everyday ways of doing things [and speaking about things] and shape the social setting in which we interrelate' (Moscovici, 1988, p. 216). But what makes SRT a theory of social knowledge? For Jovchelovitch (2007), it is the conceptualisation of knowledge as 'plural and plastic, a dynamic and continuously emerging form capable of displaying as many rationalities as required by the infinite variety of sociocultural situations that characterise human experience' (p. 70).

SRT offers a framework for the understanding of the *mobilisation* and *organisation* of knowledge in everyday life. This mobilisation and organisation draws on 'various sources, has multiple concerns and makes clear that no one thinks alone' (Bauer and Gaskell, 2008, p. 344). Underlying processes of mobilisation and organisation lay a series of first principles, if you like. First, knowing is a form of social action. Second, all social (and by implication, political) knowledge is *expressive*, not reflecting or mirroring, of subjective life worlds. SRs are not mental copies of some internal mechanism or external reality. Third, social knowledge is intimately tied to relations between people, communities and practices. Fourth, different forms of social knowledge (elite and mass public, scientific and common sense, etc.) mutually articulate each other while fulfilling different social functions and responding to, and shaping, different individual and community identity projects.[9]

---

[9] How can one ensure that all these principles are part of investigative work? By following Moscovici's advice: the only way to understanding social knowledge is to 'reimmerse' it in the 'social laboratory' where it has taken shape, i.e., 'the social setting of communication' (Moscovici, 1988, p. 215).

The overwhelming concern of political psychologists with social, and especially political, knowledge is how to *measure* it, how to account for its existence or non-existence *objectively*. There is a belief that the only way this can be achieved is by taking social and political knowledge out of its social setting of communication. For instance Zaller argues that 'granting that political knowledge is the best available measure of political awareness, there remain several questions about how knowledge itself should best be measured' (Zaller, [1992] 2005, p. 336). For political psychologists interested in the *measurement* of political attitudes and political knowledge, there is a tried and tested method. Take for instance Converse's (2006b, p. 304) 'recipe':

take a half-dozen such items, preferably with a good mix of easy, middling, and hard questions, and you can be sure that you have a measure that is quite robust, such that persons who get a perfect score will be very different political animals from those who score at the bottom. They will be much more likely to understand ideological references, to make more deft connections between political facts, and to show more stable policy attitudes. Naturally, if you can afford ten or twenty such items, so much the better for robustness.

If the 'recipe' is followed *à la lettre*, results will be robust and will allow for comparisons to be made, and causal conclusions to be drawn. Converse's 'recipe' is more a recipe for the study (and creation) of a disembodied political world and one-way, singular way of knowing. If we assume there is only one way of knowing, which in contemporary, advanced capitalist societies is associated with science, specialised and technical, elite knowledge, then investigating political knowledge and political representations becomes an exercise in reproducing the existing (elite) order, or comparing new and emerging ones with standards, patterns, that are considered to be beyond controversy. Simply following measurement 'recipes' one risks downplaying the complexity of political knowledge and political representations, as well as the rich and multifarious argumentative possibilities embedded in the social, cultural and discursive activities ordinary people enact while interacting with their social and political environments.

The debates around how best to measure political knowledge (e.g. general tests of political knowledge vs. more specific measures) misses the nature of political knowledge, its origins and its links with community, history, social identity and wider social and political processes. Studying political knowledge entails understanding how 'new knowledge is produced and accommodated in the social fabric' (Jovchelovitch, 2007, p. 44), how it is continually produced and transformed in and as part of social relations. The study of social and political knowledge is neither the listings of things that make it up, the description of the cognitive and emotional processes underlying it, nor the outcome of careful organising of questions in a survey. Rather it involves the study of how subjective and intersubjective life-worlds are expressed in social interactions and social relationships that are the basis of knowledge production, reproduction and transformation, how these life worlds project identities for self, other and community, and how they are used for acting *in* and *on* the world.

What needs to be studied is not political knowledge *per se* but systems of knowledge, social representations of knowledge, which change, transform, as they move from the context of their production and permeate different milieux. The focus of study should be on how particular individuals and societies think about their own political world and how thinking itself is framed by 'collective ideas, representations and beliefs that configure the horizons of a community of people' (Jovchelovitch, 2007, p. 41).

Political knowledge is not simply lodged in the minds of ordinary citizens, voters, and so on, ready to be collected by pollsters. The implicit image of the (isolated) cognitive knower reproduces political psychologists' search for an ideal-type of political knowledge. High political awareness points to the *correspondence* between the facts and values of politics and individual perceptions and beliefs. Low political awareness points to the lack of it. This is a view that detaches the social actor from his or her context, and from the actual social relationships where political knowledge is produced. Local, idiosyncratic, everyday knowledge of social and political issues should not be simply dismissed or classed as ignorance, distortion, error, lack of depth, or lack of insight on 'ideological references' and the political spectacle.[10] Individuals, social groups and communities are not merely vessels 'waiting to be filled by the superior knowledge and practices of experts': they are active subjects of ideology (Billig, 1991); they think for themselves and with others. If their forms of reasoning do not happen to fit the schemas and models of political psychologists or political elites driving policy issues, it does not mean that their reasoning, their thinking is not valid in its own right. For the majority of social actors, those that Converse positions as the 'confused' grass roots, society, politics, political meanings are truly 'knowledge' and 'thinking' systems, at the same time, stable and shifting, centre and periphery.

---

[10] Researching political knowledge also entails paying attention to the symbolic function of linguistic representations (see Edelman, 1977, and Chapter 7). The symbolic uses of politics are intimately linked to the symbolic function of linguistic representations that reflect complex processes of signification, connotation, denotation, as mediators between individuals, communities and the social/political world.

Representations of the political: lay constructions of political categories

One of the ways in which individuals, groups and societies understand and study their political cultures is through establishing links between political knowledge and the meaning of political categories/concepts. Assigning meaning of political categories has the power to channel 'political thought and action in certain directions' (Connolly, 1993, p. 1).

To study political knowledge and the political culture and practices of a community, one needs to define, or 're-present', political categories, link them to a wider network of concepts and political practices, and to the language and culture of that community. Moreover, one needs to understand what political categories mean to ordinary people. Political categories, such as 'revolution', 'war', 'democracy', 'dictatorship', 'human rights', 'trust', and so on carry and condense a wealth of symbolic and social meanings. They do not come with labels attached to their backs, nor are they defined in a universally accepted way.

For example, one common way in which elites and ordinary people in Eastern Europe have tried to come to terms with the 'revolutions of 1989' is through re-presenting the events by using a chain of associations of familiar (the 'revolution', as abstract political symbol, with its own history) and unfamiliar elements (what actually 'happened' in 1989).

Referring to the social and political concept of revolution, Piotr Sztompka (1994) observes that the concept belongs, at the same time, to a societal, as well as to a sociological, discourse. At the level of societal discourse, it pervades common sense: 'it evolves into a complex image strongly imbued with valuations and emotional commitments, which may be called the "myth of revolution"' (p. 302). At the level of a sociological discourse, it 'evolves into a complex theoretical construct, engendering explanatory hypotheses. It is normally called a "theory of revolution"' (Sztompka, 1994, p. 302). Both societal and scientific meanings are drawn upon by members of society as resources for anchoring and objectifying the meaning of social and political categories.

It is interesting to note how, in reporting on the early days of the revolutionary waves of protest in the Arab world in 2010, it was not uncommon for British journalists to compare what was happening in Tahrir Square in Cairo to what happened in 1989 in University Square in Bucharest. The familiar (Romanian) revolution of 1989, and the ideological context in which it took place, served as anchors to understanding the struggle for freedom in the Arab world.

Other contexts of politics offer examples where returns to familiar significations can help make the unfamiliar familiar. Take, for instance, war, the ubiquitous contemporary political phenomenon. The content of representations about the war in Iraq and about Saddam revealed/ condensed in the themes of 'war on terror' and 'weapons of mass destruction' the array of practices needed to alleviate the danger posed by the (imagined) enemy. The return to the familiar significations and familiar images of American wars and previous conflicts in the area has facilitated the construction of a purportedly legitimate case for yet another war. Talking about the 'authoritarian Saddam', the 'war with Saddam' was connected to the history of the USA's project of protecting human rights abroad, and ideas and sentiments pertaining to this. It matters a great deal how political representations come about. In each representational object 'there is a whole reality to unpack; it is a reality made of knowledges, people and practices that came before and which, gradually, solidify themselves in the texture and reality of the object' (Jovchelovitch, 2007, p. 111). Through the 'schematisation' of power relations involved and encapsulated in new notions such as 'war on terror', the US administration achieved the naturalisation of war.

The idea of 'democracy' in Eastern and Western Europe (Marková, 2001, 2004) has undergone a similar subtle process of anchoring and objectification (see also Chapter 2 for research on democratisation). Marková and colleagues have shown that different representations of democracy derive from different social realities and collective experiences. They have shown how the anchoring of democracy in the local political context and past democratic experiences is a move geared more towards the stability of a social representation of democracy, whereas the concretisation of democracy – through the creation of new meanings – is oriented towards change.

What all these examples so far have shown is that representations of political categories have the potential to support, reproduce or contest, and critique the social/political order; moreover, they have the potential to consolidate it or transform it. In essence, they express the mutual relation between social circumstances and the social construction of reality.

Other researchers have been interested in the common/shared cognitive organisation of political categories. In an extended research project, Willem Doise and colleagues have studied human rights as social representations (Doise, 2002; Doise and Staerklé, 2002; Doise et al., 1999).[11] Using multi-level statistical analysis, Doise and colleagues wanted to show how the principles enunciated in the Universal Declaration of

---

[11] For Doise et al. (1999) human rights are 'guiding principles for evaluating relationships' (p. 2). Human rights are anchored in collective realities and beliefs about aspects of reality; they are models of acceptable relationships, prototypes of fair and just relationships.

Human Rights (equality, freedom, dignity, security, equal protection under the law, freedom of movement, freedom of expression, the right to rest and leisure, duties to the community) find their way in people's perceptions and representations of social life.

Is there a common understanding of the Declaration coming from respondents of different cultural origins? What Doise and colleagues have found is that official and lay definitions of human rights have a common organisation in different countries, although common understanding did not prevent different individual positioning in relation to human rights. Although there is a general coherence in attitudes towards human rights, the strength of those attitudes may differ. Individuals sharing common references do not necessarily hold the same positions. Individuals may differ according to the strength of their adherence to various opinions, attitudes or stereotypes (Doise and Staerklé, 2002). One of their major findings was that human rights are anchored in values. Strong support for values of universalism and social harmony were systematically related to more favourable human rights attitudes.

What Doise et al. aimed to describe was not a set of disparate individual attitudes that may vary in strength and correlate with each other (as could be expected or predicted by attitude theorists) but rather social representations, 'societally anchored pattern of beliefs' (Doise and Staerklé, 2002) that have crucial implications for the way individuals, groups and communities perceive the political world. The central features of the common organisation of a SR of human rights were themes related to the political efficacy of governments and political parties, value choices and perceptions/experiences of social conflict (Doise et al., 1999). What Doise and colleagues have shown is that SRs of human rights tend to be organised around common references, 'knowledge that is shared within a community, such as common sense truisms, widely diffused political slogans, or basic legal prescriptions' (Elcheroth et al., 2011, p. 744).

In a study of SRs of human rights (Doise et al., 1998), conducted on 849 youth from Geneva, aged between 13 and 20 years of age, Doise et al. asked their participants a simple, open–ended question: 'For a number of years now, Human Rights have been a frequent topic of discussion. In your opinion, what are these rights?' They have identified four classes of individuals/four types of social positioning towards human rights: public, libertarian, concrete, egalitarian. 23.5% of respondents were classed as public (e.g. freedom of worship; freedom of belief and religion; freedom of expression; freedom of opinion; freedom of movement); 14.5% as libertarian (e.g. to think as one wishes, to go where one wants; to go out when one wants); 36.3% as concrete (e.g.

right to housing; right to own property; right to have clothing; right to eat and drink; right not to sleep outside; right to write); and 25.7% as egalitarian (e.g. everyone should have the same rights; all men are born and die equal; man and woman must be treated equally). As teenagers progress in age and scholastic experience, the authors concluded, there is a move from more personal and idiosyncratic definitions of human rights to institutionalised definitions of human rights. A communitarian political orientation was associated with a more principled and enlarged human rights definition.[12]

In their study of the French debate over the Muslim hijab, Gély and Sanchez-Mazas (2006) (partially) support Doise's idea, by arguing that shared social representations are an essential condition of democratisation. They showed how people could mobilise different versions or representations of human rights. Some social actors 'appealed to human rights in order to justify measures aimed at promoting the protection of individuals against every form of domination by the community, while others appealed to human rights to stress the fundamental rights of the individuals to express their cultural and religious identity' (pp. 388–9). The plurality of overlapping positions constituted the norm, although this did not mean that participants' SRs of human rights was not organised around common references. According to the authors, there is a moral dimension associated with the study of human rights: debates about specific human rights should be able to constitute a 'society capable of inhabiting democratically its own divisions without canceling them or radicalising them' (p. 408). Gély and Sanchez-Mazas's message is an optimistic one. Yet, political reality is much more radical and does not always heed elite and grass-roots debates over human rights.

Bauer and Gaskell (2008) have investigated what the European public thinks about modern biotechnology. Their research focuses on both formal (content analysis of newspapers and national sample survey data) and informal communication (public conversations, focus groups). They have shown that representations of modern biotechnology are

---

[12] In the same vein, Clémence et al. 1995 conducted a study of SR of human rights violations in which they found a significant amount of common understanding across national contexts (France, Switzerland, Italy, Costa Rica). In a hierarchy of agreement, Clémence et al. showed what counted as violations of human rights for participants: imprisonment without lawyer's defence (86%), parental child-beating (82%), men and women left to die of hunger (81.3%), prisoner condemned after riot without lawyer's defence (79.3%), obliging children to work in factories (79.3%), Whites preventing Blacks from renting a flat (78.9%), imprisonment due to protest against government (78.1%) to killing a burglar who broke into one's home (55.6%) and prohibiting smoking in a meeting (30.5%).

dependent on representations of science and technology.[13] The crux of their argument relates to social representations of new social objects (e.g. novel foods and crops, cloning, etc.) as the foundation for the formation of positive or negative attitudes towards new technologies.

Bauer and Gaskell (2008) show how discussions around attempts to create a genetically modified tomato led to casting an 'unfamiliar gaze on this everyday vegetable' (p. 341). Bauer and Gaskell suggest that in order to understand the debate one needs first to understand how the object of the debate was first represented (is the tomato a vegetable or a fruit?), the basics of gene technology and discussions around productivity versus food safety/public health. A previously inexistent object, the genetically modified tomato, is appropriated, understood and placed in various contexts of meaning that have to do with genetic science, agricultural science and everyday (taken for granted) perceptions. The ubiquitous and familiar tomato acquires 'many identities and possible representations and, as such, becomes an issue of re-entering and gaining a new public image' (Bauer and Gaskell, 2008, p. 342). Bauer and Gaskell show how the debate about the genetically modified tomato moves from the representation of a neutral, familiar social object to the representation of a new, strange object. The tomato becomes a political object when the discussion turns to those whose interests the 'engineering' serve, the rights, health risks involved, or the responsibilities of all the parties to the process.

Social representations and political psychology

This chapter has attempted to show how the study of social representations can become a new and appropriate object of political psychological concern. The distinctive contribution of SRT to political psychology lies in its impetus to respecifying some aspects that concern contemporary political psychology: the nature of social and political knowledge and communication processes. Political psychology needs to do more to understand the relationship between psychological processes and social practices. SRT can provide political psychology with the needed theoretical tools for analysing the links between individual cognitive functioning and general societal factors that may influence the way in which people reason and apprehend the interaction between society and politics.

---

[13] They have shown the existence of a dual process of accommodation, a two-way communication process – from science and technology towards the public, but also from the public towards science and technology.

As this chapter has shown, SRs do not simply reflect our social and political reality; they constitute an inter-subjectively agreed social and political reality. The social and political world constructs individuals, groups and communities, as much as they construct the world. Social representations are the building blocks of such a construction. SRs are forms of social action in their own right, they make and unmake relationships between individuals, groups, communities, as well as constitute what the 'social', the 'political' is for us, they define the possible and actual trajectories of social interaction and social identities. SRs, especially those of political categories, embody and define the experience of political reality and political practices, determining their boundaries, their significance for individuals, groups and communities, and their relationship to other social practices.

Through its focus on the dynamic 'unity' between psychological processes and social practices, SRT appears suitable for explaining the heterogeneity and diversity of social and political knowledge, the tensions and flows of modern social and political life. These are some of the issues that Moscovici set out to explore in *La Psychanalyse*. Continuing on the same path, but developing new insights, is the way for political psychology to show its increased relevance to the study of social and political issues. SRT can help political psychology move beyond (dualistic) debates concerning elite versus mass public organisation of knowledge, structure versus function of political practices, and form versus content of political representations to a dynamic and integrative analysis of these issues, one that does not deny their relation to commonsense knowledge.

By drawing attention to stability and change, cooperation and conflict, innovation and resistance, SRT can help psychologists, sociologists and political scientists understand social and political life as inter-subjectively experienced. Political psychology could benefit from a focus on forms of thinking that engender their own reality and are transformed and disseminated in social communication.

SRT may not correspond to the model and practice of political psychology now, especially in North America. Political psychology needs a general theory of social knowledge, and social thinking and communication. SRT can provide it. Issues of political socialisation, the development of political knowledge and political awareness can be studied profitably by drawing on a political psychology of social knowledge inspired by SRT. What is at stake in politics is not only individual cognitive functioning or rational decision-making, but also the social and political knowledge developed, owned and disseminated by individuals, groups and communities; what is at stake are not only elite but also lay conceptions of politics.

There is a great deal that goes in any 'reading' of the political world: social relations and social practices, the habits and traditions of (national) cultures, social identities, emotion and affect. Political psychology needs to be able to develop critical and potentially transformative accounts of the links between psychological and political orders. Political psychologists need to open a critical discussion of the usefulness and relevance of SRT for the study of political behaviour and the various implications for issues of political socialisation, political involvement and democratisation of politics. As it has been the case for European social psychology, SRT may well prove to be a progressive and original research programme for political psychology around the world.

range of social and political phenomena: issues and dynamics of ethnic pluralism are perceived in terms of ethnic dominance (Sidanius *et al.*, 1997) or in terms of ethnic minority–majority asymmetry in national attitudes (Staerklé *et al.*, 2010). Moreover, SDO predicts and shapes the dynamic of intergroup bias (Levin *et al.*, 2002). For example, using the SDO scale, Jost and Thompson (2000) demonstrate that 'group-based dominance' and 'opposition to equality' act as independent predictors of ethnocentrism and social policy attitudes among both African Americans and European Americans. A recent meta-review of social dominance and support for group-based hierarchy (Lee *et al.*, 2011) states instead that SDO is a 'unified construct' (p. 1046).

It could be argued that whether or not SDO is a two-factor or unified construct matters less than understanding what it reflects: a universal form of group-based inequality. Lee *et al.* contend that SDO is valid across cultures, and 'group differences in social dominance orientation are not an artefact of individualistic societies' (2011, p. 1050). Nonetheless, Turner and Reynolds argue that SDO should not be conceived of as a 'relatively stable, fixed individual difference variable but reflects specific forms of group-based inequality. It is best understood as a group attitude, which varies with self-categorisation in contemporary contexts, the meaning of group membership, group position and intergroup relationships' (2003, p. 202; see also Schmitt *et al.*, 2003). A focus on 'individual differences' in social dominance orientation can obscure the individual and group-based negotiation of social reality and the actual specificity of antecedents and consequences of politics of intergroup relations (Huddy, 2004; Reicher, 2004).

What is the importance of cross-societal differences in understanding and supporting group-based inequalities and the status quo, and explaining societal change over time? Under what circumstances is group membership translated into discrimination, consensus, or conflict? Under what conditions are group identities conducive to or hindering collective actions? What is the role of social and self-categorisation and social context in this process? When and how will a subordinated group seek (positive) differentiation in relation to dominant groups?

These are questions to which, on its own, SDT cannot provide satisfactory answers. SDT reduces the understanding of political behaviour to universal evolutionary/psychological drives and orientations, offering a vision of social and political conduct where intergroup conflict, intergroup attitudes, and so on are in some strange way *prior* to (rather than *following* from) the nature of social and self-categorisation and social relations with others (Turner and Reynolds, 2003).[2] It does not seem to take fully into account that group attitudes, as well as group identities, shape and are shaped by, rather than simply derived from, social structure and social organisation (Reicher *et al.*, 2010).

People construct and reproduce their attitudes towards self and others, and towards social objects (like inequality or group domination) depending on social categorisation and social identification concerns that arise in the context of intergroup relations (Tajfel and Turner, 1979). SDT treats social identities and the process of social categorisation as a feature of the 'objective world' (Antaki *et al.*, 1996), and less as a feature of human action and of how people categorise self and others.

Social categorisation and social identity

The complexity of political behaviour, intergroup behaviour, group and intergroup attitudes is not a function of the complexity of our psychological orientations (and their 'biological' underpinnings) but rather a function of the complexity, contingency, social structuration and dynamic of social and political life. This statement is an insight derived from ideas that have become the foundation of a distinct and original European social psychology (e.g. Israel and Tajfel, 1972; Moscovici, 1972; Moscovici and Marková, 2006; Tajfel, 1972), part of a broader desire and move towards a societal and political turn within social psychology. Henri Tajfel's seminal concern with the idea that 'there is no such thing as a social vacuum in human affairs' (1972, p. 81) is perhaps more relevant than ever, especially when one is interested in studying intergroup relations and social change from a genuinely social psychological vantage point.

Tajfel was the first to recognise and chart the (surprising) effects of simple social categorisation. The 'minimal group experiments', as they came to be known, were the first step towards building a social psychological understanding of processes of differentiation and assimilation, and the creation of psychological distinctiveness between groups. Preference and bias for fellow group members (in-group) and discrimination against those perceived as others (out-group) was 'triggered'

---

[2] A universal evolutionary/psychological drive and orientation is linked to a universal need to imbue the social, economic and political system with legitimacy (Jost and Banaji, 1994; Jost *et al.*, 2004). As Huddy (2004) argues, this entails considering the differences among individuals in terms of and 'extent to which they perceive the current economic and social system as legitimate' (p. 952).

by arbitrary group categorisation. In-group bias was found in virtually meaningless groups (e.g. Tajfel *et al.*, 1971). For example, experiments demonstrated that, on a point allocation task, participants favoured their own group and 'discriminated' against the group to which they did not belong. There was thus strong evidence that mere awareness of being in one group as opposed to another could produce intergroup discrimination.

The beginning of the work on processes of differentiation and assimilation was set by Campbell (1956) who noted that an important facet of stereotyping was the enhancement of contrast between groups. Tajfel and Wilkes (1963) have taken this idea further to derive a set of social consequences from it. They observed that, when judging a set of physical stimuli (a set of lines), participants were prone to certain kinds of 'errors': intracategory assimilation and intercategory differentiation. Later experiments found the same effects (Doise *et al.*, 1978; Eiser, 1971; McGarty and Penny, 1988). A number of explanations were offered along the way for the dynamic of social identities in intergroup contexts. For example, it was experimentally demonstrated that threats to people's social identities are responded with attempts to differentiate the in-group positively from out-groups (e.g. Bourhis and Giles, 1977; Breakwell, 1978). It may happen, nevertheless, that similarity (whether of status or attitudes) seems to promote attraction between groups (Brewer and Campbell, 1976). Issues related to the dynamics of the social identity of inferior groups, groups of subordinate status, were also approached experimentally. For example, Tajfel and Turner (1986) suggest that a possible response in cases of low self-esteem of subordinate group belonging is to abandon the current social identity or to find and promote different dimensions of comparison (see Lemaine, 1966 for a classic example).

The importance of processes of categorisation was taken a step further with social identity (Brown, 1995; Tajfel, 1981b; Tajfel and Turner, 1986) and self-categorisation theory (Turner, 1999b; Turner *et al.*, 1987). It was a step forward from the perceptualist limitations of previous research to greater emphasis on the social context of group interaction and correlate issues of power, status and differentiation between social groups (Billig, 1976; Tajfel, 1978).

Social identity theory (SIT) and self-categorisation theory (SCT) have found themselves playing on two interrelated fronts. First, a 'cognitive' front, which kept intact all the assumptions regarding the basic processes of classification and categorisation. The idea behind this was that the world is too complex an environment for individuals to be able to make sense of it without some mechanism of simplifying and ordering it (Hamilton and Trolier, 1986). According to this view, categorisation constitutes a fundamental adaptative process (Allport, 1954; Bruner, 1957). Second, a 'motivational' front, which started as a motivational theory of self-esteem, stemming from the idea that one's own self-worth is defined in the arena of intergroup comparisons. According to this view, social identity was defined as 'those aspects of an individual's self image that derive from the social categories to which he perceives himself as belonging' (Tajfel and Turner, 1986, p. 16). Group members will be motivated to maximise the differences between groups by favouring the in-group, and emphasise the positive distinctiveness of their own group on any valued dimension.[3]

A psychological shift from personal to social identity is mirrored by a behavioural shift from interindividual to intergroup action (Tajfel and Turner, 1979). The salience of social identity dictates who is treated as in-group and who as out-group. SCT goes as far as to suggest that without self-categorisation, group behaviour would not be possible. Group behaviour is dependent on an act of self-definition. Subjective self-categorisation will inform how the person sees others in terms of available and salient social identities.

Contemporary/modern developments of social identity and self-categorisation theory have shifted the focus from the perceptualism of earlier versions to promoting an identity-based understanding of political behaviour and human action, with a focus on the interrelation between social categories, social reality and social and political action (see, inter alia, Crisp and Hewstone, 2007; Onorato and Turner, 2004 ; Reicher, 2001, 2004; Reicher and Hopkins, 2001; Reicher et al., 2010). The main presupposition of such an impetus is that forms of social identity and forms of social action are conterminous. As Reicher and Hopkins argue, 'category perceptions are a sensitive and variable reflection of the changing relations between groups in our social world' (2001, p. 396). More importantly, social identity is framed as a concept that 'mediates between social context and the action of human subjects', and not 'a psychological reality that determines social reality'

---

[3] The theoretical perspectives of SIT and SCT are structured and shaped by the encounter between the individual and the social. As Hogg and Abrams (1988) contend, studying social antagonism in SCT relies on the assumption that society is constructed and structured into 'discrete social categories, which stand in power, status and prestige relations to one another' (p. 18). For Reynolds and Turner (2001), social antagonism can be described as a *psychologically rational and valid product of the way members of certain groups perceive the social structure of intergroup relations* (p. 160, emphasis in original; see also Turner, 1999a, b).

(Reicher, 2004, p. 933).[4] Modern SIT tries to rescue Tajfel's primary focus, not on discrimination, but rather on resistance. According to Reicher, Tajfel's concern was 'not with the inevitability of domination but with the possibility of change' (Reicher, 2004, p. 931; see also Billig, 2002).

Modern developments of social identity and self-categorisation theory have been concerned with how we categorise self and others, how these categorisations affect judgements and actions, how we develop social and political identities appropriate to group membership, what are the consequences of self-categorisation for social and political action. The study of these concerns is underpinned by the idea that the social world is in continuous flux, the very basis of social categorisation is in constant motion and self-perception is a highly variable and 'context-dependent process' (Onorato and Turner, 2004). According to Reicher, 'there is no given form of social categorisation or of relations between categories that obtains across all contexts, and no given context has always been stratified in terms of the same categories and category relations' (Reicher, 2004, pp. 924–5). In a world of conflicting ideologies, institutional and political constraints, and structural and social inequalities, the categorisation process is a continually shifting one. Lay and academic references to social inclusion/exclusion, social dominance, differentiation and assimilation *point to*, *index*, a variety of specific social actions. In order to understand these actions one needs to explore 'how self definitions are produced in context' (Reicher, 2011, p. 391). The social identity tradition urges us to focus on the specificity of the social world and social conduct and the multiplicity (and the social context) of social categorisations and social identifications. The self and groups, as well as the social world, are not unitary and fixed conceptions but rather complex relational systems that can be defined (and studied) at various levels of generalisation.

Multiple social categorisation and multiple identities

Researching issues of social and cultural diversity, multiculturalism, issues of discrimination and tolerance brings into view the multiplicity

---

[4] One of the most common critiques of social identity theory is that its main focus is usually on measuring in-group bias, whether in evaluative judgements or reward allocations (Huddy, 2001, 2004). Yet, what this critique misses is the nature of social identity theory. As Billig argues, 'social identity theory is not a theory of prejudice ... It is, at root, a theory of group freedom. It tells of the way that oppressed groups can find ways to challenge groups that have the power to ascribe identities and stereotypes' (2002, p. 179).

of positions, identities, social worlds that people inhabit. Experiences of society, group belonging and social identification are understood as essentially about social actors 'being multiply called upon, categorised, classified, registered, enrolled and enlisted, often in highly contradictory and antagonistic ways' (Wetherell, 2009a, p. 4). One cannot understand social and cultural diversity, multiculturalism and issues of discrimination and tolerance without taking into account the multifarious manifestations and interactions between individuals, and consequences for self- and other perception, without asking how identity is actually *at* and *in* play for social actors (Merino and Tileagă, 2011).

Identities are not constructed outside of social contexts. Intergroup, intercultural and interethnic relationships (and related issues of self- and group definition) do not simply stand in a *sine qua non* relation to in-group versus out-group distinctions, to already prescribed self-definition and social identification. As Reicher (2004, p. 934) reminds us, 'one of the key tenets of the social identity tradition is that we have a range of possible social identities and that when we behave in terms of any given social identity, we act on the basis of the beliefs, norms, and values associated with that identity'.[5] The point is to understand how social/membership categories are socially constructed, how the so-often taken-for-granted world of social and ethnic categorisation is multiple, rather than singular, and is continually produced, negotiated or contested in multiple acts of social categorisation. In doing so one should be able to describe not only how social identities weave in and out of social relations between individuals and groups, but also how social actors position themselves and others and what social actions and social consequences follow from that.

Studies of the ways in which ethnic minorities define and account for their identity (especially to members of their own group) are still relatively scarce in social and political psychology (but see Leudar and Nekvapil, 2000; Merino and Tileagă, 2011; Verkuyten, 1997, 2003, 2004, 2005; Verkuyten and de Wolf, 2002). For instance, Verkuyten and de Wolf (2002) show how ethnic minority members (Chinese residents in the Netherlands) construct different versions of identity in interactions with members of their own group through mobilising various discursive and cultural resources, and offering both deterministic (the significance of appearance, the possession or non-possession of critical ethnic attributes and the importance of

---

[5] Reicher's statement is supported by Brewer who writes, 'in the modern, complex social world … singular ingroup-outgroup differentiations (dramatic and powerful as they may be) may be more the exception than the rule' (2010, p. 11).

early socialisation) and agentic accounts of their identity as minority group members (the active and constructive role of personal self in identity construction).

Merino and Tileagă (2011) show how the ethnic minority category Mapuche in Chile is not simply invoked as a normative ethnic reference, but rather actively constituted through its use in specific interactional contexts. Mapuche adolescents manage issues of self-definition and group identification by making flexible use of their understandings of category-bound knowledge, attributes and activities attached to 'being' and 'feeling' Mapuche. In their study of disidentification and disavowal of identity of young Somali refugees in the UK, Valentine and Sporton (2009) demonstrate how different spatial and social contexts and ethnic signifiers, such as skin colour, accent or dress, can mediate the weight placed on the perceived 'importance and availability of certain identities, such that they become particularly salient or irrelevant in specific spaces' (p. 171). Muslims' talk about their religious and national identities also reveals a complex picture of social identification (Hopkins, 2011; Hopkins and Kahani-Hopkins, 2004, 2006; Hopkins et al., 2007). Hopkins and Kahani-Hopkins (2004) point to contested and strategic dimensions of identity construction with reference to how Muslim identity in Britain is talked about in different ways 'so as to promote different conceptions of collective interest' (p. 339). Versions of Muslim identity can be built around a sense of superordinate commonality, as well as a sense of subgroup distinctiveness. Hopkins and Kahani-Hopkins show how identities are always constructed in a context of justification and criticism and serve strategic interests of self-presentation.

In all these studies, issues of ethnic self-definition and social identification are understood as the result of a range of constructive processes that express fluid and contextual self- and group definitions. What these studies show is not just how participants talk about and construct their own ethnic minority identities, but also how ethnic social categorisation is far from a singular process, but rather multiple and relational. Minority group members themselves are very much aware of the implications of identity constructions for self- and other definition and are its active producers, contesters and disseminators.

Experimental social psychological research within the social identity and self-categorisation tradition also supports the idea that intergroup, intercultural and interethnic relationships (and related issues of self- and group definition) depend on conceiving of social categorisation as a multiple, cross-category cutting process. According to Brewer (2010) individuals in multifaceted, complex societies 'have multiple ingroup memberships that are, objectively, crosscutting categories' (Brewer, 2010, p. 12; see also Roccas and Brewer, 2002).[6]

The study of social and cultural diversity is a case in point. It implies the recognition that persons are 'differentiated along many meaningful social dimensions' (Brewer, 2010, p. 11; see also Azzi et al., 2011). Social life offers us so many examples of perceived membership overlap and cross-categorisation. Experimental social psychology has shown the existence of such a phenomenon in the laboratory. For instance, Hall and Crisp (2005) show how introducing multiple criteria for social categorisation can lead to the reduction of intergroup bias (Crisp et al., 2001; Crisp and Hewstone, 2000, 2006, 2007).[7] Considering alternative ways in which people can be classified was conducive to reducing bias and associated with more positive evaluation of out-groups (cf. Schmid and Hewstone, 2010). It was shown, for example, that exposure to diversity encourages identification with superordinate categories. In a study conducted in Northern Ireland, Schmid et al. (2010) have demonstrated than those in mixed neighbourhoods were more inclined that those living in segregated ones to self-categorise in terms of common in-group category (Northern Irish).

Improving attitudes towards former out-group members (what is termed 'recategorisation') can also lead to reduced bias (Gaertner and Dovidio, 2000). Experimental research has identified various forms/ strategies of recategorisation: dual identity and one-group representation (Dovidio et al., 2007, 2009; Hopkins, 2011). For Dovidio et al. (2007), majority and minority groups display different preferences for these strategies. Majority group members are more inclined to 'endorse recategorisation as a single superordinate group' (Dovidio et al., 2007, p. 305), whereas minority group members may opt for a dual identity, 'specifically one that reflects both their subgroup identity and common group connection' (p. 312). A consequence of multiple social categorisations is that tolerance of other groups has many different facets. Rijswijk et al. (2009) have shown how social context and

---

[6] Some of these multiple in-group memberships can be perceived as potentially incompatible or incoherent identities. For instance, Jaspal and Cinnirella (2010) have investigated identity aspects of British Muslim gay men of Pakistani origin in non-gay religious contexts. The study showed that a repudiation of the religious institution could act as a psychological lever against incoherence. Being gay and Muslim was not always perceived as incoherent. What mattered most was the 'individual's subjective perception of compatibility between their identities' (p. 865).

[7] Getting people to think of others along multiple dimensions may lead to reduced intergroup bias. One can potentially increase perceptions of diversity through multiple classifications and open the way for interventions based on psychological theories and principles (Cameron and Turner, 2010).

social categorisation can influence the perception of migrants. Where Poland migrants' Catholicism was salient, Northern Irish Protestants expressed less welcoming attitudes of Polish migrants. Van der Noll *et al.* (2010) also argue that tolerance is context specific. They show how their Dutch participants tend to take into account 'various aspects of what they were asked to tolerate and the sense in which they should be tolerant' (Verkuyten, 2010, p. 151). Van der Noll *et al.* found that their participants expressed prejudicial attitudes towards Muslims, but also show acceptance of some activities of members of that group, in some cases. One can distinguish between prejudice towards Muslims *and* intolerance of public activities by members of the same group as two separate dimensions.

Social identities, mobilisation and social solidarity

As so many examples of social and political psychological research are showing today, it is becoming increasingly problematic to theorise and analyse identity as a fixed object, as something that is simply given (Benwell and Stokoe, 2006; Reicher and Hopkins, 2001; Wetherell, 2009a, b). There is a much needed and innovative move towards 'how individuals are assembled, defined and positioned ... how identities authorise, anticipate and guide social action' (Wetherell, 2009a, p. 1). We live in a world where identity displays and identity complexity is a feature of both ordinary and media lives and stories. From the controversy around the birthplace of American President Barack Obama, or the Mormon faith of American politician Mitt Romney, to the August 2011 London riots or Europe's current financial crisis, identity is perceived, constituted and self-constituted as 'both contingent and yet organised, open and predictable' (Wetherell, 2009b, pp. 4–5). There is an intimate link between the construction of identities and social action. The unthinking reproduction of national identity, collective mobilisation, helping and pro-social behaviour and crowd behaviour are perhaps the most salient examples of such a link.

Daily, nation-states are reproduced as nations and their citizens as nationals in banally mundane ways. This phenomenon has been called *banal nationalism* (Billig, 1995), a notion that starts from the assumption that 'nationhood is not something remote in contemporary life, but it is present in "our" little words, in homely discourses which we take for granted' (Billig, 1995, p. 126). It is usually argued that national symbolism evokes psychological attachment to the nation as an abstract entity (Schatz and Lavine, 2007) and that one can distinguish between different varieties of national attachment (Schatz *et al.*, 1999). Yet, what one witnesses is how nationhood manifests itself in discursive and social practices one takes for granted (Wodak *et al.*, 1999). Society constructs and embodies routine practices that reproduce the nation as taken for granted. The US or the European Union (EU) flag hoisted up on a pole, unnoticed and unheeded by most of us, offers a constant reminder of nationhood and collective identity. The routine practices of the media, the framing of national news, the ubiquitous weather report and the sport headlines are all discursive sites for the unthinking reproduction of the nation. Routine words ('we', 'us', 'here'), visual representations, symbols, spatial metaphors, 'flag' the homeland (Abell *et al.*, 2006; Wallwork and Dixon, 2004; Yumul and Özkirimli, 2000).

The effectiveness of nationalist rhetoric relies on the construction of the nation as something inalienable. Politicians are most skilled at reifying national identities, presenting them as natural or eternalising them through reference to history (O'Doherty and Augoustinos, 2008; Tileagă, 2008). Definitions and constructions of national categories can shape political action. For example, in their work on the construction of national interest in Scotland, Reicher and Hopkins (2001) noted how politicians used national identity to provide the values on which national interest could be based and pursued. Although all politicians invoked Scottish identity, not all invoked the same understanding of what it means to be Scottish. For instance, the notion of Scots as 'silent and downtrodden' was connected to support for political projects linked to independence and a voice for Scotland. There was an apparent agreement on the national traits attached to being Scottish (these were used by both Labour and Conservative Scottish MPs). Yet, as Reicher and Hopkins argue, this apparent agreement was also hiding a 'profound dissensus concerning the nature of social relations that characterise Scottish society' (p. 389).[8]

The effectiveness of nationalist rhetoric also relies on rhetoric used to expand the boundaries of the in-group. The relation between collective (political) mobilisation and political categories such as national identity is a case in point. Reicher *et al.* (2006) offer a social identity interpretation of helping behaviour, in the specific case of the mobilisation of Bulgarians against the deportation of Jews in the Second World War. Focusing on the analysis of documents cited in Todorov's *The Fragility of Goodness* related to opposition to the 'Law for the Defence of the Nation' (modelled on the infamous Nuremberg laws), Reicher *et al.* reveal the pivotal role of three types of arguments (ranging from the national to universal). First, *category inclusion* arguments

---

[8] For other examples of category construction in political discourse, see Chapter 8.

that position Jews as part of a common in-group rather than separate out-group (Jews are Bulgarians; Jews are fellow professionals; Jews are fellow human beings). Second, *category norms* arguments that put forward the idea that helping behaviour is a core aspect of in-group identity (Bulgarians are humane; politicians should uphold the values enshrined in the Bulgarian constitution; human beings should act in a civilised and humane way). Third, *category interest* arguments that suggest that the in-group will suffer negative consequences if Jews are persecuted (Bulgaria and Bulgarians will be harmed if it chooses to pass anti-Semitic measures; the Church will be unable to recruit Jewish converts).

According to Reicher *et al.* the predominant (yet not exclusive) mode of argumentation is based on the invocation of national identity ('we, Bulgarians'). The banal ideology of nationhood (Billig, 1995) provides speakers with powerful rhetorical and argumentative resources to justify the inclusion of the Jews in the national body politic. Reicher *et al.* have shown the existence of a subtle relationship between having a national identity (and possessing ways of talking about nationhood) and mobilisation and social solidarity. Talking about nationhood, constructing and expanding the boundaries of (inclusive) national categories mediated the significant mass mobilisation against the deportation of Jews in 1940s Bulgaria.

The manipulation of category definitions in experimental studies has shown how category inclusion and drawing the boundaries of the in-group are positively related to helping behaviour and bystander intervention. For example, Levine *et al.* (2002) have shown how bystanders are more likely to help victims that are described as in-group. Levine *et al.* (2005) have documented the link between emergency intervention and identity. An injured stranger wearing an in-group soccer team shirt is more likely to be helped than one wearing an out-group/rival team shirt or unmarked shirt.[9] As Levine *et al.* have argued, 'it is by exploring the social meanings of the intervention situation in terms of the way bystanders make sense of category relations in social contexts that new insights about helping behavior will emerge' (2005, p. 452).

Levine and Thompson (2004) have extended social identity insights to the role of social categories in the likelihood of helping after natural disasters. The likelihood of intervention is dependent on 'whether disasters, however upsetting they may be, are perceived to occur in in-

---

[9] In certain conditions, as Hopkins *et al.* 2007 have shown, strategic identity concerns (e.g. improving the group stereotype) may result in out-group helping.

group places and to in-group people' (p. 241). In another study (Subasic *et al.*, 2011), solidarity with disadvantaged groups (sweatshop workers) was seen as related to co-victimisation and inclusive social identity.[10] Understanding issues of mobilisation and social solidarity turns on questions of social identification and drawing the boundaries of the in-group. The clearer and more straightforward the identification with the group, and the more widely the boundaries of the in-group are drawn, the more people are likely to help.

The work of Drury and Reicher (2000) on the social psychology of crowd behaviour shows how crowd members act in terms of salient social identities. Crowd events are analysed as intergroup encounters. They show the importance of understanding the nature of collectivities and collective identities in terms of different phases of crowd events and dynamic social categorisation. Stott *et al.* (2001) argued that 'hooliganism' at the 1998 World Cup finals was a narrow explanation of participation in collective disorder. Taking into account spatial and temporal orientations and accounts of participants Stott *et al.* have shown how an 'ongoing process of inter- and intragroup interaction functioned to generate and then change the nature of supporters' collective identities' (p. 376) and how, paradoxically, 'violent action toward out-group members came to be understood as legitimate and sometimes even necessary by those who had previously seen it as inappropriate' (p. 376). In an ethnographic study of the 1990 poll tax riot in the UK, Stott and Drury (2000) give an account of the role of dynamic categorisation processes at different stages in the unfolding of the event. As the two authors argue, 'at each stage in the event the contours of crowd action reflected the rational acting out of the defining dimensions of the collective identity (at first in relation to the poll tax; and later in relation to the illegitimate action of the police)' (p. 266). What the study shows is that when the social interaction context changes, so too does self-categorisation: in the early stages of the event the social identities of the participants were defined in terms of anti-government protest; later, these were defined in relation to the illegitimate actions of the police.

Collective identities, participation and collective action

We live in a time where the images of the protesters in Tahrir square, the 'Occupy' movement, the Spanish 'indignados', and so on conjure a

---

[10] For Subasic *et al.* solidarity is predominantly about the 'redefinition of some higher level, superordinate identity whose norms and values define whether or not the relevant intergroup relations are appropriate and legitimate' (2008, p. 332).

variety of images and manifestations of some kind of collective identity. The omnipresent protester was declared in December 2011 the 'person of the year' by the US magazine *Time*. *Time* wrote then as follows: 'No one could have known that when a Tunisian fruit vendor set himself on fire in a public square, it would incite protests that would topple dictators and start a global wave of dissent. In 2011, protesters didn't just voice their complaints; they changed the world.'

The 'revolutionaries' of Tahrir square, the 'occupiers' of Wall Street, the 'indignados' of Madrid, are enacted collective identities that have become the subject of societal and media controversy and commentary. They show how individuals can express and harness agency, political energies, and strive for social change. Collective (political) identities are created and affirmed as one participates in and performs political acts and as one displays verbal, cultural and political stances associated with these.[11]

We also live in a time when the actions of groups and communities are vilified or seen as dangerous by policy makers or politicians. The August 2011 London riots are a case in point. Here is an excerpt from the position taken by former British Prime Minister Tony Blair, writing in the *Guardian*'s online section, 'Comment is free':[12]

The big cause is the group of alienated, disaffected youth who are outside the social mainstream and who live in a culture at odds with any canons of proper behaviour ... In my experience they are an absolutely specific problem that requires a deeply specific solution ... This is a hard thing to say, and I am of course aware that this too is generalisation. But the truth is that many of these people are from families that are profoundly dysfunctional, operating on completely different terms from the rest of society, either middle class or poor.

Blair's commentary portrays a social world where the boundaries between groups are not permeable, and where there are strict divisions in society; it is a society of 'us' (the righteous, civilised citizens) versus 'them' (the dysfunctional individual and family). Blair's exhortation can be said to be typical of a view of society and social relations that does not take into account the idea that social and political actors actively

---

[11] For instance, it can be argued that activist identities are not automatically imbued with political meaning and given once and for all. In their work on life histories of extreme right activists, Linden and Klandermans (2007) have shown how 'becoming an activist' is a complex process that involves processes of identity continuity (links with earlier political socialisation), conversion (break with the past) and compliance (identity linked to circumstances beyond their control).

[12] *Guardian*, 20 August 2011, 'Blaming a moral decline for the riots makes good headlines but bad policy' (www.guardian.co.uk/commentisfree/2011/aug/20/tony-blair-riots-crime-family?intcmp=239) (last accessed July 2012).

construct personal and collective identities rather than passively acting out some cultural or political prescription of identity. He seems to miss the multiple nature of identity, and the complex affiliations people express and bring to social relations.

One of the central questions around the August 2011 UK riots was: who were the rioters? This was the question which Tony Blair sought to answer. The initial, widespread political assumption was that the rioters were largely young, Black gang members (with a criminal record). *Reading the Riots*, research conducted by *The Guardian* newspaper (in partnership with the London School of Economics and Political Science) has challenged this vision by showing the diversity of participation to the riots.[13] The study reported that although, overall, there were more Black participants,[14] ethnicity varied significantly from area to area. For example individuals interviewed in Salford and Manchester were predominantly White, whereas in other areas there was a larger proportion of ethnic minority (Black, Asian) or mixed race. Also, 32% of those interviewed declared that they did not have a previous conviction.

The independently commissioned report (2011) written by the Riots Communities and Victims Panel (5 *Days in August*) investigating the causes of the riots supports the view that rioters were not a homogeneous group of individuals whose actions stemmed from the same reasons. It concluded that 'no single group was responsible' (p. 13). According to the report, 42% of participants were White, 46% were Black, 7% were Asian and 5% were classified under Other. Five categories were identified by the report: organised criminals, violent aggressors linked to arson and violent attacks on the police, 'late night shoopers' (looters), opportunists ('people caught up in the moment'), and 'spectators' (people who just happened to be present). It is interesting that ethnicity was given here less prominence in drawing the social profile of the rioters. The report contends that these were not race riots and that the majority of subsequently convicted rioters were not gang members.

---

[13] The *Reading the Riots* research, inspired by the 1967 study of the Detroit riots in the USA, has drawn on data collected from 270 confidential interviews with people directly involved in the riots, as well as the analysis of 2.5 million riot-related tweets. In contrast to the Detroit study that has used quantitative research methods, it was thought that a qualitative framework of analysis would be the most appropriate method to understand the August disturbances. For more details on the *Reading the Riots* study, see www.guardian.co.uk/uk/series/reading-the-riots (last accessed July 2012). For an interactive timeline of the riots see www.guardian.co.uk/uk/interactive/2011/sep/05/england-riots-timeline-interactive (last accessed July 2012).

[14] According to *Reading the Riots* the overall ethnic composition was 47% Black, 26% White, mixed race/other 17%, Asian 4.5%.

Reading the Riots also noted a contradiction between what 'rioters' were saying and what the government saw as the main cause of the riots: gang culture. Instead of a gang-driven riot, the study noted the emergence of a sense of togetherness among people categorised as 'gang members': 'a sense of a common enemy, a common cause, brought members of gangs from different territories – gangs partly defined by their defence of territory and hostility to those from other turfs – to co-operate for as long as the disturbances lasted'.[15]

The nature of these events cannot be understood outside a social psychological framework that highlights the mutual interpellation of collective identity and collective action. Political conflict, as well as political consensus, revolves around identity categories and participation. As Klandermans (2003) argues 'movement participation has become a common way of doing politics' (p. 670). Major social and political movements have been created, oriented and led through the construction and affirmation of categories. A focus on collective identity reasserts the role and significance of the agency of social actors.

Reicher expresses this idea aptly when he writes, 'identities may be better seen as projects' (Reicher, 2004, p. 935). Collective identity displays, categorical descriptions and their taking-up in societal and media commentary (e.g. 'revolutionaries', 'indignados', 'dysfunctional families', 'gang members', etc.) are the very stuff of politics. Politics is about the creation of identities, publics, allegiances, the mobilisation of political synergies, and the making of new collective identities. Collective action can be undertaken by members of high-status and low-status groups, or a mixture of the two (van Zomeren and Iyer, 2009; van Zomeren and Klandermans, 2011). People participate for various reasons (Klandermans, 2003).

One of the key insights of the relation between collective identity and collective action is that when group identity becomes politicised willingness to engage in collective action is greater (Simon and Klandermans, 2001). For instance, in a study of support for political Islam and political action among Turkish and Moroccan second-generation people in Europe, Fleischmann *et al.* (2011) point out how perceptions of discrimination politicises young Turkish and Moroccan Muslims by increasing their willingness to engage in political action. There is not one single 'profile' of politicised Muslims. What counts as a politicised Muslim

---

[15] *The Guardian*, 7 December 2011, *The four-day truce: how gangs put hostilities aside during the riots* (pp. 6–7). The conclusions of *The Guardian* and London School of Economics researchers support the findings of collective action researchers. The formation of a superordinate common identity and goal can succesfully drive collective action.

is a 'function of differential levels of support for political Islam and/
or political activism' (p. 645). Focusing on social actors' own frameworks of understanding of 'moderation' and 'extremism', Hopkins and
Kahani-Hopkins (2009) show how, in community speeches, Muslims'
identity descriptions 'reflect their own identity projects and the forms
of collective action that they wish to organize' (p. 111). Different constructions of 'extremism' (e.g. as antithetical to Islam) were seen as
driving social and political arguments against the establishment of a
'benchmark against which deviant or distorted versions of identity may
be judged and extremism identified' (p. 111) and against essentialist
constructions of Muslim identity.

A study by Wills (2009) on the London Citizens Living Wage
Campaign showed how political action and support for change can
be fuelled by creating superordinate identities, as well as managing
diversity in a multicultural metropolis. According to Wills, different
forms of 'scaling-up' identity and managing political action were used.
These included replacing divisions by new identifications, and fostering the coexistence of multi-layered identifications through superordinate categories (the 'wider society' or the imagined community of
the nation). Wills suggests that issues of policy, mobilisation, individual and collective empowerment, and social change can be conducted
through the management of social identity. Political action for social
change depends on managing social identification across differences
of experience.

Seemingly different definitions of identity carry implications for the
forms and manifestations of collective mobilisation and action.[16] The
social psychology of protest (Klandermans, 1997; Klandermans et al.,
2008) offers further insights into the relationship between collective identity, social identification and collective action. For example,
Simon et al. (1998; see also de Weerd and Klandermans, 1999) show
that identification with members of a movement organisation is crucial. A strong identification with a group makes participation in protest
more likely.

According to Simon and Klandermans (2001) there is a link between
what they call 'politicised collective identity' and the struggle for power
through political action. According to them politicised collective identity needs to be understood as a 'form of collective identity that underlies

---

[16] As Chapter 4 has shown, collective beliefs play a crucial role too. For instance, Jodelet
([1989] 1991) demonstrated how collective representations of madness protect community identities against the threat of madness, and regulate social action towards
people defined as others.

group members' explicit motivations to engage in such a power struggle' (p. 323).[17] Anger is one of the commonly listed motivations for participation in collective action. Nonetheless, according to Stürmer and Simon (2009) there is a limited role of anger and participation in protest. Anger works only for 'hostile protest' (reducing individual negative state) but not for 'instrumental protest' (achievement of collective goals). As the authors argue, it is more important to translate anger (about collective injustice, for example) into politicised collective identity.

There are several consequences of emphasising politicised collective identity. Politicised collective identity provides 'group members with a meaningful perspective on the social world and their place in it' (Simon and Klandermans, 2001, p. 327). For instance, according to Klandermans et al. (2008), immigrant collective action and participation (turning discontent into action) can be fuelled by a sense of integration into society, and the construction of a politicised collective identity linked to being able to act on one's grievances (see also Simon and Grabow, 2010 on the politicisation of Russian migrants in Germany). It has also been shown that participation in protest reinforces identification and induces collective empowerment (Drury and Reicher, 2009). Klandermans et al. (2002) have shown how a sense of collective identity of farmers from Spain and the Netherlands can stimulate and predict preparedness to take part in farmers' protest. Van Stekelenburg et al. (2009) explored whether motivational dynamics of individual protesters were moderated by the social movement context. The findings pointed to a positive answer. According to van Stekelenburg et al. 'the wish to express one's view when one's values have been violated influences someone's motivation to take part in protest' (2009, p. 831).

The power of 'politicisation', 'mobilisation' (or, for some, the 'radicalisation') of group identity depends on the ways collective identities are constructed, and the social context in which they are displayed or played out. This is a process that functions at two levels: at the level of individuals participating in collective action (people, social movement activists) and at the level of those (usually politicians, lobbying groups, etc.) who wish to influence collective action for political purposes. In the arena of politics, politicised interests (cf. Huddy, 2003) meet collective

---

[17] A politicised collective identity is the outcome of three crucial aspects: awareness of perceived shared grievances, blaming and adversarial rhetoric, and the involvement of other sections of society. Social identity, cognition, emotion and motivation are seen as mediating between collective identity and collective action (van Stekelenburg and Klandermans, 2010).

identities and interests. Politicisation is an outcome of the interaction between the two. For instance, the politicisation of a 'hate crime' can lead to altering or transforming group members' perception of discrimination. An interesting finding points to the idea that some expressions of prejudice are less likely to be perceived as deriving from group-based inequality and, as a consequence, elicit less feelings of anger, protest, and collective action (cf. Ellemers and Barreto, 2009).

Exploring identities and social action

This chapter has argued that social and collective identity is critical to the myriad ways in which human collective action is structured. Identities are produced in interaction with others, within intragroup and intergroup relations. Social action is a 'function of context because the operation of psychological processes depends on social parameters' (Reicher, 2004, p. 921). Rather than claiming that intergroup political behaviour is determined, in its entirety, by social hierarchical and social dominance orientations, political psychologists need to be able to explain what conditions lead to the creation and affirmation of social and collective identities, and how identity and social action involve and facilitate each other. A vision of social hierarchy and social dominance defines, and works with, a notion of identity as the product of individual psychology, societal and evolutionary constraint. Yet, social and political life reflects both stable and fluid identity positions (Huddy, 2001, 2004). The basis of social and political behaviour is the constant effort at forming, defending, rejecting and affirming identity positions; at its heart lie the processes of social categorisation and social identification. Social identities and their intricate link to social action reflect the social structure, social organisation and culture of which they are part.

Constructions and reconstructions of identity arise in the context of social practices and are produced to manage social situations and organise (collective) action. Social actors themselves play out and develop conceptions of intergroup relations (including dominance, inequality, inclusion and exclusion, etc.). Different constructions of identity authorise and facilitate particular courses of action. Political psychological research needs to be able to describe and understand the social psychological relationship between how social groups and communities are imagined and organised, and types, forms of collective social and political actions, that follow from that. Political psychological research needs to include and develop visions of social and political conduct where intergroup conflict, intergroup attitudes, and so on do not *precede* but rather *follow* from and *constitute* the nature of social identification and social relations. The primary task of political psychology of identity is to offer an understanding of 'how people come to share understandings and to act together in the world' (Reicher, 2011, p. 392; see also Hopkins, 2011). It is too often assumed that 'society divides neatly into homogenous cultures, communities and groups with clearly marked external boundaries, where these communities are distinguished by a large number of shared and essential characteristics and clearly marked cultural traditions' (Wetherell, 2009b, p. 9). Political psychologists need to resist the temptation to treat and isolate social and political categories as distinct, stable and one-dimensional categories. This is a crucial insight that can make a meaningful contribution to research on psychological foundations of identity politics.

A healthy democracy depends on questioning how it produces and reproduces self- and other categories, political divisions, political categories, and social and political identities that are relevant to political activities, collective mobilisation and action. This is the concern of both elite and lay social actors. If political psychology claims to be interested in the study of the democratic political process then it should study more closely how social and collective identities are produced in contexts of social and political action. Social and collective identities, and political categories, reproduce external (social and political) constraints, as well as organising social and political action from within. If one takes political categories and identities for granted one risks sliding into conservative and undemocratic politics. If one considers them as open-ended and dynamically shifting one opens the way for liberal and progressive politics.

The classical insights of Tajfel and Turner, and modern developments in social identity, self-categorisation theory and the social psychology of collective action, can offer political psychology a transformed impetus in research on intergroup relations, the formation of social and political identities, and collective action. This new impetus should rely on two aspects: (a) an innovative way of thinking about groups and their role in social structure and organisation, the link between group behaviour and shared social identity; (b) a new manner of thinking about intergroup relations, as psychological realities, an 'expression of how people define themselves socially and of their understanding of the reality of their intergroup relationships' (Turner, 1999b, p. 19).

This new impetus entails understanding the cross-sectional nature of identity, the complex webs of social identifications individuals articulate within and across identity categories, and the multiplicity of positions in response to intragroup and intergroup categorisations. If political psychology is to study satisfactorily how political behaviour (and social action, more generally) can be a vehicle for producing, transforming and changing social relations, then the notion of identity must be a central part of its theoretical and empirical language.

From the archive model of memory to lived experience

Memory is at the centre of human experience. Memory is what makes us human. The past is a site of social meaning. These are statements with which the majority of psychologists agree. The truth of these statements rests on two fundamental questions: (a) how to study memory by incorporating the tension and interplay between preservation and loss, remembering and forgetting, the relationship between memory, identity and narrative: and (b) how to reconcile the distinction between memory as individual faculty, and memory as collective or social phenomenon. This chapter outlines some of the issues that arise from various attempts to find answers to these questions, especially those with particular relevance to political psychology. This chapter presents the main tenets of a sociocultural approach to researching social memory, with an emphasis on political narratives, commemoration and national memory of socio-political events and coming to terms with the past. The chapter ends with a brief outline of implications (and recommendations) for a political psychology of collective memory.

In his book *The Sense of an Ending*, British novelist Julian Barnes writes: 'As the witnesses to your life diminish, there is less corroboration, and therefore less certainty as to what you are or have been.' The quotation expresses, in a nutshell, the contingency of selfhood. What it intimates is that biographical time does not correspond exactly to biographical reality, but to the multiple reconstructions of the unfolding past/time by people. What Barnes has found, as so many of us have, is that what we call 'individual memory' about one's life appears only apparently as a 'property' of the self. Instead we find it *distributed* beyond one's own person, 'beyond one's head' (Bruner, 2001), as it were, and *mediated* by personal and social relationships, and the material environment. Our relationship to the past and others is an unfinished business. Our memories (and identities) are not essences we carry within us, but _ner a result of particular configurations and constellations of the subject in relation to networks of distributed and mediated activities. Our memories are located within mental, material and cultural spaces. Our personal and group history, our self-definition and that of others, the artefacts and objects that we encounter or produce, the cultural patterns we socialise in, and so on are all aspects that point to memory as a *relational* process at the intersection of individual and social frameworks of meaning.

When one turns to the academic and scientific study of memory, one is faced with a conceptual and epistemological difficulty: how does one start to think about memory? As Brown argues, this is 'not just a matter of settling upon agreed definitions or concepts, but of questioning what the substantive is to which this word refers' (2008, p. 262; see also Danziger, 2008). One of the most entrenched ways of thinking about memory is based on the idea of memory as encoding, storing and retrieving of information, the idea of memory as (an) *archive*. According to Brockmeier (2010), 'Western common sense, both in everyday life and in science, assumes that there *is* a specific material, biological, neurological, and spatial reality to memory – something manifest – in the world' (p. 6, emphasis in original). Memory is seen as being located in the mind, 'in the head' and in the brain of an individual. It has a precise delineation given by the strict, unfailing interplay of encoding and retrieving processes, activation and accessibility, and the sequence of different mental states. The archive is one of the metaphors 'we live by', to use Lakoff and Johnson's (1980) words, a metaphor constitutive of everyday and scientific meanings of memory around the permanency and solidity of memory. Contemporary neuroscience (with its imaging techniques) can offer us actual 'images' of how the mind works. Coupled with the suggestive power of the image and representation, the model of encoding–storing–retrieving of information for memory is the most powerful (and evocative) there is.

The model of encoding–storing–retrieving of information poses several problems for the conceptualisation of memory. There is a tendency to reduce memory to an entity 'that is as good and desirable as it is powerful, and it is as powerful as it is capable of storing ("saving") information in an ultimately all-encompassing storeroom' (Brockmeier, 2002, p. 16). There is also a tendency to reduce memory to the problems of experience and recall. What matters to neurocognitive sciences is the *correspondence* between experience and representation, that is, the 'saving', and subsequent 'recall' of experience in, and from, the material interstices of the brain. Individual consciousness (and brain activity) takes the centre-stage; anything else is an epiphenomenon. 'Recall' is usually the dependent variable, with other factors acting as independent variables.

One of the major consequences of this is that social contexts of experience remain not only unaccounted for, but also 'undertheorised' (Olick, 1999, p. 341). There is no sense in which people are embedded in social contexts when they are remembering and forgetting. There is no sense in which it is *people* who are doing the remembering and the forgetting, and not automatic or constructive processes in *brains*. Lived experience – the open, fleeting, socially and culturally imbued frameworks, cultural practices and artefacts, in and through which people think, relate to others – are not given attention in their own right. The archive model is firmly grounded in an individualistic and positivist outlook of human nature. As Brockmeier argues, what is lacking from the archive model of memory is a perspective on 'human beings as persons who remember and forget, embedded in material, cultural, and historical contexts of action and interaction' (2010, p. 9).

The discursive (Harré and Gillett, 1994), narrative (Bruner, 1986) and sociocultural (Valsiner and van der Veer, 2000) turns have led to researchers taking important steps towards the study of memory embedded in cultural frameworks (artefacts, signs and symbol systems – language and narrative) (cf. also Hammack and Pilecki, 2012). The most recent revival of a culture of commemoration, the public uses of museums and monuments, and the inflation of political apologies for past wrongdoings have also challenged the idea of memory as an archive of the past. Yet, despite all the critical insights offered by the narrative, discursive and sociocultural approach, such insights are conspicuously absent from the agenda of political psychology. The focus is on individual memory and models of memory firmly grounded in the archive model: memory is either studied as an appendage to rational decision-making (Hastie and Dawes, 2010; Lau and Redlawsk, 2001), as a resource for motivated cognition (Taber, 2003), or as the outcome of 'online-models' of processing information (Lavine, 2002).

One example is that of political socialisation, where political psychologists have been slow to recognise and include the phenomenon of mnemonic socialisation[1] as part and parcel of political socialisation (but see Sapiro, 2004). Mnemonic socialisation gives rise to 'mnemonic communities' (Andrews, 2007; Zerubavel, 2004) and is mediated by

---

[1] Mnemonic socialisation is a phenomenon that refers to the totality of the practices of a particular culture – formal (museums, history textbooks) and less formal settings (families co-reminiscing, the various manifestations of popular culture) – where explicit and tacit lessons in what is memorable and forgettable are carried out.

'mnemonic practices' (Olick and Robbins 1998) at different levels of social organisation.[2]

Families are such settings of mnemonic socialisation. It is through the family as a framework of social memory that early political social-isation can take place. Younger members of families learn not only *how*, but also *what* must be remembered or forgotten. Kids or younger adults learn to express as well as repress, remember as well as for-get, and recognise what can and cannot be uttered in polite company inside and outside the family (Billig, 1999). They are also introduced to, and participate in, discussions about political issues of the day, or past history. Family reminiscence and conversation are tools and mechanisms for the enculturation and political socialisation of chil-dren and families (Fivush, 2008; see also Rigney, 2008). In a similar vein, Paez *et al.* (1997) have demonstrated the importance of social sharing especially within the family for knowledge and attitudes towards the Spanish civil war. Paez and colleagues have shown how the presence of a *social climate* in which people socialise can lead to stronger re-evaluations or intentional and committed thinking about a past socio-political event.

Billig's (1998) study of British families talking about the British royal family shows how talking about a particular event in the history of the nation (e.g. the Coronation) is also an opportunity to link it with the history of the family itself. Billig has shown that when recounting his-torical events or positioning themselves towards members of the royal family, families are recounting their own histories, and, as a conse-quence, are enacting political socialisation as families.

A study by Gordon (2004) has shown how a 'family political iden-tity' – 'democrat' and 'supporter of Al Gore' – was constructed dur-ing a family conversation during the week of the 2000 US presidential election. This was achieved by creating discursive closeness or distance with candidates (G. W. Bush and Al Gore) ('that 'W' guy' vs. 'Al'), referring to family members as 'democrats', using negative descriptions of G. W. Bush and people around him, and emphasising humiliating or embarrassing incidents (e.g. the G. W. Bush drink-drive arrest). These studies show that political socialisation is enacted as we perform social acts and as we display verbal, cultural and political stances asso-ciated with these. Political socialisation is an ongoing process produced through mnemonic socialisation, during storytelling and in interaction with others.

---

[2] There is no story of socialisation (political or otherwise) 'that transcends community, context, and discursive tradition' (Gergen, 2005, p. 117).

Another example is that of the study of the collective memory of socio-political events. Here political psychologists have had a lot to say, although they have treated collective memory more as the aggregated individual memories of members of a group, what Olick (1999) has called *collected memory*.[3] Most of the research focus has been on the memorability and ability of recall of 'emotionally evocative events' (Finkenauer *et al.*, 1997). It is usually argued that in order to be memorable and have a lasting effect, a political event needs to induce a significant emotional experience (e.g. JFK assassination, 9/11, the death of Lady Diana).

Pennebaker *et al.* (1997) provide another example of how political psychologists have sought to approach the collective memory of socio-political events. In their volume, the social nature of the creation and maintenance of collective memories of socio-political events is addressed in a variety of ways. Conway (1997), for instance, studies collective memory in terms of autobiographical memory. Construction, distortion and forgetting (e.g. Baumeister and Hastings, 1997) or construction and transition of collective memories (e.g. Igartua and Paez, 1997; Iniguez *et al.*, 1997) are other issues of interest to memory scholars. This tradition of social psychological study of socio-political events tends to focus on individual or social factors, which are seen to influence the process of individual memory formation. In so doing, these particular perspectives seem to sidestep the relevance of focusing on actual instances in which memories of significant socio-political events are constructed and anchored within collective frameworks of meaning.

It is sometimes not enough to say that social memory reflects the influence of social factors on individual memory, as Pennebaker *et al.* (1997) argue. The meanings that people attach to the past and the ways in which people make use of and construct different versions of the past in various argumentative contexts can be said to be more complex than the above-mentioned positions allow. The issue is not simply how the past is mediated by memory, emotion or cognition (at both individual and group/generational level). It also makes sense to focus on exploring argumentative contexts in which representations of the past are negotiated, and the discursive and cultural resources drawn upon for the individual and public articulation of the meaning of socio-political events. The aim should not be solely to describe the function of collective

---

[3] Sociologist Jeffrey Olick distinguishes between individualist and collectivist understandings of collective memory. On the one hand, he writes about *collected memory*, 'based on individualistic principles: the aggregated individual memories of members of a group' (Olick, 1999, p. 338); on the other hand he refers to *collective memory*, where 'certain patterns of sociation not reducible to individual psychological processes are relevant for those processes' (p. 341).

memories in terms of inner psychological processes. Collective memories of socio-political events need not be *explained* using pre-established, abstract models of how cognition, emotion, representation and experience interact and determine one another but rather *described* in their actual, public articulation and their implications for political and ideological concerns.

A sociocultural approach to researching collective memory

As Chapter 1 has illustrated, public opinion does not reside in the heads of individuals ready to be collected by opinion pollsters, but rather it acquires its form from the 'social framework in which it moves and from the social processes in play in that framework' (Blumer, 1948, p. 543). Blumer's insight has its roots in a thought expressed much earlier by the Durkheimian sociologist Maurice Halbwachs on how people acquire their memories. Halbwachs believed that 'it is in society that people normally acquire memories. It is also in society that they recall, recognise, and localise their memories' (Halbwachs, [1952] 1992, p. 38). What Halbwachs alludes to is the existence of an individual 'sensible' natural order of happenings, people, social relations, emotions and cognitions that lay members of society can fully apprehend and make available to themselves and others,[4] and a social and collective order: beliefs, representations, and group and institutional practices produced and reproduced by the language, customs and social rituals of a community. Halbwachs was not the only one interested in showing how individual and social frameworks shape and acquire memories, how social and cultural meanings are constructed. In *Remembering*, Frederic Bartlett ([1932] 1995) also studied how cultural meanings are put together and was concerned with 'problems of remembering and its individual and social determination' (p. 314).[5]

---

[4] The cultural 'anchor' of an interpretative/sociocultural approach to memory is perhaps the most famous study of memory and its recovery ever written, Marcel Proust's *À la recherche du temps perdu*. The tea and 'la petite madeleine' are the initiators of a journey into the past, embodied experience of time and space. It is with Proust that we start to realise that the past is present in every field of social experience, and that it can feature in intentional and unintentional ways in how we live our lives and relate to others.

[5] As he so very convincingly puts it, 'I have never regarded memory as a faculty ... narrowed and ringed round, containing all its peculiarities and all their explanations within itself. I have regarded it rather as one achievement in the line of the ceaseless struggle to master and enjoy a world full of variety and rapid change' (Bartlett, [1932] 1995, p. 314). Bartlett showed how cultural (and community) meanings are not fixed, and how social conventions, social representations, social institutions, play a pivotal role in the process of remembering.

Both Halbwachs and Bartlett argue for a *presentist* vision of remembering, where the preservation and loss of memories becomes an active construction and reconstruction of the past from the standpoint of the present. They both treat social memory as a receptacle of social standpoints, social representations and social/cultural identities. They have opened the way for sociocultural and interpretative perspectives on collective memory that expound a view of social life where individuals create life worlds and actively use language games that are 'saturated' by the implicit or explicit presence of others, relational, discursive and dialogical resources, narrative tools and wider social frameworks of meaning making and meaning interpretation.

Such a perspective implies three things. First, one needs to be able to describe the circumstances (e.g. political, sociocultural, discursive) under which collective memory becomes a public affair: how does 'memory' *actually* 'matter' to people (Brown, 2008; Campbell, 2008; Middleton and Brown, 2007). This entails treating collective memory as a 'relational process at the intersection of different durations of living' (Middleton and Brown, 2005, p. vii). Collective memory is best appraised in terms of the interplay of multifaceted social positions, visions and interests. Collective memory is best understood on a continuum that extends from the creation, circulation, distribution/redistribution of personal and societal meanings from face-to-face and small group interactions to the use of official 'instruments of memory' (Olick, 2007; Wertsch 2007). If it is true that memories belong to an 'intersubjective' past (a past 'experienced' and 'lived' with and in relation to others) then it makes sense to study collective memory from the perspective of intersubjectively constituted meaning and meaning-making practices.

Second, interpretations and understandings of the recent past are as much a concern of professional academics as they are for ordinary people. It is in and through language practices that both academic experts and lay people give meaning to collective memory and construct representations of (troubled) recent history. Professional academics and lay people make use of and apply various (general and particular, universalist and individualist) interpretive schemes to the understanding and interpretation of recent past. The key task of a sociocultural approach to memory is to describe the variety of interpretative practices and study the dilemmatic, and often contradictory, nature of social and political stance taking (Billig, 1996).

Third, collective memory does not simply reflect nor expresses 'a closed system for talking about the world' but rather 'contrary themes, which continually give rise to discussion, argumentation and dilemmas'

(Billig *et al.*, 1988, p. 6). Political psychologists have approached collective memory with a concern of documenting the individual cognitive and emotional processes, their stability and permanence, but have failed to account for its contingency, context-related and context-dependent emergence. Collective memories are contingent, intersubjective and inter-textual. Political psychologists can learn from anthropologists, ethnographers and some cultural historians who have pointed to the moral ambiguities and vagaries of (collective) memory that often stem from the idea that the (collective) memory of social and historical 'realities' can be placed by academics, politicians, ordinary citizens, and so on within different social frameworks and networks of interpretation (Bucur, 2009; Gallinat, 2009). The genuine 'collective' nature of collective memory comes from its being articulated in and through language (narrative and conversation). Narrative is a human practice, social tool, a 'unique cultural practice' (Brockmeier, 2010, p. 22) of social and temporal localisation for individuals, groups and nations, and a response to such a challenge (Wertsch, 2011).

The importance of a sociocultural perspective for the understanding of social memory may be clearer if we consider some central concerns in recent political psychological research on collective memory: the study of political narratives as memory and identity projects, commemoration and collective memory of political events, and coming to terms with the past.

Political narratives as memory and identity projects

How does memory actually matter to people is the central question for understanding political narratives. As Campbell (2008) argues, memory matters because it is the foundation on which (and through which) our sense of political identity is accomplished. According to this view, political identity is relationally shaped, and achieving political identity means searching for (and drawing upon) a narratable past. It is too often (or too hastily) assumed that it is only natural for individuals and groups to have (an) identity(ies) or memory(ies), and too often forgotten that it is through constructing, negotiating or resisting identities that individuals are able to acquire, make sense of and recall their memories.

For both individuals and communities collective memory is the 'active past that forms our identities' (Olick, 1999, p. 335). This idea applies more stringently to researching the collective memories of nations. Nations have to create their own histories and interpretations of themselves – they are not only 'imagined' but also 'interpretive communities'

(Billig, 1995). They have to continually narrate their past, present and future, and continually reproduce themselves as nation-states in an international world of nations. Contemporary democracies are subjected with regularity to what Pierre Nora has called 'tidal waves of memory' (Nora, 1998): returns of a repressed past (e.g. colonial past, communist past); searches for roots and national heritage; the increasing importance of commemorations and museums. Collective memory has an important positive function for democratic community: 'to guarantee justice, to achieve its potential and to secure its continuation' (Misztal, 2005, p. 1,320).

In order to serve this function it needs to be cast as a narrative that serves some identity project. Collective memory, as narrative, can function as 'orchestrated cultural practices to guarantee reproduction of a political order' (Misztal, 2005, p. 1,332). Yet memory, and different forms of its narration, can constitute a threat to societal cohesion and consensus. Political narratives embed both progressive and conservative functions of collective memory for democratic communities.

The positive and negative functions of collective memory can be brought together under the more general phrase, 'politics of memory'. The phrase 'politics of memory' is an umbrella term for different manifestations and instantiations of memory, both those grounded in lived experience or more formal symbols and representations (Assmann, 2008; Huyssen, 2003; Olick, 2007). It is often used as a label for transitional justice processes in democratising societies (e.g. de Brito et al., 2001), narrative clashes over monuments and sites of memory and collective meanings attached to it (e.g. Wertsch, 2008), conflicts over the meaning given by 'mnemonic communities' to events of national importance (e.g. Wertsch, 2002; Wertsch and Karumidze, 2009), 'mnemonic resistance' of minority or repressed groups or antagonisms between formal historical discourses and vernacular ways of meaning making and representing reality (e.g. Andrews, 2007).

From post-apartheid South Africa to post-communist Eastern Europe, national/political narratives about the recent past have mediated both empowering and progressive as well as limiting and conservative representations of recent history, identity projects and political action. The process of creating official political narratives usually informs or accompanies political process and supports national identity projects (Olick, 2007). If nations are 'imagined communities' of memory and forgetting (Billig, 1995), then we have to take seriously the notion of a 'public' or 'national memory'. This is not something that nation-states just have, but rather something they create from the historical 'big narratives' of the national group and the 'little narratives' of individuals (Rowe *et al.*, 2002). National memories and political narratives around them participate in the ongoing, unfinished identity project of the national collective. A variety of public forums, such as public commemorations, museums, monuments, truth commissions, and so on, mediate the conflict around and negotiation of national memory 'in the service of providing a usable past that serves some identity project' (Wertsch, 2007, p. 650).

Commemoration and the national memory of socio-political events

In order to study the formation of collective memory, one must study the practices of communication, and of transfer of societal meanings, that make remembering in common possible (Connerton, 1989). Many such social practices, usually considered traditional, are in reality recent inventions that serve particular political and ideological ends (Hobsbawm and Ranger, 1992). The Royal jubilees, Bastille Day and the Olympic Games are all recent inventions that attempt to forge and facilitate the creation of collective identities to fix and solidify social and political meaning. As Connerton writes, 'their intention is reassurance and their mood is nostalgic' (1989, p. 64).

According to Nora (1998) one is witnessing an unnoticed passage from the 'historical to the remembered and the remembered to the commemorative' (p. 626). One of the most common and most powerful social practice is public commemoration.

Commemoration is one of the means of directing public attention to an event through the construction of collective experience or emotion. As Pennebaker and Banasik have noted, 'the creation and maintenance of a collective or historical memory ... involves the ongoing talking and thinking about the event by the affected members of the society or culture' (1997, p. 4).[6] Although the ritualistic 'Today we commemorate + event' does not seem to be more than a reiteration of similar rituals performed earlier, commemoration can be seen as constantly testifying to the fact that 'the event was a true event, with a true emotional impact and true importance' (Frijda, 1997, p. 111). It places the event and interpretations of it above subjective interpretations, constituting it 'as an objective fact in the world' (1997, p. 111).

---

[6] This process contributes to turning the event into a collective narrative. One could argue that this process is also a political and ideological process, which may involve the posing of 'questions about the present, and what the past means in the present' (Hodgkin and Radstone, 2003, p. 1).

In terms of national commemoration, mainly coming from individuals with representative duties, one can identify an attempt to put forward a, sometimes, non-controversial *representative* view (Ensink, 1996).

The main objective of commemoration involves the construction of a 'unitary and coherent version of the past' (Misztal, 2003, p. 127). Commemorations can also be used as opportunities to respond to criticism, to build (rebuild) positions of political legitimacy and representativeness, to 'authorise' a *preferred* version of specific events and history. The commemorative ritual is part and parcel of instituting a political and historical 'reality'. Socio-political events like revolutions, or the fall of communism, do not speak for themselves; they need to be constituted as true and meaningful objects of commemoration. What is usually at stake is the meaning of what is commemorated. The meaning of what is commemorated might be placed within an argumentative context, a context of justification and criticism (Billig, 1996; Tileagă, 2008).[7] Commemorative discourses interlink with various genres of political discourse (neoliberal economic discourses, individualistic and collectivist discourses of justice, discourse of national priorities, etc.).

Commemorative discourses do not allow a plurality of views on the events, but rather encourage and reproduce a 'dogmatic commitment to one – and only one account of the past' (Wertsch, 2002, p. 125). For instance, the commemorative rituals of 9/11 in the USA have produced it as a 'signifier' that unifies a stable, non-controversial, 'politico-ideological field' (cf. Laclau, 1993). The events of 9/11 have become an unquestionable given. This is a similar process to the one identified by Barthes ([1957] 1993, p. 143) when writing about 'myth'. In 'passing from history to nature', political events acquire 'the simplicity of essences'; myth 'organises a world which is without depth, a world wide open and wallowing in the evident, it establishes a blissful clarity: things appear to mean something by themselves'.

In post-communist Eastern Europe, commemoration and narration of nationally significant political events (especially those linked to the break-up with the communist regime) are central to the construction of foundational political narratives and national identity. For example, the commemoration of the Romanian revolution in the Romanian parliament engendered a political struggle over the meaning assigned to

---

[7] For the outsider, the meaning assigned to a particular political event, the *categorisation* of the event, is not necessarily placed within a context of controversy. For example, according to the British historian Timothy Garton Ash, 'nobody hesitated to call what happened in Romania a revolution. After all, it really looked like one: angry crowds on the streets, tanks, government buildings in flames, the dictator put up against a wall and shot' (1990, p. 20).

events (true revolution?, coup d'état?). One of the ways in which this struggle was negotiated by former president Ion Iliescu (a controversial figure of December 1989) in a series of commemorative speeches was to argue that 'the events' belong to the political category of 'revolution', whose 'existence' is historically undeniable and associated with very particular characteristics or features. It is through establishing the categorial meaning of a socio-political event that individuals and communities orient themselves to social memory, making it 'salient as a "memorable" and "tellable" event and engage with others in ... debate' (Middleton and Brown, 2005, p. 21). In extracts 1 and 2 Iliescu is responding to increased criticism from the liberal public sphere on finding out the truth about the events (for more details, see Tileagă, 2008).

Extract 1
The Romanian revolution was the achievement of the Romanian people, it belongs to the Romanian people. The Romanian revolution has not been an artificial act, decided in I don't know what offices, by I don't know what subversive organization. The Romanian revolution, like all revolutions in general, like in all other countries, in 1989, has been the result of a profound crisis of the old system and the impossibility of government to offer realistic and acceptable solutions to the problems that the Romanian society was facing. (18 December 2003)

Extract 2
A revolution changes radically the political and social system and consecrates the irreversibility of fundamental changes in society, it goes by itself that it does not resolve from the very beginning and definitively all the problems. It opens the way to evolution and ensures the premises for offering solutions. (21 December 2000)

In Iliescu's case, constituting the categorial meaning of the December events *as* 'revolution' provides for side-stepping political accountability for past actions, knowing the truth and delegitimising critical voices. As Edelman has argued 'categorisations give meaning both to what is observed and to what is assumed ... shape both what we see and what we do not see in the political world' (Edelman, 1977, p. 23). According to Iliescu, it is the *nature* and exceptional character of the 'events' that should point to how the nation collectively remembers and reconstructs the recent past. In doing so, he *disconnects* the Romanian revolution from its controversial particulars, which allows for reframing, controlling the various public interpretations of the events. In such a context, finding out the truth about the past is a category of special knowledge: truth can only be a *possibility* but not an *actuality*. As Tileagă (2008, 2010) has shown, it is the struggle over the 'grammar' of 'essentially contested' concepts of political discourse (Connolly, 1993) that plays a pivotal role in understanding how communities construct their own memories and 'communities of memory' get formed, reproduced and disseminated.

Coming to terms with the past: the legacy of former authoritarian regimes

The fall of communism and transition to democracy has put Eastern European societies in the position of needing to fashion and give an account of themselves and their recent, often tumultuous, transformation. The various manifestations (successes and failures) of a politics of memory in Eastern Europe (positions and debates on the nature and function of democracy, justice and reconciliation with the past, trials, amnesties, laws of condemnation, etc.) point to the vagaries and difficulties of a clean and ultimate break with the recent communist past (Galasińska and Galasiński, 2010; Stan, 2006; Tileagă, 2009b; Waśkiewicz, 2010).

One of the ways in which the legacy and consequences of social and political change (the collapse of communism) was understood was through the creation of convincing images and representations of the recent communist past. One category of such proposals about reality were the official/elite attempts at 'mastering' and 'coming to terms with' the communist past, and interpreting the legacy and the *nature* of the communist regime (e.g. Tismăneanu, 2008).[8] The ultimate aspiration of official attempts at representing recent history was to provide a rational and synthetic, unique and unified collective memory, to generate non-controversial (historical) knowledge and truth-telling perspectives capable of overriding individual, lay experiences or perspectives (Tismăneanu, 2007).

In most former communist states reckoning with an evil and traumatic communist past has entailed a very strong dimension of recuperating and re-writing communist memory and history through the voices of the victims, identifying the victimisers and revealing the nature and extent of the perpetrated crimes (see Stan, 2007; Tismăneanu, 2008). It has also meant asking the question: does the recent communist past lend itself to any emplotment? Or does it belong to a special class of events such that it must be viewed 'as manifesting only one story, as being

---

[8] The essence of official attempts at 'mastering' and 'coming to terms with' the communist past was to get society 'to come to a common mind' (Taylor, 2004, p. 91), and to propose and ratify a moral and political vision of collective memory around a normative 'morality tale'.

emplottable in one way only, and as signifying only one kind of meaning?' (White, 1992, p. 38). The report of the Presidential Commission for the Analysis of the Communist Dictatorship in Romania (also known as the 'Tismăneanu Report') – henceforth the 'Report' – condemning the crimes and abuses of communism in Romania (1945–89) was such an attempt.[9]

The leading author of the Report was Professor Vladimir Tismăneanu, an internationally renowned expert (political scientist and historian) of communism. The Report consisted largely of an account of communism's political methods and institutions. It aimed to convey the repressive and criminal nature of totalitarian society and give an exhaustive account of communism as a self-perpetuating political system. In December 2006, in front of the Romanian Parliament, the Romanian President, Traian Băsescu, officially condemns the crimes and abuses of the communist regime, declaring communism as 'illegitimate' and 'criminal' (see extracts 3–5 for some excerpts from the Report):

Extract 3
Condemning communism is today, more than ever, a moral, intellectual, political, and social duty/obligation. The democratic and pluralist Romanian state can and ought to do it. Also, knowing these dark and saddening pages of 20th century Romanian history is indispensable for the younger generations who have the right to know the world their parents lived in.

Extract 4
Against the facts presented in this Report, it is certain that genocide acts have been committed during 1945–1989, thus the communist regime can be qualified as criminal against its own people.

Extract 5
Taking into account the findings of this Report, the President can say with his hand on the heart: the Communist regime in Romania has been illegitimate and criminal.

The attributes 'illegitimate' and 'criminal' that are attached to communism do more than describe communism, 'they place it in a class of objects ... and define the perspective from which it will be viewed and evaluated' (Edelman, 1967, p. 131). By emphasising the criminality and illegitimacy of communism, the Report creates, affirms and legitimates a narrative for an ethics of memory: (collective) remembering transmits responsibilities (Poole, 2008). As argued previously, the hallmark of creating and reproducing collective memory in the public sphere is

---

[9] For more details on the structure, scope and reactions to the Report, see Cesereanu (2008), Ciobanu (2009), Hogea, (2010), King (2007), Tănăsoiu (2007) and Tismăneanu (2007, 2008).

represented by a dogmatic commitment to a singular, non-controversial account of the past (cf. Wertsch, 2002). A process of 'canonisation' of a *unique* representation of recent history requires that alternative experiences, perspectives, interpretations are actively 'repressed or radically downplayed' (LaCapra, 1994, p. 6).

As Tileagă (2009a) has argued, throughout the Report communism is described in general terms as a 'regime' and 'ideology', 'utopian conception', 'enemy of the human race', instituting 'the physical and moral assassination', and having survived 'through repression', but also in national terms, where communism is seen as a '(foreign) occupation regime', 'criminal towards its own people', 'anti-national', and so on. To talk and write of communism means to talk and write of national identity, narrate the nation, its past and future. The Report is proposing a specific method of reasoning about society, history and memory that constitutes communism as 'Other', not 'us'. The narrative of communism is not self-condemnatory or self-blaming, but rather communism is distanced from (the national) self.

Extract 6
The total sovietisation, through force, of Romania, especially during the period 1948–1956 and the imposition, under the name 'dictatorship of the proletariat' of a despotic political system, ruled by a profiteering caste (nomenklatura), tightly united around its supreme leader.

Extract 7
Pretending to fulfill the goals of Marxism, the regime has treated an entire population as lab mice in a nightmarish social engineering experiment.

Extract 8
...the imposition of a dictatorial regime totally surrendered to Moscow and hostile to national political and cultural values.

Extract 9
The Romanian Popular Republic, who has come into being through diktat, or more exactly, through a coup d'état, symbolises a triple imposture: it wasn't even a Republic (in the full sense of the phrase), it wasn't popular, and, most certainly, it wasn't Romanian.

In extracts 6–9 one can see how legitimating communism's existence, forms and experiences is portrayed as the effect of someone else's *doing*: 'the total sovietisation, through force, of Romania' and 'the imposition of ... a despotic political system' [6], 'dictatorial regime' [8], fulfilling the 'goals of Marxism' [7]. Communism (and its effects) is treated not as something of 'our' own making (reproduced and sustained by Romanians themselves), but rather as an emergence and outcome of other people's desires and actions that are hostile to national values

(the 'soviets' and 'Moscow'). The categorisations of 'despotic political system' [6] and 'dictatorial regime' [8] suggest that communism
is a clearly definable phenomenon, political form and ideology that, in
the last instance, 'must be seen to appear in the same way to anyone'
(Smith, 1978, p. 35). The coming into being of the 'Romanian Popular
Republic' is said to be the result of external forces and influences ('diktat', 'coup d'état') [9].[10] Communism is also found to be 'responsible'
for crimes 'against the biological makeup of the nation'. Through references to physical and psychological effects (e.g. 'psychological weak-
ening and disheartenment of the population', 'decreased capacity for
physical and intellectual effort') communism is *externalised* and *objec-
tivated* (van Leeuwen, 1995) as a *sui generis* political ideology that has
worked against the Romanian nation.

Notwithstanding the Report's attempt to construct the political
memory of communism around its illegitimacy, criminality and otherness, the issue of how people experienced and lived communism still
remains. Bucur expresses this idea when she writes: 'if the picture of
Romanian communism viewed from the inner sanctum of the Politburo
in Bucharest is one of unchanging authoritarianism with grotesque
elements of a cult of personality, this angle provides very little insight
into how people lived it' (2009, p. xiii). Communism was not just an
external ideological order governing or influencing the behaviour of
elites and population. Communism was, for most people, 'lived reality'
(Bucur, 2009; Gallinat, 2009; Mark, 2010), and essentially 'incommu-
nicable' to those who have not lived it. When the professional historian
of Eastern Europe, or sociologist of transition describes the communist
social and political order, he or she is describing a social and political
object 'that has already been described, namely by lay society-members
themselves' (Watson, 2009, p. 1). Communism is *already* socially *constituted*, *distributed* and *circulated* in 'documentary' form (Smith, 1974).
Communism is 'an administratively constituted knowledge incorporated into records, files, and other forms of systematic collection of
"information"' (Smith, 1974, p. 261). Communism is also a confes-
sionally constituted knowledge incorporated into various types and
kinds of witnessing and testimonies, and various other public sources
of memory.

---

[10] Further attributes are attached to the communist dictatorship project. The report
describes it as 'antipatriotic', the Romanian communist leaders are portrayed as lacking 'patriotic sentiments', and Romanian politics not being the affirmation of a 'patriotic spirit/will'. What matters politically for the condemnation of communism is to
construe communism as not reflecting Romanian values and national interests.

Members of a national community will not tell the same stories. The hope of linear, consensual national narratives is upset by the unevenness, ambivalence and contradictory nature of individual positioning in relation to the past, and individual attempts at challenging public 'master narratives', official versions of the past (Andrews, 2007).[11] There is an implicit tension between the formalisation and conventionalisation of (collective) memory and the naturally occurring diversity of experiences, perspectives and interpretations. Investigating political narratives as memory and identity projects should not automatically presuppose a search for 'grand narratives' and ultimate truth but rather a closer engagement with the intricacies and idiosyncrasies of different life worlds, a multitude of local voices, and a variety of means of expression and relations to the body politic.

The tension between the formalisation of (collective) memory and the naturally occurring diversity of experiences, perspectives and interpretations is present in studies that look at how individuals themselves understand the controversial political times in which they were living, and how they sometimes choose to position and locate themselves. In a study of commemorations of war in Europe, Bucur (2009) shows how grand, hegemonic narratives of war (especially the Second World War) are 'disrupted' by a vast array of regional, religious, ethnic and gender features that point to how war (and death) itself can be understood in terms of and through the various spoken, written and spatial products and practices of 'average people at the local level' (Bucur, 2009, p. 2). She points to how both the communist and post-communist 'official commemorative calendars' of the Romanian state have attempted to create national commemorative rituals (around a 'heroes cult' and commemorative sites such as the Tomb of the Unknown Soldier and the Mărăşeşti Mausoleum) that implicitly or explicitly clash with local communities' own ways of remembering and constructing social memories.

The troubled history of reconciliation in South Africa is another relevant example here. Andrews (2007) shows how in the context of testimonies and responses to the Truth and Reconciliation Commission (TRC) there was no unique or collective narrative model that was used by the social actors. Although citizens recounting tales of suffering was indeed a unique (and successful) model of rebuilding a 'broken' nation,

---

[11] There is no 'natural end' to understanding the recent past; there is no ultimate story. The study of collective memory and coming to terms with the past must not make the following mistake: 'to use consensus to cure the diseases of consensus' (Rancière, 2007, p. 106).

it was far from being a uniform one, with different stories being told, sometimes as the result of pressures on victims to tell certain kinds of stories while testifying, or as the outcome of different experiences and perspectives of victims and perpetrators, and various other individuals and groups challenging official versions of the past and demanding redress. As Andrews argues the concern of TRC was more with the creation of acceptable, believable, pragmatic versions of memory rather than with truthful collective memory, developing realistic and usable images of the past history of race relations rather than truthful ones. In a similar vein, Olick (2003, 2007) notes how the official memory of German politics since 1989 has suffered a shift that has led to the 'normalisation' of Nazi past. Olick identifies a subtle move from problems of genocide and German accountability for the Holocaust to problems of state violence, triggered by the fall of the Berlin wall, the dismantling of it and confronting the legacy of the Stasi. He has shown how older, more traditional events for commemorating and recognising German crimes have been replaced with commemorations of the fall of the Berlin wall and German unification. New public debates on the more recent country's past, unification and the legacy of the socialist regime take centre-stage and fashion a different version of collective memory for new generations.

Barbara Miller (1999, 2003) analyses narratives of 'guilt and compliance' of former Stasi collaborators in East Germany and offers a socio-psychological framework for describing and explaining attempts of 'coming to terms with the past'. Issues of regret, guilt and compliance are interpreted using psychological categories and theories such as cognitive dissonance, selective memory, and common explanations in terms of socialisation, double morality, double standards and accepting political lies.

If for Miller memory is simply an issue of selectivity, storage and retrieval of significant details relevant to telling stories and positioning the self, for Gallinat (2009) individual and social memory are inextricably linked, a site where moral ambiguities are expressed and managed. In ethnographic studies of the social construction of the socialist past in East Germany, she shows how the answer to several moral questions thrown in the mix by the study of individual and collective memory and identity do not have a straightforward answer. Who was who back then? Who was I? What am I now? Who can pass judgement? How do you approach the issue of betrayal of trust? She shows the existence of a tension between universal and particular versions of morality that are alive in people's accounts of past events, of self and others, of social and political realities. As she argues, 'the memories arising from these lives continue to shape people's relationships in the past, present and future, and these relationships are as complex and, at times, paradoxical' (p. 197).

In another study, Gallinat (2006) focuses on the narrative work of a group of former political prisoners in their attempt to communicate their experiences of the past. She notes that, in most of the cases, participants could not move their stories beyond general phrases like 'horrible', 'awful', or 'unbearable'. Very particular episodes of abuse in Stasi prisons were not mentioned, although other aspects were mentioned (lack of hygiene, privacy, sleep deprivation, etc.). Their narratives were also punctuated by heavy silences and difficulties in finding the right words. For Gallinat all this shows the 'tension between wanting to transmit the extraordinariness of the episode and a feeling of failing to do so' (p. 354).[12]

Gallinat's interviewees were not finding it easy to be themselves, they were jockeying for positions in a struggle to find both socially and individually acceptable (rational and moral) identities. Understanding the process of narrating the post-totalitarian past and uncovering the implications of such a process for social memory have to do as much with the interpretative talent of the researcher, as with the 'reality' of memories of the past that are inexorably linked to texts – the 'testimony', the 'archive', the 'document' – of any kind. The struggle to find socially and individually acceptable, rational and moral identities is inexorably linked to a textual reality (the file, personal notes, etc.) (Tileagă, 2009b, 2011a; see also Skultans, 2001) and the different activities and relations of which people are part.

Towards a new political psychology of collective memory

This chapter has tried to show how collective memory can be rendered as a proper object of political psychological concern by folding it into notions of experience, narrative and social frameworks, and overcoming the duality between individual and collective memory. Memory

---

[12] She also shows how these stories 'limited the space for self-narration' due to the various constraints placed on the person by the social/public climate of opinion, and the demands of an official politics of recognition of past wrongdoings. A similar argument is made by Mark in relation to post-communism. He argues most people had to 'contend with the complex lives they had lived before 1989 but also with the dominant expectations of the post-communist period that they would relate their experiences in terms of persecution and suffering' (2010, p. 183; see also Skultans, 1998).

manifests itself and takes various forms at different levels of social and political organisation, in public and in private, in elite discourse and lay meanings, as personal remembering as well as commemoration. Each of these forms is important and needs to be studied in its own right. By understanding first how individual and social memories work in juxtaposition one can also understand how repertoires of political knowledge, political beliefs and political identities are constructed. In order to overcome successfully the duality between individual and social memory, one needs to consider memory as being a social and cultural product, and remembering/forgetting as social and cultural practices.

Political psychologists may find that there is much to be gained from incorporating some of Halbwachs's crucial insights into the social character of memory. There is more to Halbwachs's contribution than his *presentist* approach. Halbwachs has been concerned with the various locations of memory (from the religious landscape to the family), and, essentially, with memory as being rooted in practices and social relations. As this chapter has shown political psychologists are more inclined to study collective and historical memories of individuals and groups through revealing the cognitive and emotional mechanisms of storage, encoding and retrieval of information. The archive model of memory limits our vision of how individual and collective memories are formed, how they are affirmed and how they are resisted or transformed. It is not always (literal) recall or accurate representation that matters, but also how individual and collective memories are embodied and located within the mental and material spaces of society. By widening its approach to memory to include sociocultural and interpretative aspects, political psychology will run less the risk of proposing a type of psychological and political science where one does not deal closely and systematically with lived experience, and the life worlds of social relations and social meanings.

A move away from the archive model implies the rejection of the naive notion of 'the past', memory, being preserved in a mental (or material) archive. Political psychologists need to study memory for the social functions it fulfils, how it assumes collective relevance in the cultural, social and political web in which it is entangled. They need to study the various social sources of memory, as well as people as 'memory consumers' (Kansteiner, 2002, p. 180). Individual and collective memories are neither fixed nor given once and for all, but can be pushed into certain forms by cultural, societal and political constraints; they can become the foundation for certain types of stories, imbued with the ideology of the social/political context and individual experiences. Individual and collective memories (and identities built through and around them) are sources of dispute and moralising. As this chapter has intimated, the formulation of arguments, representations, or attitudes towards the recent past presupposes that counter-arguments, counter-representations or counter-attitudes are not only possible, but are the make-up of how personal and societal meanings are created, sustained and circulated in society.

7   Discourse and politics

Visions of politics and discourse

In his book, *The Symbolic Uses of Politics*, the American political scientist Murray Edelman is offering his own description of politics. He argues that 'because politics does visibly confer wealth, take life, imprison and free people, and represent a history with strong emotional and ideological associations, its processes become easy objects upon which to displace private emotions, especially strong anxieties and hopes' (1967, p. 5). Edelman's 'definition' of politics proposes a vision where politics is the agent and driver of a transformation of society's order: a politics that *does things to people*. This is a vision of politics shared by many a political scientist and political psychologist. It is the power of its symbolism that leads most researchers to focus more on politics as *process* rather than on politics as *social action*, more on what politics *does* to people rather than on how politics is *done* by people in and through discursive and social practices. This chapter is an attempt at showing how the balance can be profitably shifted towards understanding politics and political discourse as a complex form of social activity. This chapter outlines the relationship between politics and language. It argues that political language is a multifaceted form of social activity that justifies careful study in its own right. Chapter 8 expounds on some propositions developed here, using empirical analyses of political rhetoric.

For discourse analysts, language is central to (the conduct of) politics. As Chilton and Schäffner argue, 'it is surely the case that politics cannot be conducted without language, and it is probably the case that the use of language in the constitution of social groups leads to what we call "politics" in a broad sense' (1997, p. 206). For researchers interested in the ethnography of political processes, 'true' politics is what happens behind the scenes, the 'backstage' of politics (Wodak, 2011).[1]

---

[1] At the root of this vision of politics lies the distinction between the glamorised and fictionalised world of politics and 'real', daily politics. According to Wodak one cannot

To Edelman's definition of politics, one can also add the most commonly used (metaphorical) contrast in defining politics, that between 'struggle' and 'cooperation' (Tilly, 2002; Tilly and Tarrow, 2006). Arguably, perspectives on politics, whether they originate in political science or linguistics, pay attention, in some way or another, to language and communication, and how they participate in or are an integral part of political processes. The only problem is that some of these perspectives are more inclined to rely on a *referential* theory of language that sees it as a neutral, passive medium between thoughts and actions.

One of the distinctive features of recent European approaches in social and political psychology is to recognise the importance of analysing discourse for understanding politics and political attitudes (Billig, 1996; Condor, 2000; Potter, 1998). According to van Dijk (1997, p. 2, emphasis in original), discourse is defined as a

> *practical, social* and *cultural,* phenomenon ... language users engaging in discourse accomplish *social acts* and participate in *social interaction,* typically so in *conversation* and other forms of *dialogue.* Such interaction is in turn embedded in various social and cultural *contexts,* such as informal gatherings with friends or professional, institutional encounters.

Discourse is the site where social and political representations, political knowledge, interpretative repertoires and other social and discursive resources come together to build political world views, of cooperation or antagonism, fair or unequal distribution of power and resources, morality or immorality, security or insecurity, and so on.

If one recognises that politics operates through language, and that language is constitutive of social activities, then one must also recognise that politics is not a surrogate image of the social world but is an integral part of that world and a productive and constitutive element of social life and social activities. One can go as far as to suggest that politics is established in people's doings, activities, actions, as these are organised in social relations and social practices (cf. Smith, 2005).[2] The ordinary person is not a dupe, whose mind is being constantly filled by outside, social and political forces, and who reacts unthinkingly. The 'subject' of politics is a discursive being who thinks and argues with politics (Billig, 1991). The relationship between politics and language

---

understand how politics is actually 'done' or 'performed' if one does not focus on the social practices that constitute politics as a profession.

[2] Central to understanding the variety of manifestations of politics and political language is 'the ambiguous and relatively open-ended interaction of persons and groups who share a range of concepts, but share them imperfectly and incompletely' (Connolly, 1993, p. 6).

in use is essential and ineluctable. As a consequence, it is more useful to view political language less as a particular *collection* of discourses, and more as a particular cluster of *effects* and *consequences of* discourses.

Discourse analysis and political discourse

We live in a world where we are constantly bombarded with verbal messages of many kinds, from detergent adverts to party conference speeches. Electronic media (Jamieson, 1988) and the rhetoric of the political image (Barthes, 1977) have changed the nature of contemporary political oratory (Billig, 2003). The intricate visual and verbal rhetoric of contemporary politics acts as a mediator between organisations and publics, politicians and their voters, and so on. As Chilton and Schäffner argue, 'the opportunity for the reception, interpretation and critique of political texts and talk has vastly increased' (1997, p. 206).

According to Edelman, 'politics is for the most of us a passing parade of abstract symbols, yet a parade which our experience teaches us to be a benevolent and malevolent force that can be close to omnipotent' (Edelman, 1967, p. 5). We are 'cued' into social and political beliefs by the language of politics. As he argues, 'symbolic cues ... go far toward defining the geography and the topography of everyone's political world' (Edelman, 1977, p. 41). Edelman has shown the political implications of our most mundane ways of naming and classifying 'social problems': poverty, drug abuse, crime, and so on, from the use of terms that evoke the 'alleged weakness and pathology of the individual' (Edelman, 1967, p. 27) to dubious and highly ambiguous terms that can create misleading beliefs.[3]

Edelman's image of politics is a cogent one, although incomplete. It only draws attention to symbolic aspects of politics. Yet, politics can also be thought of as a sequence of discursive accomplishments. Today's (political) journalism all around the world is a telling example of how the 'deeds' of politicians are not some external dimension that needs to be scrutinised separately from the 'words' of politicians. Words and deeds are one. The rhetoric of politicians themselves (not

---

[3] Edelman argues that what we take for politics and political processes is no more than the result of a 'linguistic segmentation' of the political world (Edelman, 1977). It is 'our mode of referring to problems' (p. 41), our ways of talking about them that creates such separations, that can lead to anxiety, relief or hope, can present social and political issues in one way and not in another. For political scientists like Edelman, 'linguistic fragmentation' is an issue of the symbolic uses of politics, whereas for linguists the same 'fragmentation', the existence and reproduction of binary oppositions in contemporary politics, is the upshot of lexical choices.

just that of commentators) reflects this. The various political themes that constitute 'normal' politics in Western democracies (e.g. immigration, employment/unemployment, economic crisis, apologising for past injustices, etc.), do not come with labels attached to their backs and nor do they automatically point to a 'reality' that is, somehow, *beyond* that of how social and political actors routinely agree to talk about or choose to construct, debate, defend or critique these issues.

When one stops at how political language has been explored in political psychology, one can notice that political psychologists and political scientists seem to be mostly interested in *quantifiable* accounts of political language (see, e.g., Lasswell's *et al.*'s (1949) investigations into quantitative semantics, Osgood's (1978) 'semantics' of international politics, or Tetlock's (1983) 'integrative complexity'). What political language *accomplishes* and *how it does so*, and what (particular) political statements *communicate* do not constitute the focus of analysis (but see Finlayson, 2004, 2007).

For example, Tetlock, the exponent of what is known as cognitive integrative complexity theory, found that 'conservative senators presented issues in significantly less integratively complex ways than their liberal or moderate colleagues' (Tetlock, 1983, p. 123).[4] What matters here is the putative complexity of an individual's information-processing cognitive system, and not the actual *use* of language in its social, cultural and ideological context.[5] This kind of analysis can obscure more than it reveals of the pragmatics of political language. It proposes and reproduces a realist vision of both politics and language. What Tetlock's integrative complexity theory overlooks is that people (especially politicians) may have 'rhetorical stakes' when talking about the causes of social and political events or defending an ideologically informed position. As Billig argues, the strength of discourse perspectives is that they can provide 'both the theoretical apparatus and the methodological tools for examining in detail how ... "rhetorical stakes" are accomplished' (1996, p. 21). Qualitative analysis of political language as social action, based on careful and detailed discursive analysis of social interactions or texts, is considered non-essential by Tetlock.

This propensity reflects not only an epistemological and methodological positivist and objectivist inclination, but also an apolitical vision of politics. It is time for political psychologists to move from

---

[4] See also Chapter 8 for a detailed critique of Tetlock's integrative complexity theory in the context of researching political rhetoric.

[5] This tendency is part of a larger move to treat language in general as an independent variable, and working in settings and with materials where the variability of individuals' talk is mostly ironed out (see Potter, 2012).

studying quantifiable and realist aspects of (verbal) political language towards qualitative and social interaction aspects. Political language ought to be studied as social interaction and social practice, and in terms of its various functions constitutive of political contexts and political culture. A focus on discourse as a form of social action is needed to describe the mutual articulation and constitution of language and politics.

One can (needs to be able to) *show* empirically how various organisations of talk and text around grammatical and syntactic structures, semantic and pragmatic constructions and conversational turns or phrases can *describe*, and say something meaningful about the mutual constitution of discourse and politics. As van Dijk (1997, p. 5) puts it,

an interaction between doctor and patient, between teacher and student, as well as a parliamentary debate or a courtroom session, are not only complex forms of institutional dialogue. They constitute, and are inherent parts of, the more complex discursive and social practices of teaching, providing health care, legislation and "doing" justice.

The relationship between discourse and politics is complex, and requires empirical analysis in its own right. In its contemporary form, political psychology is more interested either in the individualistic *psychology* of politics (e.g. Taber, 2003; Tetlock, 2005) or the macro *political* patterns of international relations (e.g. Herrmann, 2003), but pays less attention to the discursive nature of politics and to how its various forms and functions are the outcome of intricate interactions and social practices.

The crucial contribution of discourse analysts in the social sciences is to offer perspectives on unpacking the discursive organisation of political discourses. For discourse analysts discourse is constitutive of and constituted by social and political 'realities' (Fairclough, 2010; Fairclough and Wodak, 1997; van Dijk, 2008, 2009; van Leeuwen and Wodak, 1999; Wetherell and Potter, 1992; Wodak, 2011). As Fairclough and Wodak (1997) argue, 'discourse is socially *constitutive* as well as socially shaped: it constitutes situations, objects of knowledge, and the social identities of and relationships between people and groups of people' (p. 258, emphasis in original). This chapter is not the place to give justice to the variety of discourse analytic approaches,[6] but rather to focus on the most influential: critical discourse analysis and discursive psychology (see also Chapter 8 for some additional remarks on discursive psychology).

---

[6] For an account of the variety of discourse analytic approaches in the social sciences see Schiffrin *et al.* (2003).

Discourse analysis in linguistics: critical discourse analysis

Critical discourse analysis (henceforth, CDA) is a style of discourse analytic research that 'studies the way social power abuse, dominance and inequality are enacted, reproduced, and resisted by text and talk in the social and political context' (van Dijk, 2001, p. 352).[7] CDA sees discourse as a form of social practice and action. The idea of discourse as a form of social practice and action can be found in a vast body of research programmes in (critical) linguistics and social theory (see Fairclough, 2010; Wodak, 2011 for overviews). Research on political discourse (Chilton and Ilyin, 1993; Chilton and Schäffner, 1997; Wilson, 1990, 2001; Wodak, 2002, 2011) and media discourse (Fairclough, 1995b; Fowler, 1991; Fowler et al., 1979; van Dijk, 1988, 1989, 1991) has been a constant preoccupation of CDA researchers.

The study of ethnocentrism, anti-Semitism and racism has also been a central concern for critical discourse analysts (using a diverse range of material such as conversations, interviews, parliamentary debates, news reports, scholarly text and talk, images) (see, inter alia, Reisigl and Wodak, 2001; van Dijk, 1997; van Leeuwen, 2000; Wodak, 1996, 1997a, b; Wodak and van Dijk; 2000 Wodak et al., 1999). Critical discourse analysts ask questions about the ways in which specific discourse structures are deployed in the reproduction of social dominance. It is one of the main presuppositions of CDA that discursive practices are intimately linked to ideological effects. According to Fairclough and Wodak, 'they can help produce and reproduce unequal power relations between (for instance) social classes, women and men, and ethnic/cultural majorities and minorities through the ways in which they represent things and position people' (1997, p. 258).

For example, Fowler et al.'s (1979) seminal work on the role of power and control in language also included an analysis of a press coverage of an 'ethnic' event (the disturbances at the Notting Hill festival in London). Among other things, Fowler et al.'s findings pointed to how the syntactic structure of the sentences reflected the 'White' dominant perspective of the journalists and the active and passive agency and responsibility of participants to the event was managed through the use of passive forms, particular syntactic and semantic choices. The study of Sykes (1985) on discrimination in discourse comes to similar

---

[7] See also Chouliaraki and Fairclough (1999), Fairclough (1992, 1995a, 2010), Fairclough and Wodak (1997), van Dijk (1993b, 2001), Wodak and Meyer (2002) for summaries of the main tenets of CDA.

conclusions involving the role of grammatical forms in the textual presentation of 'us' and 'them'. In a series of studies, Teun van Dijk examined the ways majority group members in the Netherlands and the USA talk about minorities and ethnic relations in everyday conversations, the press and parliament and elite discourse (van Dijk, 1984, 1987, 1991, 1993a). Van Dijk shows how 'difference' is constructed by speakers along the lines of positive self-presentation and negative-other presentation, together with the use of specific grammatical and syntactic strategies to rationalise prejudice against minority groups. As he suggests, these strategies serve in various ways to legitimise and enact distinctions from those designated as 'others'.

Part of an extended and laborious programme of critical discourse studies, Ruth Wodak and her associates from the University of Vienna have engaged in a series of inquiries into the social, political and historical dimensions of anti-Semitic discourse in Austria (Wodak, 1990, 1991; Wodak and Matouschek, 1993; see also Fairclough and Wodak, 1997). Wodak and colleagues are the proponents of a discourse-historical approach to the rhetoric of racism and anti-Semitism. This discourse analytical approach to the study of prejudice and racism is based on a more context-sensitive approach, including, among other dimensions of context, the broader socio-political and historical context, but also the history of the discursive practices that reproduce dominance and racism.[8] Wodak and colleagues have shown how racist or anti-Semitic beliefs and ideologies are expressed and used for different aims. These have historical traditions and multiple roots, and therefore need to be studied in that context. Discourse analysis is the tool that allows one 'to make explicit the whole range of linguistic devices used to code such beliefs and ideologies as well as the related practices' (Reisigl and Wodak, 2001, p. 266).

Other critical discourse studies, focused on anti-immigrant discourses, have shown how metaphors can be used to dehumanise immigrant workers in the USA (Santa Ana, 1999), and how various discursive strategies are used to treat immigrants, and the poor, as adversaries (Wodak and Matoushek, 1993; see also Edelman, 1977). The use of pronouns and deixis ('we', 'here') and the creation of a contrast between 'us' and 'them', appeals to personal self-interest and apocryphal stories have the power to direct policy and shape political

[8] The discourse-historical perspective has not only confirmed the complexity of prejudiced discursive patterns, but has also suggested that the prejudicial content which expressions of prejudice transmit is largely determined by the historical and linguistic contexts of their emergence (cf. Wodak and Matouschek, 1993; Reisigl and Wodak, 2001).

processes and discourses around immigration, poverty, and so on. Van der Valk (2003) analyses right-wing parliamentary discourse of immigration in France showing that this discourse tends to be organised around a broader trope of negative-other presentation, which includes not only immigrants but their allies too, the most prominent being the parties on the left.

Most notable and more recent concerns in CDA have been foundational, with a re-orientation towards theorising and empirically documenting the triangle society–cognition–discourse (Chilton, 2004; van Dijk, 2008, 2009). At the core of these concerns lies the problem of integrating theories on cognition in critical discourse analyses of talk and text. The assumption is that there must be something underlying our production, organisation and understanding of (political) discourse: mental representations and mental models that guide the process of tying new information to already amassed information. Since the work of van Dijk and Kintsch (1983), there was a strong suggestion of integration. The key idea here is that 'sense is made by readers or hearers, who link their knowledge and expectations stored in long- and short-term memory to the processing of the language input' (Chilton, 2004, p. 154). Chilton goes further to affirm, 'there may exist a deep link between the political and the linguistic' (p. xi). The link is provided by a cognitive theory of language and politics. Cognitive, 'mental' or 'context' models and schemas are, according to van Dijk, fulfilling mediating work (van Dijk, 2009).

Whether or not cognition is seen as playing a pivotal role, the aim of CDA is, on the one hand, to consider the specific *political purposes* to which language is put; and, on the other hand, to chart the particular linguistic means that are used 'by people speaking politically' (Chilton, 2004, p. 200). For critical discourse analysts the task of analysis 'is to relate the fine grain of linguistic behaviour to what we understand by "politics" or "political behaviour"' (Chilton and Schäffner, 1997, p. 211). What is defined as 'political" are those discursive social actions (and social activities) that involve (and reproduce) unequal power relations, dominance, but also resistance, conflict.

There are two crucial strengths of a critical discourse analytic approach. First, it offers an approach to political discourse that allows the linking of individual linguistic and discursive practices with the broad political and historical context (which is seen as underlying their production and reception). Second, it offers a platform for analysing discourses in connection to other discourses, produced synchronically or diachronically. The latter is referred to as 'intertextuality', which comprises a dynamic between 'contextualisation' and 'recontextualisation' (see Fairclough, 2010; Reisigl and Wodak, 2001; Wodak, 2011). This is seen as one of the key features that underlies political discursive practices. According to Wodak (2011, p. 39), intertextuality

refers to the linkage of all texts to other texts, both in the past and in the present. Such links can be established in different ways: through continued reference to a topic or to its main actors; through reference to the same events as the other texts; or through the reappearance of a text's main arguments in another text. The latter process is labelled *recontextualisation*. By taking an argument out of context and restating it in a new context, we first observe the process of decontextualisation, and then when the respective element is implemented in a new context, of recontextualisation ... hence arguments from parliamentary debates, from political speeches or in the mass media are recontextualised in a genre-appropriate way related to specific discourse topics, genres or texts.

For instance, studies by Erjavec and Volcic (2007) on Serbian recontextualisation of G. W. Bush's discourse on 'terrorism', and by Hodges (2008) on 'discursive competition' between journalists and White House officials, have shown how 'recontextualisation' works in practice and how it can prove to be a very useful analytic tool. Erjavec and Volcic (2007) show how G. W. Bush's discourse on 'terrorism' is recycled, used and applied uncritically to all violent actions by Muslims irrespective of the local political/historical context. Hodges (2008) offers a commentary on the power of a politics of 'recontextualisation' between journalists and White House officials over the words of an American general that has seemingly cast doubt on Iran's involvement in Iraq. Hodges demonstrates how recontextualisation is achieved by using reported speech frames/sequences, focalisations and erasures of speech elements, reformulations supposedly serving as clarifications, or reframing the 'gist' of the controversial position. Studies such as these (and many others) demonstrate that it matters how discourses and texts are being circulated and recycled by participants to serve local, interactional business, as well as ideological purposes.

Discourse analysis in social psychology: discursive psychology

The work undertaken in Britain by Michael Billig, Margaret Wetherell, Jonathan Potter, Derek Edwards and others (Billig, 1985, 1998; Billig *et al.*, 1988; Potter and Wetherell, 1987; Wetherell and Potter, 1992; see also Augoustinos and Tileagă, 2012) was a firm step towards establishing discourse analysis as a useful tool in the analysis of social and political practices of various kinds. The development of what is now known as 'discursive psychology' (henceforth DP) was facilitated by the intellectual climate created by the works of Gergen (1973), Harré and Secord (1972) and Shotter (1977), and earlier orientations in the philosophy of language and analytic philosophy (Austin, 1962; Wittgenstein, 1953).

The moment that marked the steady development of the discursive perspective in social psychology was the publishing of *Discourse and Social Psychology* by Jonathan Potter and Margaret Wetherell in 1987. In the same year, Michael Billig's *Arguing and Thinking* was published. The contributions by Potter and Wetherell, and Billig, have rekindled social and political psychologists' interest in language, rhetoric and the argumentative nature of thinking. Their concern with language is not one for language's sake. It stems from the realisation that many of the notions and problems addressed by modern social psychologists can be profitably explored in terms of discursive and social interactional practices.

DP has offered, over the last twenty-five years, original and critical insights into the empirical project of psychology (Augoustinos and Tileagă, 2012; Billig, 2012; Potter, 2012). There is a plethora of books and articles that presents the general characteristics of DP (e.g. Billig, 1991; Edwards and Potter, 1992a, 1993; and more recently, Edwards and Potter, 2001; Hepburn and Wiggins, 2007; Potter, 2012; Potter and Edwards, 2001; Wiggins and Potter, 2008). DP is a broadly constructionist approach associated with a relativist meta-theory (Edwards *et al.*, 1995; Gergen, 1994). DP is constructionist in two ways. On the one hand, it starts from the assumption that individuals construct their own reality through the intermediary of the descriptions they use. 'Reality' is part of our practices through the categories and descriptions, which are part of these practices. As Jonathan Potter (1998, p. 235) argues, reality is 'constituted in one way or another as people talk it, write it, argue it and undermine it'. On the other hand, these very descriptions and accounts that people use in various situations 'are *themselves* constructed; that is fabricated in occasions of talk, or in specific texts, from words, metaphors and a range of discursive resources' (1998, p. 235, emphasis in original).

Arguably, the potential appeal of DP to social and political psychologists is best understood in relation to intellectual debates and social psychological notions and topics that it sought to respecify. Discursive psychologists have offered a range of critical reinterpretations of some of the basic psychological notions such as, attitudes (e.g. Wetherell and Potter, 1992; Wiggins and Potter, 2003), memory (e.g. Edwards and Potter, 1992a, b; Middleton and Edwards, 1990; Tileagă, 2011a), emotion (e.g. Edwards, 1999), cognition (e.g. Edwards, 1997, 2006; te Molder and Potter, 2005), identity (e.g. Benwell and Stokoe, 2006; Merino and Tileagă, 2011; Stokoe, 2009) or the gender problematic (e.g. Edley and Wetherell, 1997, 1999).[9]

Discursive psychologists have focused their study on the subtle, complex, context-sensitive nature of talk and its orientation to social action. People *do* things with their talk: they make accusations, justify their actions, ask questions, excuse, persuade and so on. People use language to do things and to construct versions of the world, depending upon the function of their talk. As Billig (1997) has rightly observed, discursive analysis 'is more than following procedures for collecting and categorising discursive data; it involves a theoretical way of understanding the nature of discourse and the nature of psychological phenomena' (p. 43). DP does not propose a 'method' of analysis (conversational or otherwise) that can be applied in every instance, but constitutes an *epistemological* turn. DP treats talk and texts as social practices and, as Edwards (2003, p. 1) suggests, studies the 'relationships between mind and world, as psychology generally does, but as a discourse topic – as a participant's concern, a matter of talk's business, talk's categories, talk's rhetoric, talk's current interactional concerns'.

Political language, and especially the mutual articulation of politics and language, is a domain where discursive psychologists have made important contributions; yet their insights have passed unnoticed in political psychology.

One of the most fruitful avenues for the examination of the mutual articulation of politics and language is the study of the language of racism. Since the pioneering work of van Dijk (1984, 1987) and Billig (1985) on the links between discourse and racism, discourse has come to be seen as a 'prominent way in which ethnic prejudices and racism are reproduced in society' (van Dijk *et al.*, 1997, p. 144). The work of Margaret Wetherell and Jonathan Potter (Wetherell and Potter, 1992) on the language of racism in New Zealand has been of central importance in investing discourse analysis with the power to question unequal relations of power and document the reproduction of dominance through talk. Among other things, they have shown how constructions of tolerance and denials of feelings of prejudice are part of the common identity work of contemporary racist discourse and how liberal and practical

---

[9] They have also provided critical insights into the psycho-sociological study of notions such as categories (e.g. Widdicombe and Wooffitt, 1995), the attribution process (e.g. Edwards and Potter, 1992a, 1993), social representations (e.g. Billig, 1993; Potter and Edwards, 1999) or racism (Edwards, 2003; Tileagă, 2005, 2007; Wetherell and Potter, 1992).

arguments can be used flexibly alongside conservative and prejudiced ones (Augoustinos and Every, 2010; Rapley, 1998, 2001).

Following on the path opened by *Discourse and Social Psychology* (Potter and Wetherell, 1987), *Mapping the Language of Racism* was the first systematic, empirical attempt at viewing opinions, beliefs and attitudes ('prejudiced' or otherwise) not as a-priori phenomena that need explanation, but rather as resources that members can, flexibly, draw upon in talk, in order to achieve contextual relevant rhetorical and social action. Wetherell and Potter (1992) opened the way for the study of attitudes as 'evaluative practices' (flexibly produced for particular occasions – Speer and Potter, 2000). Also, they paved the way for a completely different understanding of political discourse. For Wetherell and Potter, discourse is not inherently political, it becomes so in 'argument, debate and application' (Wetherell and Potter, 1992, p. 139).[10]

For instance, Tileagă (2005, 2007) has revealed how notions of depersonalisation and dehumanisation can be respecified through a focus on racist social practice and discursive aspects of extreme prejudice. He has shown how talk about ethnic minorities (the Roma minority in Romania) is constitutive of a (potentially eliminationist) discourse that places Romany people beyond a, purportedly, civilised moral order. He has shown how extreme prejudice directed at ethnic minorities is not the outcome of some deep-seated disposition of the speakers, but rather stems from particular clusters and patterns of discursive organisation and accounts that treat Romany people essentially 'unlike us'.

Discursive psychologists do not try to see whether the speaker is 'really' prejudiced, whether openly or behind the camouflage of his talk. Prejudice is approached analytically as something that may be attended to in various ways, in talk itself (Speer and Potter, 2000). The aim is to avoid conclusions such as that the speaker is basically prejudiced, but camouflaging it in the way they talk and that analysis can reveal their true beliefs and attitudes (cf. Edwards, 2003). The discursive approach has helped the process of mapping the production of 'prejudice' as an everyday phenomenon as it is produced by members in social interaction. What counts as 'racism' is inextricably and locally produced, as such, in talk.

---

[10] Discourse research on ethnic relations has demonstrated the social-action level of attitudes. Racist attitudes are seen as interpretative effects of descriptions and explanations (Potter and Wetherell, 1988; Tileagă, 2007; Wetherell and Potter, 1992). People's talk is not 'just' talk. For instance, providing an evaluation *for* something is, often, implicitly providing an evaluation *against* something else (Billig, 1988). As discursive psychologists have argued, it is better to treat evaluative talk in terms of its role in interaction rather than trying to characterise it using notions such as attitudes and opinions (e.g. Puchta and Potter, 2002; see also Chapter 1).

Racism is not a psychological dimension that can be applied to some individuals and, by extension, not others. The analysis of social interaction considers the local codes of argument and practices of rhetorical organisation of selected interactions. Discourse analysis of racism in social psychology goes beyond the semantic, pragmatic, grammatical and propositional levels of linguistic analysis and the simple interpretation of complex discursive strategies. For example, as van Dijk put it (1987), 'talk about ethnic groups involves complex strategies and moves aiming at positive self-presentation within the overall of negative other-description' (p. 22). When delicate topics are under discussion and when social norms are rather strict, face saving is essential. In discussing van Dijk, Billig (1988) argued that the assumption of a contradiction between racist attitudes and interactional strategies should be seen as a contradiction within the different ideological themes people draw on. Billig *et al.* (1988) suggest that common sense is dilemmatic and people possess contrary themes as part of their common stock of knowledge. The argumentative nature of (racist) attitudes is stressed, as attitudes represent positions in a matter of controversy (Billig, 1996). The rhetorical and argumentative context of attitudes implies that people will justify their stance and criticise competing views.

Other strands of discursive work have focused on construction and reproduction of opinions, political attitudes and ideology (e.g. Billig, 1991, 1998) and the management of political categories in political discourse (e.g. Tileagă, 2008, 2010). Billig's (1998) investigation of British families talking about the British royal family is a fascinating investigation of ordinary talk and what it can reveal about the study of opinions, political attitudes and ideology. Billig shows how, when invited to talk about the greatest 'family' in the country, British families are also talking about themselves. The context of their evaluations of the royal family was the context of a family discussion where comparisons, analogies, metaphors and humour are the ingredients of political socialisation (see also Chapter 6 on discursive aspects of political socialisation). The opinions, attitudes and ideologies that British families express do not come ready formed but rather are the result of the 'creative dialogue' between family members, pushing 'speakers into new realms of talk and thought' (Billig, 1996, p. 28).

Tileagă (2008, 2010) has offered detailed discursive analyses of the various conceptual/discursive contests over political categories in Eastern Europe, with a particular focus on how the Romanian 'revolution of 1989' was discussed and defined in elite accounts and attempts at constructing an ideological representation of the event in a succession of commemorative speeches. Focusing on the political rhetoric of former Romanian president, Ion Iliescu, Tileagă has shown that one can only successfully understand the mutual constitution of language and politics, and how language functions as a form of social action, if one focuses on the contested and contestable language of the polity (Connolly, 1993; Gallie, 1956). He has made a strong case for a detailed investigation of how social and political categories are actually *used* and *defined* by people in different settings, and how these uses and definitions are consequential for managing (public) controversies and building support for 'preferred' representations of social affairs. The category 'revolution' is not a neutral label for the events of 1989. Social and political categories come with a range of presuppositions, common category-based knowledge and category-bound attributes.

Tileagă argues that one needs to pay careful attention to how these categories are defined and the uses to which they are put in a variety of argumentative contexts (Billig, 1996). Tileagă demonstrates how Iliescu's discourse on the Romanian revolution is incorporating unre-flectively the contours and confines of the conventional meaning of 'revolution' in an attempt to delegitimise the increased challenges from the political opposition and wider public regarding the 'truth'. Iliescu's chosen way of managing controversy leads to a perspective on politics and political accountability that takes for granted and assumes uncrit-ically the very terms and stakes of public controversy around the mean-ing of the '1989 revolution', political action, responsibility and truth. Political categories and concepts are not universal; they are relative to the language and culture of a polity.

In the same vein, Augoustinos *et al.* (2011) show how apologising for past injustices is a complex social and discursive practice, where speak-ers and audience orient to various issues of (historical) truth, identity, emotion and national identity (see also LeCouteur *et al.*, 2001). Their analysis of the prime minister's apology to indigenous Australians highlights how emotion and reason are used by the Australian prime minister to present his discourse *as* a political apology and manage public controversy. Issues of 'empathy' and 'humanising the other' were realised through the discursive construction of collective emo-tion, through the subtle use of different levels of self- and national categorisation.

What both Tileagă and Augoustinos *et al.* show is that the social cat-egories and identities speakers invoke can be used as strategic political tools for managing political controversy. Both give support for the notion that category contests, and the discursive realisation of psychological states, provide an argumentative space for political interaction. Both Tileagă and Augoustinos *et al.* treat political language as a complex form of social activity, *as* social practice, clusters of various organisations of social actions. Political language does not appear and reproduce itself in a vacuum. It functions in an argumentative context of controversy, where categories, categorisations, identities 'shape both what we see and what we do not see in the political world' (Edelman, 1977, p. 24).

Discursive social psychologists have laid the foundations of an analytic trend that has attempted to show that what social and political psychologists are, in fact, studying are phenomena constituted in and through social interaction (Edwards, 2012; Potter, 2012). There are two implications arising from this. First, discursive psychologists have offered an alternative and transformation of the social psychological study of psychology's topics without relying on the conventional socio-cognitive assumptions contained in much of existing social psychology. For instance, the notion of 'cognition' (see, inter alia, Antaki, 2006; Edwards, 2006; te Molder and Potter, 2005) is treated as participants' accomplishment in talk and not as something pre-existing, preforming and predetermining language choices and mental states. No assumption is made as to 'what goes on' in participants' heads, but rather cognition, emotion, mental states are something that are seen as publicly *inspectable* and *analysable* in and through the details of everyday or institutional talk. DP stresses the importance of language as a topic of inquiry in its own right, and not a pathway to something that lies behind it. Most of the psychological phenomena, which psychologists have traditionally considered to be 'internal states', are constituted in and are an integral part of social activities.[11]

Second, DP has championed the systematic and rigorous use of records of actual interaction and behaviour, and considered the way in which naturalistic[12] materials provide access to participants' own orientations and displays. DP has been at the forefront of a new way of doing social psychology, based on meticulous and specific analyses of actual instances of discourse (Potter, 2012). The majority of contemporary

[11] For instance, Edwards (2006, 2007) shows how cognitive terms (*think* or *feel*) and modal verbs (*would*) are used in police interrogations by both police and suspects to manage 'factual' versions of reality: what happened, who is responsible, who acted, and so on. Edwards points to how these terms do not index mental states but rather are constitutive of social actions: blaming or deflecting blame, managing personal or group accountability for actions, stake or interest.

[12] As Potter (2012) argues, the term is used by discursive psychologists 'to mark the contrast from the "got up" materials that have been at the centre of social psychology's development in North America and much of Europe – vignettes, experimental protocols, survey responses' (pp. 437–8).

social and political psychology approaches focus on human conduct as essentially dependent on (putative) mental entities. In contrast, discursive psychologists start with mundane and institutional social interaction and social practices. Most of contemporary social and political psychology fails to take seriously the social interactions and social practices within which social actors situate their social and political behaviour. In contrast, DP underlines the central role and function of those social practices.

DP argues that the variety of social interactions and social practices represents an intricate and contingent social order. Political psychology has moved away from studying the normative organisation of social interaction and social life, and the systematic use of records of actual human action (talk and text). The possibilities that DP opens for the study of politics, for both psychologists and political scientists, are endless. Instead of collecting observations through scales or experimental set-ups, mostly in an attempt to test theories or cognitive models, the aim would be to generate discursive records of particular domains (and study their discursive organisation) – interaction in news interviews, panels, political speeches, lay meanings of politics expressed in focus groups, for instance – which could then be used to generate more hypotheses and for the study of other political phenomena.

Families talking about the royal family, majorities talking about minorities, national apologies and political speeches that debate political categories are only some examples of how DP has been used in the study of political language. All these settings and contexts are rich sources of naturalistic data from which one can examine a number of important issues related to political language: first, its pragmatic and linguistic features; second, its anchoring and constitutive role in broader social practices, and in a conception of human and social action that does not treat language as a peripheral or epiphenomenal dimension. Discursive psychologists urge political psychologists to examine the 'rich surface' of language and social interaction (Edwards, 2006). Researching political language as a network of mental representations will inevitably lead to treating discourse as the *expression* of cognitive states and schemas. In contrast, what DP suggests is that political language is examined as *performative social action* in the details of its discursive organisation.

Political discourse – complex form of social activity

Although there are many points on which critical discourse analysts and discursive psychologists interested in political language disagree, what is key for both approaches is that political discourse is a complex form of human/social activity to be studied in its own right. This chapter argued that this focus can constitute the core, if not the foundation, for a distinctive and original political psychology. Some social psychologists have recently expressed a feeling of disquiet with social psychology increasingly becoming a 'science of self-reports and finger movements', and uneasiness with how social psychology chooses to eclipse the study of behaviour, the study of what people actually do (cf. Baumeister *et al.*, 2007). Political psychologists have followed suit, by acknowledging that political psychology cannot just rely on cognitive models to understand political behaviour (Kinder, 2003).

A focus on discourse as a phenomenon of politics, studied in its own right, could transform the empirical and epistemological landscape of political psychology. Researching political language in its own right needs to claim (re-claim) its place at the centre of political psychological inquiry. Such a shift would also re-situate and redefine political psychology as a science of social and political practices. It will move it away from an almost exclusive focus on mental processes and processing, mental organisation and overreliance on cognitive models, experimental scenarios, imagined situations, towards the study of actual behaviour. Contemporary political psychology represents an academic institutionalised structure of meanings that has the power to influence psychological and political thought and action in certain directions and not in others. Those researchers who simply rely on established/ conventional frameworks and concepts to get to the 'facts' of political life, to the 'psychology' behind political behaviour, and those who act unreflectively within the confines of established methods and methodologies, actually have the perceptions and modes of inquiry available to them limited in subtle and unnoticed ways.

Researching political language in its own right is not simply a matter of charting the 'linguistic fragmentation' of social and political life. It is a matter of the *constructive* and *constitutive* role that language plays in social and political life. This position has wider implications for the analysis of political language. The analysis moves the study of the inner realm of the cognitions and emotions of the individual towards the study of outward expressions of political meanings, and of the public and accountable ways in which political realities are constructed when we talk about ourselves and others, home or international affairs, towards the study of discursive practices that constitute, enact and reproduce politics, political meanings and political realities.

Both CDA and DP, with their sustained focus on the mutual articulation and constitution of language and politics, can provide an original alternative to describing and understanding the relationship between language practices, political action and reality. By pointing to how actual political language is constituted by a series of action-oriented accomplishments and ideological forms, socially organised clusters of discursive practices, can facilitate and enrich the study of the meaningful relationship between psychological processes and political practices.

8 Political rhetoric

Political discourse and the relevance of rhetoric

The preceding chapter has discussed the relationship between discourse and politics. It has outlined the crucial and original contribution of discourse analysis in linguistics and social psychology to the study of political language. In this chapter the discussion is broadened to how social and political psychologists have traditionally approached the issue of persuasive communications, and some examples are given of how they treat language and rhetoric. The remainder of the chapter includes a discursive analysis of two selected aspects of political rhetoric: the use of metaphors and identification with an audience. The chapter closes with a discussion of the crucial task of moving towards a genuine political psychology of political rhetoric by anchoring it in the detailed study of the public *use* of language.

It is perhaps a truism to affirm that in politics, as in other realms of social life, rhetorical commitment and debate are necessary ingredients. Arguably, the political importance of rhetoric and dialogue is a position that does not often require justification. What does require justification is the way in which one thinks about and approaches it empirically. The term 'political rhetoric' refers both to the ways in which politicians try to persuade various audiences and to the (academic) study of such oratory (see Billig, 2003; Condor *et al.*, in press). This chapter approaches political rhetoric in the spirit that Aristotle (trans. 1909) first championed. This is an analytic spirit, where the focus is on discovering 'the available means of persuasion in each case' (p. 5). This chapter suggests that the phenomenon of political persuasion 'calls for a psychological approach that is itself rooted within the study of rhetoric' (Billig, 2003, p. 223).

A widely held assumption is the one that claims that 'political discourse is the use of language in ways that humans, being political animals, tend to recognise as "political"' (Chilton, 2004, p. 201). The only problem with such definitions of political discourse is that they are circular. They start and end with Aristotle's 'political animal', positing, in an evolutionary fashion, a direct correspondence/relationship between human nature and political discourse. But it is debatable whether there is something inherent in this relationship. The rapport between human nature, language and politics is necessary, functional and yet sometimes unexpected and not at all obvious (Moscovici, 1988; Billig, 1987). To be able to speak of 'political discourse' requires not only some notion of how human beings go about recognising things and features as 'political', but also what is behind (or *what goes with*) this process of recognition. Here political psychologists have had much to say.

As Chapter 7 has shown, political discourse can be described as a complex form of social activity. For some, it is the expression of information-processing complexity (Suedfeld *et al.*, 2001; Tetlock, 1984), political impression formation and management (McGraw, 2003), the satisfactory or unsatisfactory political explanations given by politicians (McGraw, 2001), the interplay of linguistic and pragmatic (Fairclough, 2010; Wodak, 2011) or rhetorical and discursive factors and features (Billig, 2003; Tileagă, 2008, 2010). One could place these concerns on a continuum from informational inputs and cognitive processing complexity to linguistic, rhetorical and discursive features of discourse. When the focus is on informational 'input–output' models, questions concerning political discourse take the following form: 'When does political discourse rise enough above the informational din of modern life for citizens to take notice? What types of political information provoke more thought than others?' (cf. Taber, 2003, p. 446).

When the focus is on rhetoric, questions take on a different emphasis: What makes speeches/messages persuasive? How are they constructed and what are some of their most striking rhetorical features? What is the function of 'little words' such as 'us' ('we') and 'them' ('they')? And, more broadly, how can people's political thinking be analysed and understood by examining political discourse? 'Informational input' and 'cognitive processing' questions tend to focus on the 'when' (conditions, constraints) and the 'what' (content) of political communication and persuasion. The questions on 'rhetoric' focus on 'how' (social action), that is on how language is organised rhetorically to elicit certain effects and how social actions are accomplished using various rhetorical and discursive/cultural resources. The latter questions have originated in a 'way of doing' psychology that, alongside other critical social science perspectives with roots in linguistics and social theory (Fairclough, 2010; Wodak, 2011), has revived an interest in rhetoric and language use (Billig, 1987, 1996; Edwards, 1997; Potter and Wetherell, 1987; Wetherell and Potter, 1992; see also Chapter 7).

Consider, for instance, an extract from Barack Obama's Nobel lecture in December 2009 at the Oslo City Hall in Norway.

The service and sacrifice of our men and women in uniform has promoted peace and prosperity from Germany to Korea, and enabled democracy to take hold in places like the Balkans. We have borne this burden not because we seek to impose our will. We have done so out of enlightened self-interest – because we seek a better future for our children and grandchildren, and we believe that their lives will be better if other peoples' children and grandchildren can live in freedom and prosperity.

Barack Obama's wise words on American foreign policy can be seen to reflect a vision of politics, where politics itself is the agent and driver of the transformation of society's order. In this case, the politics of one nation is the agent and driver of the transformation of the world order. In order to achieve this rhetorical effect, Obama needs to position himself as speaking from within the community of reasonable politicians whose interest is not only that of his own community. President Obama can be seen as being engaged in an attempt at political persuasion, defending and justifying the USA's humanitarian wars. In order to achieve that he needs to establish himself as exhibiting a certain democratic 'character' (he does the same for the policies he is advocating), he needs to put the audience into a certain frame of mind (by making reference to national self-interest in the service of the world of nations) and advance rational and substantive arguments to support the thrust of his political case. Obama embodies patriotism and duty in the way that other American and British leaders have done in the past.

There is no doubt about what 'we' refers to here. The use of 'our men and women in uniform' seeks to establish a relationship between the representative of the nation and an imagined audience sharing the same political interests. There is also a clear distinction between 'us' (Americans) and 'them' (others, named and unnamed). If what is at stake is political action of a particular sort ('humanitarian intervention'), then 'we' (Americans) are the agents and drivers of that action; 'other' nations are the recipients of this action; they are the recipients of 'our' noble goals (see Billig, 2003 for an extensive discussion of the rhetoric of 'us' and 'them' in political discourse). Thus, policies of national self-interest are made to coincide with policies of international self-sacrifice.

'Enlightened self-interest' stands like an abstract political symbol that legitimates American foreign policy throughout time. Through his choice and use of pronouns, Obama signals and discursively operates political distinctions. His political message intermingles the rhetoric of power with one of solidarity (Brown and Gilman, 1960). He relies on pronouns of distance ('us' vs. 'them') to convey a political message of solidarity. The distinction between 'us' and 'them' is needed for political action and persuasion to work. Without it, there would be no politics of intervention and no persuasion. What is the strategic function of Obama's use of language? Is it producing a common view around basic, common values as an intrinsic part of constituting a togetherness repertoire and the legitimation of political action (humanitarian intervention)? Arguably, Obama appeals at the heart of what is contemporary politics: persuading others to partake in a common view on what is universal or particular, virtuous or corrupt, warranted or unwarranted. As history shows us, such an attempt can be used for both progressive and conservative ends.

Persuasive communications

Social psychological research associated with the now famous dictum: 'who says what to whom and with what effect' was the first systematic and comprehensive attempt to understand the relationship between communicators (sources), communication (messages) and audience (recipients) (Hovland et al., 1953). When Hovland agreed to work for the US War Department, towards the end of the Second World War, German propaganda was a living example of how the masses could be persuaded to rally behind Hitler and support the war effort. The US government was concerned with propaganda (and its effects), and it wanted to see how propaganda (especially in the form of films) could persuade American troops to consider that the end of the war might not come as soon as they wished. What started as a practical and political issue was soon turned into a psychological programme of research at Yale University aimed at discovering 'general laws of persuasion'.

For instance, it was discovered that experts are more persuasive than non-experts (Hovland and Weiss, 1952), or that popular and attractive communicators seemed to be more effective than unpopular and unattractive ones (Kiesler and Kiesler, 1969). It was noted that one is more easily persuaded if one thinks the message is not deliberately intended to persuade or manipulate (Walster and Festinger, 1962), that people with low self-esteem are persuaded more easily than people with high self-esteem (Janis, 1954) and that when the message is simple, people are more susceptible to persuasion when distracted than when paying full attention (Allyn and Festinger, 1961). It was highlighted that persuasion can be increased by messages that arouse fear in the audience (Leventhal et al., 1965), although results were mixed (see Janis and Feshbach, 1953; Leventhal et al., 1967).

As Billig (2003; see also Billig, 1987) argues, the Yale studies of persuasion 'tended to assume a separation between the independent or rhetorical variables and the psychology of the recipients' (p. 224). Nonetheless, other approaches such as McGuire's (1964) inoculation theory and Petty and Cacioppo's (1981, 1984) dual-process models of persuasion proposed that the relationship between messages and audiences could be conceived of as a form of rhetorical and argumentative dialogue. McGuire started with the practical problem of the brainwashing of American soldiers taken prisoner in the Korean War. The experiments that he designed and performed (Anderson and McGuire, 1965; McGuire and Papageorgis, 1961) have tried to demonstrate the importance of attitudinal 'inoculation' as a technique of resisting persuasion. He showed that by providing his participants with small doses of arguments they could build stronger 'defences' to counter-arguments. In McGuire's research, argumentation is a characteristic of the receivers' internal thought processes. By actively creating or looking for counter-arguments, participants built defences. McGuire's recipients have had to imagine and rehearse both sides of the argument.

Petty and Cacioppo's (1981, 1984, 1986) dual-process model of persuasion draws on developments from cognitive psychology to consider how source and message may play well-defined roles, and how together with motivation and the amount of cognitive effort expended on the message, they can determine the specific outcome of attempts at persuasion. According to the model, when people are motivated to attend to a message and deal with it thoughtfully they are more likely to use a central route to process it. When attention (and motivation) is reduced and people become cognitively lazy they are more likely to use a peripheral route.

The two routes to persuasion suggested by Petty and Cacioppo match 'classical rhetoric's distinction between persuasion by content and persuasion by form' (Billig, 2003, p. 224). Persuasion models have been mainly applied to advertising, not to politics. The difficulty comes when one tries to apply these models to contemporary politics. Petty and Cacioppo's distinction between form and content does not map easily onto the complex visual and verbal rhetoric of contemporary politics that permits individuals to let their motivation and attention *float* and work with finer and looser distinctions. The engagement and study of contemporary politics are more akin to a gestalt psychology of parts and wholes than to strict distinctions between form and content. There are also different styles and forms of politics. The formal and informal conversational gambits of television politics or the ceremonial and ritual of parliamentary debates pose problems for the traditional distinction between form and content. Depending on the context, the 'character' that speakers are keen to present (*ethos*) stops being a peripheral matter and becomes a central element, especially for those political observers who know where to look, and who and what to scrutinise. At the same time, the arguments that the speakers are advancing (*logos*) can fade into the background.

Complex political issues do not come with labels attached to their backs, and it is up to the citizens/viewers to make sense of what is going on. *Ethos*, *pathos* and *logos*, the three ingredients of classical rhetoric, can shift from background to foreground, from part to whole. For example, presidential campaigns have their different ratios of ethos, pathos and logos, as other more complex political manifestations will have theirs. A televised debate involving the leaders of three major parties, such as that between Gordon Brown, David Cameron and Nick Clegg in the UK in 2010, involved all three elements to a different degree, than say, the fierce debate around the invasion of Iraq in the House of Commons.

Cognitive integrative complexity

The assumption behind both McGuire's and Petty and Cacioppo's models is that thinking can be intrinsically rhetorical. Other social and political psychology perspectives have tried to consider the relationship between personality, cognitive structure and cognitive style when considering political rhetoric. The focus here will be on integrative complexity theory, as developed by Tetlock, Suedfeld and colleagues (Suedfeld *et al.*, 1992; Suedfeld *et al.*, 2001).

The issue of cognitive complexity is usually thought of in terms of different ways of processing information.[1] In Tetlock's (1983, pp. 119–20) own words, the focus of integrative complexity theory is on

the cognitive differentiation and integration of information. Differentiation refers to the variety of aspects of an issue that a person recognizes ... A more differentiated politician would recognize that policies have multiple, sometimes contradictory, effects that cannot be easily classified on a single evaluative dimension: effects on diverse political constituencies, various parameters of the economy, defense posture, and the strategies of one's allies and opponents. Integration refers to the development of complex connections among differentiated characteristics. The complexity of integration depends on whether the individual perceives the differentiated characteristics as operating in isolation

---

[1] One of the guiding questions for this programme of research has been, 'do leaders process information in simplistic ways, focusing only on a single perspective or black-or-white alternatives, or do they recognize different points of view, perhaps even integrating them into broader complex perspectives?' (Winter, 2003, p. 124).

(low integration), in simple patterns (moderate integration) or in multiple, complex patterns (high integration).

The focus of 'cognitive complexity' research is on elite political discourse – different groups of political actors: US presidents (Tetlock, 1981b), senators (Tetlock, 1981a, 1983), members of the British House of Commons (Tetlock, 1984), United Nations (UN) general assembly speeches concerning the Middle East (Suedfeld et al., 1977), Middle East leaders during the Persian Gulf crisis (Suedfeld et al., 1993), Canadian prime ministers (Suedfeld et al., 2001), Soviet politicians during the 1980s (Tetlock, 1985; Tetlock and Boettger, 1989), American and Soviet policy rhetoric (Tetlock, 1988) and the rhetoric of selected politicians, such as Bill Clinton (Suedfeld, 1994) or Mikhail Gorbachev (Wallace et al., 1996).

For instance, Tetlock (1983) looked at congressional speeches given by senators during 1975 and 1976. Material collected from archives was coded for integrative complexity in terms of both 'differentiation' and 'integration'. Tetlock (1983, p. 122) concluded that

liberals and moderates both advanced more complex policy statements than did conservatives ... there was no statistically detectable difference between liberals and moderates ... Republicans tended to be less complex than Democrats ... and political ideology emerged as the only significant predictor of integrative complexity. More liberal senators tended to be more complex.

Tetlock introduced a qualification – a very significant one, but one whose implications have been ignored – 'the less complex policy statements of conservative senators may not so much reflect variation in cognitive style as in rhetorical style' (p. 124). For Tetlock rhetorical style is a function of political roles (opposition vs. policy-making roles). Tetlock et al. (1984) tested the cognitive versus rhetorical style hypothesis. It was discovered that 'where liberals and moderates were in politically dominant roles, they were more integratively complex than conservatives; by contrast, when conservatives were in politically dominant roles, they did not become more integratively complex than liberals and moderates' (1984, p. 988).

In Tetlock (1983) and Tetlock et al. (1984), the distinction between 'simple' rhetoric and 'more complex' rhetoric is not accounted for in rhetorical terms, but rather in cognitive/information processing terms. Although the importance of specific rhetorical contexts is not dismissed, Tetlock's model does not take into account the argumentative context in which political accounts are given and the rhetorical actions they fulfil. In a study looking at the 'integrative complexity' of American and Soviet policy rhetoric (Tetlock, 1988), Mikhail Gorbachev's political rhetoric was found to be significantly more complex than that of his predecessors.[2] His 'rhetoric' was perceived as being 'very consistent with the emerging impression of Gorbachev in the West as a pragmatic, albeit forceful, leader with an acknowledged ability to argue for his policies in flexible and reasonable ways' (Tetlock, 1988, p. 125). Gorbachev's political rhetoric is reduced to the analysis of decontextualised statements that can then be compared with other statements from other politicians on the two dimensions of differentiation and integration. The richness and intricacy of political language are reduced to *statements* that can be easily categorised according to a framework that downplays (or even ignores) active processes of (political) communication. It is acknowledged that 'integrative complexity is more appropriately viewed as a measure of knowledge in use in a particular situation, not a measure of intellectual ability or understanding' (Tetlock, 1983, p. 125); yet there is no sense in which this is studied in a *situated context* of communication.

Within the theory of cognitive complexity, what political communication itself *does* and what specific statements *communicate* does not seem to matter; it is solely an issue of individuals who process information either in integratively simple or complex ways. Although seemingly geared towards an understanding of political processes, integrative complexity proposes an apolitical view of politics. The complexity of political messages and the rhetorical process of identification with an audience do not seem to matter. Instead, it is the putative complexity of an individual's information-processing cognitive system that is the focus. In political terms, these kinds of analyses can obscure more than they reveal.

It is acknowledged that research on information-processing complexity needs to be 'sensitive to both representational and instrumental functions of language' (Tetlock *et al.*, 1984, p. 989); yet language is not studied or treated in its own right and there is virtually no concern with its situated and rhetorical nature.[3] There is a slight recognition that it is language that allows us to have, express and reproduce ideologies, but language is only treated as a 'transparent' vehicle for expressing attitudes and cognitive states.

---

[2] It was argued that Gorbachev's rhetorical style 'resembles that of moderate Western reformers who seek not to dismantle the systems within which they work, but to make the systems function more effectively and equitably' (Tetlock, 1988, p. 124).

[3] For instance, if one looks at the scoring manual used to code integrative complexity (Baker-Brown *et al.*, 1986), one notices that features of rhetoric are, in a way, undesirable, and can lead to 'unscorable' statements. Rhetoric poses problems for the scorers. Unscorable statements are removed from data analysis. Among the indicators that may render a statement 'unscorable' are mentioned: clichés or idioms, satire and sarcasm, descriptions.

Discourse analysis and political rhetoric

Social and political psychological research that focuses on persuasive communications and information-processing complexity has not been particularly concerned with the discursive details of politicians' rhetoric. As Billig (2003) argues convincingly, for a continuous interest in rhetoric one has to turn to conversation and discourse analysis.

Of particular interest are conversation analyses of political communication (Atkinson, 1984; Clayman and Heritage, 2002; Heritage and Greatbatch, 1986). In *Our Masters' Voices* (1984), John Maxwell Atkinson has tried to understand the discursive organisation of applause. How could one explain the fine coordination of politician's addresses and audience reaction? How do politicians communicate with their audiences in order to achieve instant coordination? He noted that politicians used so-called rhetorical 'clap-traps' to get coordinated applause. In order for this to work, politicians delivering speeches need to communicate that an 'applaudable message is under way' (Atkinson, 1984, p. 50); they need to give their audiences a sign that this is a place where an audience response would be appropriate and expected. For example, by using a 'three-part list' (see Jefferson, 1985) politicians can communicate to their audiences that they have reached a completion point where applause might be in order. Consider the extract from the Conservative Party conference in 1980, in which the then British Prime Minister Margaret Thatcher introduces her deputy (extract 1).

Extract 1 (from Atkinson, 1984) [4]

Thatcher: I am however (0.2) very fortunate (0.4) in having
            (0.6) a <u>mar</u>vellous deputy (0.4) who's wonderful
            (.) in <u>all</u> places (0.2) at all times (0.2) in all things.
            (0.2)
            Willie White [law – – – – – – – – – – – – – – – – – (8.0)
Audience: [x-xxX X X X X X X X X X X X X X X X X X X xxx-x
            (applause)

Notice how the three-part list 'in all places (0.2) at all times (0.2) in all things' followed by the name of her deputy, is used to project a completion point. Note also how the audience's applause comes in overlap with her turn.

---

[4] See the list of transcription conventions used by conversation analysts at the beginning of this book.

Heritage and Greatbatch (1986) have documented the importance of rhetorical packaging of addresses for obtaining coordinated applause. Contrasts, three-part lists and puzzle solutions are the most common. These have to be used appropriately, with timing, intonation and delivery playing a great part. The focus is on the form, accuracy and coordinated nature of delivery and response. Rhetorical properties of political speeches are a feature of how the speech itself is organised (a matter of discursive organisation and oratorical skill). If all the elements are in place, the effect is achieved.

Conversation analytic techniques are also well suited to understanding the turn-by-turn organisation of political discourse when politicians are held to account 'for their own deeds or words or for the actions/statements of the institution with which they are associated' (Montgomery, 2008, p. 262). Political news interviews are one such setting, and are increasingly used to express, validate and negotiate political views. Political news interviews can be thought of as settings where researchers can unpack the 'interactional accountability of answering questions' as Clayman and Heritage put it, which is seen as 'the fundamental basis for the public accountability of public figures' (2002, p. 235; see also Hutchby, 2006). What is at stake in conversation analytic studies is not making assumptions about the psychological states of the audience or of 'wishes', 'desires', 'intentions' of politicians making the speeches. The focus is more on rhetorical form rather than content.

A shift from a focus on rhetorical form to content is made by analyses of discourse that have been using the techniques of critical discourse analysis, especially those that combine linguistics and pragmatics with critical theory and those offering socio-cognitive analyses of political discourse (turn to Chapter 7 for a detailed discussion). For researchers trying to integrate insights from linguistics, pragmatics and critical theory, understanding and analysing political discourse implies identifying and analysing a range of *presuppositions, insinuations, inferences* and *implicatures* that are active in political texts (Wodak, 2011) and the *recontextualisation* of politics in and through the media (Fairclough and Fairclough, 2011; Schäffner, 2010). This chapter focuses on the former aspect, leaving the latter for Chapter 9.

A telling example is offered by Ruth Wodak (2011) when discussing ways of 'doing politics' in Europe. An account of her analysis of Romano Prodi's speech (Romano Prodi was the President of the European Commission from 1999 to 2004) to the European Parliament in 2000 (see extract 2) is included here.

Extract 2
The challenge is to radically rethink the way we do Europe. To re-shape Europe
… If we act boldly and decisively together, we can shape the new Europe our
citizens want and that we owe to our future generations. A just, human, inclusive Europe. An exciting, energetic, enterprising Europe. Everyone's Europe.
Let us work together to make this decade a decade of outstanding achievement
and success. A decade history will remember as the decade of Europe.

For Wodak, there are a series of presuppositions in Prodi's exhortation.
First, there is the implication that 'things have gone wrong' and that everyone must be 'involved in a common effort to make things better' (Wodak,
2011, p. 29). The political category 'Europe' is being attached to various
predicates: 'new Europe'; 'just, human, inclusive Europe'; 'enterprising
Europe'. These are presented as one political vision of renewal under different guises. Second, linguistically and pragmatically, doing European
politics is tied to 'a combination of material and mental verbs and processes' (p. 29): 'doing', 'thinking', 'shaping'. Third, Wodak observes how,
in order to work, Prodi's visionary political rhetoric needs to be accompanied by references to 'innovation, creativity, skills and knowledge' (p. 29).
The means of 'doing Europe' are not specified; there is a presupposition
of shared knowledge of activities, courses of action, and so on.

There is an assumption of shared 'collective will' (see also Fairclough,
2000 on the use of a similar rhetorical strategy in New Labour discourse). What is at stake in Prodi's speech is defining an abstract collective entity. Wodak (2011) shows how Europe is used by Prodi as a
'metaphor for a quasi static and stable entity which could be shaped
and constructed by the politicians (*we*) who work for *them* (European
citizens and future generations, *ergo* everyone)' (p. 30, emphasis in original). Europe is no longer an abstract, transnational socio-political system, but rather a 'discursively construed governable territory' (p. 30).

Also, the speech posits a 'temporal sequence' of change. The *topos* of
'change' (and implied notions of 'challenge' and 'obstacles') is constitutive of Prodi's speech and a feature of most European Union (EU)
'agenda setting' documents. As Wodak (2011) argues, '*topoi* are part
and parcel of any political speech, and – when used in this context –
are of interest for their specific persuasive function' (pp. 30–1). What
Prodi's 'visionary speech' does is to bring into focus another dimension of doing politics. Although change requires the participation of all,
the public is usually 'excluded from negotiations, from conversations
taking place in the corridors of the buildings of various institutions
… from relevant decision-making bodies, and from the crises and the
stress which necessarily occur in political life' (pp. 31–2). What Wodak
refers to as 'politics as usual' is designed and conducted in such a way
that participation and real debate are stifled.

But discourse analysts do not stop at the analysis of linguistic and pragmatic presuppositions. Inspired by developments in cognitive science, some researchers have moved towards cognitively inspired discursive analyses of political discourse. It is believed that one should focus on the 'processes of our minds in order to enhance our understanding of human nature, including our political nature' (Chilton, 2004, p. 205). The cognitive revolution in psychology and linguistics (Johnson-Laird, 1983; Lakoff and Johnson, 1980) has firmly grounded the study of language as a mental capacity in association with the other mental capacities (e.g. long- and short-term memory, mental schemas, mental models). For example, in the discipline of cognitive linguistics a focus on social and political cognition, mediated by the notion of 'mental model', has become a distinctively original approach (Chilton, 1996). According to Teun van Dijk, one of the major proponents of the international discipline of discourse studies, to analyse fully political meaning making in political speeches, conversations, and so on, 'we need not only experts in interaction, but also experts in cognition' (van Dijk, 2009, p. 102).

Van Dijk's own research on political discourse (see, inter alia, van Dijk, 1993a, b, 2008, 2009) is an example of building discursive analyses and theories based on the foundation offered by the notion of 'mental model'. For van Dijk, the notion of 'mental model' is the conceptual joint that holds in place the triangle society–discourse–cognition (Tileagă, 2011b). To hone in on the point of a socio-cognitive analysis of political discourse, van Dijk offers the example of Tony Blair's speech defending a motion intended to legitimate war against Iraq in the House of Commons (18 March 2003 – see extract 3; see also Chapter 5 in van Dijk, 2009 for an extensive account).

Extract 3
At the outset, I say that it is right that the House debate this issue and pass judgment. That is the democracy that is our right, but that others struggle for in vain. Again, I say that I do not disrespect the views in opposition to mine. This is a tough choice indeed, but it is also a stark one: to stand British troops down now and turn back, or to hold firm to that course that we have set. I believe passionately that we must hold firm to that course. The question most often posed is not 'Why does it matter?' but 'Why does it matter so much?'. Here we are, the Government, with their most serious test, their majority at risk, the first cabinet resignation over an issue of policy, the main parties internally divided, people who agree on everything else –
[Hon. Members: 'the main parties?']
Ah, yes, of course. The Liberal Democrats – unified, as ever, in opportunism and error
[Interruption]

Van Dijk argues that

> Blair will be able to speak and say *what* he says and (especially) say it *how* he says it, because in his context model he more or less consciously represents and ongoingly monitors … setting; position in House; his personal identity; his personal attributes as being democratic, tolerant, etc.; his communicative identity as (main) speaker; his political identity as Prime Minister, Head of Government, etc.; his political identity as leader of the Labour Party, his national identity as being British; the respective identities of the other participants: addressees, MPs, politicians. (2009, p. 122, emphasis in original)

All these elements (and others) are presented as (plausible) elements constitutive of a mental model. The basic requirement for analysis is to start (and end) with identifying the 'mental' or 'context' model of the speaker, which is the only dimension seen to control the production and understanding of discourse. One cannot do adequate political discourse analysis if one does not consider the presence of all the above-mentioned features as analytically relevant in terms of being a cognitive representation of context in the mind of the speaker. 'Context' models account for both content and form of communicative situations.

Linguistic-pragmatic analyses and socio-cognitive analyses can only take one so far in the analysis of political discourse. What people (politicians) say is either talked about in cognitive terms ('mental' or 'context' models) or in linguistic-pragmatic terms ('presuppositions'). What is strikingly absent from both conventional psychological studies of political rhetoric and discursive studies is attention to the fact that whatever makes up the language of politics (propositions, assessments, descriptions, etc.), what is usually referred to as 'micro-level behaviour' (Chilton, 2004), is in reality kinds of rhetorical and social action (Hepburn and Wiggins, 2007; Heritage, 1984). What is also missing is careful attention to the rhetorical nature of 'shared patterns of belief' (Billig, 1998). As Billig has cogently demonstrated, common sense is not unitary but dilemmatic, as it contains and accommodates contrary themes (Billig, 1996; Billig *et al.*, 1988). The dilemmatic aspect of common sense is an essential ingredient to understanding the regularity, as well as the variability, of manifestations of social and political behaviour.

The remainder of this chapter focuses on discursive psychology (see also Chapter 7) as an original psychological approach to understanding the nature of political rhetoric. It focuses on two aspects of discursive psychological work on political discourse: metaphors and the issue of political discourse, and rhetorical identification.

Discursive psychology starts from the assumption that thinking is intrinsically rhetorical (Billig, 1987). The central proposition is that people's political thinking can be understood and analysed by examining political talk. For instance, discursive psychologists have argued that in order to understand the meaning of political attitudes one needs to examine the process of opinion giving and stance taking within the context of controversy and argumentation (Billig, 1991; Potter, 1998). One also needs to understand the constructive and constitutive power of discourse (political discourse) and chart how people construct versions of the world, perform actions with their talk (e.g. explain, justify, assign blame) and use rhetoric to achieve various effects (cf. Potter, 1996). One of the issues that interested discursive psychologists in the early days of discourse analysis in social psychology concerned managing 'stake' and 'interest' in political discourse (see Edwards and Potter, 1992a, b; see also the discussion of 'defensive' and 'offensive' rhetoric in Potter, 1996). Discursive psychologists have identified various ways in which speakers can manage issues of stake and interest, how they can build positions as based on 'facts' rather than prejudice, bias or any particular stake; for example, by invoking the parliamentary official record (Antaki and Leudar, 2001), by drawing upon established/categorical definitions when accounting for controversial political events (see Tileagă, 2008 on accounts about the Romanian revolution of 1989), by using reported speech when discussing controversial political matters (LeCouteur et al., 2001), or by appealing to a 'failing' memory (Edwards and Potter, 1992b).[5] What all these studies show is that political rhetoric is made of the various rhetorical tactics that are tailored to their occasions of use.

Metaphors and rhetorical identification in political discourse

The use of metaphors in political language has attracted particular attention in recent years, especially in the area of cognitive linguistics (e.g. Chilton, 1996; Chilton and Ilyin, 1993; Lakoff, 2002; Musolff, 2004). According to Charteris-Black, metaphors fulfil a variety of functions: from managing and ultimately consecrating a politician's *ethos*, intensifying the tone of the speech, explaining actions and policies to creating political and personal myth (cf. Charteris-Black, 2005). Some other researchers believe that in political discourse 'metaphors are often

---

[5] See also analyses of European politicians' discourse on immigration (e.g. Wodak and Matousheck, 1993) and van Dijk's work on elite discourse and racism (e.g. van Dijk, 1993a) for other discursive ways to construct reasonableness and positions based on 'facts' vs. political stake.

not just embellishments of literal propositions, but modes of reasoning about, for example, the future and about policies' (Chilton, 2004, p. 203). Metaphors can have very serious political implications: they can frame exclusionary, as well as inclusionary, policies (Wodak, 2011), they can frame political issues and inform local and national politics (Skinner and Squillacote, 2010), or they can feed wider discourses of threat and defence (Lakoff, 2002). Metaphors transform themselves and are transformed through their use; they have their own particular semantic and historical careers (Billig and MacMillan, 2005; Musolff, 2010).

Politics itself is apprehended in metaphorical terms (see, e.g., Fairclough, 1992 on 'politics as war'). Take, for instance, the metaphor of Europe as a 'common house' (see Chilton and Ilyin, 1993), a metaphor designed to help to break with the old European order and feed a new and renewed discourse of 'integration' (see also Wodak, 2011 on contemporary metaphors and visions of Europe). In order to understand the political implications of metaphors one needs not only to establish the pervasiveness of metaphor in political discourse, but also to explore the semantic and historical career of concepts/metaphors (see Musolff, 2010 on the semantic history of the 'body politic' metaphor, and Billig and MacMillan, 2005 on the transformation from metaphor to idiom of the 'smoking gun' phrase in relation to political controversy around the search for weapons of mass destruction in Iraq). One needs to take a historical approach to understand how metaphors have entered or might enter the political language.

Billig and MacMillan contend that 'any analysis of political metaphors needs to draw upon more general theories of metaphor. Regarding political metaphors, it is necessary to see how the two aspects of metaphor – the creative and the idiomatic – might be connected' (Billig and MacMillan, 2005, p. 460). On this matter, discursive psychology has something to say. The issue of transformation of metaphorical meaning should not only be treated in cognitive but also in discursive terms. Transformation occurs in and through language: 'what was once sharp and novel becomes through usage ordinary and indistinct. One might say that the living metaphor starts dying once it begins to live within language' (Billig and MacMillan, 2005, p. 461). One should look at how language is used to see what speakers and writers are doing with their discourse.

Billig and MacMillan (2005) report and discuss the exchange between the broadcaster Dan Rather and US Secretary of State at the time, Colin Powell, from the American television programme '60 minutes' on 5 February 2003:[6]

---

[6] The context of the exchange was Powell's address to the UN where he had made the case for the existence of a 'present and clear' danger of Iraq's weapons of mass destruction.

Extract 4

Dan Rather: And to those who say, 'Well, there's no smoking gun,' would you argue with that?

Colin Powell: What do you mean by a smoking gun? How about lots of smoke? I think I put forward a case today that said there's lots of smoke. There are many smoking guns. When we say that he has had thousands of litres of anthrax, and we know it – he's admitted it, it's a matter of record, there's evidence, there's no question about it – is that a smoking gun? Is it a smoking gun that he has this horrible material somewhere in that country and he's not accounted for it? And the very fact that he has not accounted for it, I say could be a smoking gun. It's been a gun that's been smoking for years.

Billig and MacMillan show how the appropriateness of the idiom ('smoking gun') can be contested by problematising its meaning. According to Billig and MacMillan, Powell manages to do that by, on the one hand, suggesting a 'diversity of legitimate interpretations' (p. 475), and on the other hand, 'metaphorizing the idiom in a different way' (p. 475). Through the use of a series of rhetorical questions Powell manages to challenge the 'unambiguous proof of culpability' that the idiom is usually used to denote. The idiom itself is not questioned, but there is a suggestion that 'different people could use it in different ways' (p. 476). Powell shifts from 'smoking gun' to 'smoke'. As the authors argue, 'with this shift, the 'gun' part of the 'smoking gun' is returning to literality: it refers generally to weaponry, rather than to tapes and memoranda' (p. 476). The anthrax to which Powell is referring, or 'rather its non-discovery, can smoke dangerously for years and years' (p. 476).

Billig and MacMillan warn against the temptation to 'divorce' metaphors from their 'particular contexts of their usage', and speculate, in abstract and general terms, what experience or experiences they express. Instead, one should examine 'what the users of such metaphors are doing rhetorically and pragmatically' (p. 462).

One major contribution of discursive psychology is the reconceptualisation of variables routinely treated as internal cognitive processes. Discursive psychologists argue that 'identification' is one such variable and can be treated as a 'rhetorical' rather than an 'internal process' (Billig, 2003, p. 232).[7]

One of the common ways of politicians to identify rhetorically with their audiences is by drawing on *commonplaces* (Billig, 1987), repertoires or moral values shared by audiences ('justice', 'mercy', 'freedom', 'responsibility'). Edelman (1977) analyses the language of poverty as a mixture of repertoires of blame and sympathy, where poverty is both

[7] The analysis here is confined to elite political discourse, but the discursive approach is not solely concerned with the analysis of formal political discourse – see Condor and Gibson (2007) and Wetherell and Potter (1992) for examples of rhetorical/national identification of ordinary society members.

deplored and tolerated. Augoustinos *et al.* (1999) point to the presence of repertoires of blame and sympathy in their analysis of discourse on Aboriginal land rights, where politicians and ordinary people are seen as sympathising with the plight of Aboriginal people, while criticising their lack of effort.

Political speakers often declare identities to achieve specific rhetorical ends (e.g. constructing a common identity with the audience). For instance, Reicher and Hopkins (1996a, b) have shown that in social identity terms the success of any meaningful attempt at political persuasion is dependent upon three conditions: the salience of the social identity of the audience group; the perceived relevance of the political message and arguments to the salient social identity of the audience; and the success of the speaker in presenting himself or herself as incumbent of the relevant social identity. This can be achieved through the way social and political categories are defined and the way the speaker categorises or constructs his or her self-identity. But definitions and categorisations of social and political categories, and self-categorisations are 'dynamic and fluid within the course of a single interaction, being locally crafted, or worked up, in an occasioned manner, to meet the moment-by-moment exigencies of conversational interaction' (Rapley, 1998, p. 328; see also Antaki *et al.*, 1996). What Reicher and Hopkins (1996a, b) refer to as 'mobilisation discourse' is nothing more than an attempt at discursive construction of inclusive in-group identities. Social identity is a 'flexible resource ... which may be deployed in talk to a speaker's argumentative, or rhetorical, advantage' (Rapley, 1998, pp. 328–9). The interactional and political goal of political rhetoric that addresses political contentious issues is to accomplish commonality of interest through identifying with a rhetorically constituted audience.

The discursive construction of inclusive in-group identities can be illustrated with two examples from discourse analytic studies: Mark Rapley's (1998) analysis of right-wing and populist Australian politician Pauline Hanson's maiden speech to Parliament and Tileagă's (2008) analysis of the former Romanian President's commemorative address celebrating the Romanian 'revolution'.

Rapley (1998) notes that Hanson's political rhetoric is carefully designed to highlight her ordinariness, reasonableness and to implicitly justify the mass appeal of her highly contentious views of immigration. The (political) self is discursively constituted through a specific declaration of identity, 'ordinary Australian-ness' (see extracts 5 and 6).

Extract 5 (renumbered)

1	Mister Acting Speaker, in making my first speech in this place,
2	I congratulate you on your election and wish to say how proud I am to be here
3	as the independent member for Oxley. I come here not as a polished politician
4	but as a woman who has had her fair share of life's knocks. My view on issues
5	is based on commonsense, and my experience as a mother of four children, as
6	a sole parent, and as a businesswoman running a fish and chip shop.

As Rapley argues, Hanson constructs her in-group by using a contrast pair (people with a fair share of life's 'knocks' vs. politicians). This is a rhetorical move that allows her to voice subsequently her entitlement to in-group membership by virtue of her life experience. 'Experience' or 'what one has experienced' is a powerful rhetorical device to manage stake and entitlement to say things. Her experience is predicated on what is commonsensically attached to categories such as 'mother', 'sole parent' or 'businesswoman' (lines 5–6). She lays claim to an 'epistemological entitlement' by virtue of constructing herself as the 'prototypical representative of the social category of "ordinary" or "mainstream" Australian' (Rapley, 1998, pp. 331–2). The next move is to put forward a claim to membership in the category 'ordinary Australian', and as a politician, to construct herself as a representative of that category. In doing so she 'naturalises' the very categorical construction she is using (ordinary Australian) by ensuring that other alternative political constructions and categorisations are excluded.

Extract 6 (renumbered)

80	Anyone with business sense knows that you do not sell off your assets
81	especially when they are making money. I may be only 'a fish and chip
82	shop lady', but some of these economists need to get their heads out of the
83	textbooks and get a job in the real world. I would not even let one of them
84	handle my grocery shopping. Immigration and multiculturalism are issues
85	that this government is trying to address, but for far too long ordinary
86	Australians have been kept out of any debate by the major parties. I and
87	most Australians want our immigration policy radically reviewed.

A series of contrastive pairs ('economists' – professional experience vs. 'fish and chip shop lady' – personal experience) and ('ordinary Australians' – common people vs. the 'major parties' – the politicians) are used by Hanson to 'claim a common in-group membership with ... ordinary Australians whom she has rhetorically constructed as disenfranchised – indeed "most Australians"' (Rapley, 1998, p. 333). Her own political position (a review of the immigration policy) is made to coincide with the wishes of a prototypical ordinary Australian. By the use of common slang ('fed up to the back teeth') and idiomatic formulations ('a woman who has had her fair share of life's knocks'), she adopts the demotic voice of those she seeks to influence. She formulates her personal and political identity 'within the lexicon of the social category to which she claims a membership entitlement' (p. 340). The effect of this is that her 'in-group' is rhetorically enlarged to encompass 'most Australians'. At the same time, the 'out-group' is narrowed down to (economic) experts and politicians, which are constructed as being out of touch with reality.

Tileagă (2008) focuses on how rhetorical identification with an audience can be the precursor of an ideological representation of a national event (the Romanian revolution of 1989). Tileagă analyses commemorative addresses in the Romanian parliament of the former Romanian president Ion Iliescu. The analysis included here shows how a particular type of rhetorical identification with the audience can serve argumentative political goals. Consider extracts 7 and 8.

Extract 7 (21 December 2000)

1	Mr President of the Senate and Chamber of Deputies
2	Ladies and gentlemen senators and deputies
3	Dear friends from the days and nights of the December revolution
4	Esteemed audience

Extract 8 (18 December 2003)

1	Mr President of the Chamber of Deputies
2	Distinguished members of the legislative bodies
3	Distinguished members of the Government
4	Ladies and gentlemen representatives of diplomatic missions
5	Honourable guests
6	Dear revolutionary friends
7	Dear fellow countrymen

Notice how the speaker's use of formal forms of address indexes an institutional rather than personal identity. Yet, at the same time, Iliescu also manages to position himself within and rhetorically identify with the community of 'revolutionaries' (participants to the revolution) by using politically relevant categories to the context in which he is speaking: 'revolutionary friends' (extract 8, line 6) and 'friends from the days and nights of the December revolution' (extract 7, line 3). A particular (political) moral order is thus framed. The membership category 'friends' carries with it a set of category-bound activities. The 'friendship' is defined *through* the event, through *taking part in the event*: friends *of* the revolution. The president is not only speaking from within the national community of which he is the political representative, but also from within the community of revolutionaries, the community of the (active) participants in the revolution. One could argue that this is not a simple rhetorical move of identifying with the audience, but a move of managing entitlement issues and framing a particular (political) moral framework in order to construct an ideological representation of the Romanian revolution (see more on this in Tileagă, 2008 and 2010). These ways of addressing the audience organise the categorial features of the address, and can be seen as preliminaries to the relevance of warrantability, entitlement and accountability issues. The official warrant (President of Romania) is seconded and embedded in a sense of (personal) solidarity and camaraderie with the community of the participants in the revolution. In so doing, the speaker is not presenting himself as merely a commemorator, a witness; he presents himself as a *participant*: he is to be seen as claiming co-membership in the category 'revolutionary'. This is a very strong move of warranting an epistemological and speaking entitlement and a preface to offering and authorising his own politically preferred version of the Romanian revolution.

In both examples, the presentation of the self and identity is managed in very specific rhetorical contexts. Subtle political positioning and rhetorical effect is accomplished by the careful use of rhetorical devices and categories, the construction of personal and social identities, and identification with both distant and proximal audiences. Discursive psychologists argue that the study of such features requires analysis that goes beyond the cognitive functioning of individuals. The project for scholars of political discourse is to 'show how ideological, rhetorical, and psychological factors are contained and reproduced within the details of political talk' (Billig, 2003, p. 243).

Reclaiming the role of language for politics

The analysis of political discourse is hardly a new topic of inquiry; yet it is conspicuously absent from the agenda of political psychologists. This is not to say that social and political psychologists do not have theories or applied models on political discourse. It is just that their research agenda has historically not been directed towards studying political discourse in its own right by considering the relationship between language and politics. Language is routinely treated as yet another independent variable to manipulate, alongside other meaningful socio-psychological variables for the study of politics. Language is largely seen as a mental faculty/phenomenon and stripped of its constructive and constitutive properties. The public *use* of language is seen as a property and emergence of cognitive systems and means of organisation of information, and not an intrinsic feature of social interaction between people.

For politicians and political psychologists interested in political discourse, language seems inherently designed to enable one to communicate political representations. But one should not stop there. One should not only consider how language is a vehicle for political representations but also look at how language is used to see what speakers and writers are doing with their discourse, what social actions are being performed and what political 'realities' are thus being constituted. By proceeding in such a way there is less of a risk that we come to accept the rhetoric of politics as an objective description of reality of politics.

In order to understand and analyse fully and faithfully the nature of contemporary political language, one needs to move from cognitive and information-processing theories and models towards a more linguistic, rhetorical and discursive perspective, which takes account of how political language is constructed, negotiated and distributed, its rhetorical properties and functions, and its intended audience. When a discursive perspective is applied to matters of politics (especially to the analysis of elite political discourse) it hopes to provide not only a detailed and language-orientated way of examining the intricate rhetorical nature of political messages but also demonstrates how political psychological theory can be transformed in the process.

Mediated politics: political disco
      political communication

Mediated politics and political communication

The spectacle of contemporary politics around the world is intimately bound to a 'multiaxial' (Delli Carpini and Williams, 2001) media and communication environment. The nature of contemporary political communication is in continuous transformation (Bennett and Iyengar, 2008). This chapter offers a summary of the main tenets of a discursive approach to political communication. It starts by charting the strengths and weaknesses of contemporary psychology of political communication. The chapter then moves on to discuss how political communication can be conceived of as a social accomplishment, and an outcome of, as well as influence on, complex forms and networks of social practices. After offering some empirical examples drawn from work on the ethnography of political processes, discursive research on politicians' communicative style, political advertising and political humour, the chapter closes with an outline of an alternative approach to political communication that relies specifically on the importance of investigating how political communications are actually produced, circulated and consumed in society. In doing so, this chapter argues that political psychologists can borrow creatively and learn from media, communication and discourse theorists interested in the complexity of political communications.

The rise of 'self-expressive politics' (Stanyer, 2007), the increased 'personalisation' (Castells, 2011) and 'professionalisation' of politics and political communication (Negrine, 2008; Wodak, 2011) are only some examples of how political phenomena do not exist outside communication processes, outside information and communications of and about politics. Politics and political processes need to be 'packaged' (Cappella and Jamieson, 1997; Franklin, 2004) in some communicative form or other in order to reach imagined, proximal or distal audiences. In most Western and Eastern European democracies, this is usually the job of politicians themselves, the mass media, 'spin doctors' and the easingly powerful political public relations industry. Their role is to onstruct, direct, circulate and disseminate political communications (McNair, 2011).

Understanding the notion of 'mediated politics' requires taking seriously the idea of how much communication technologies (especially new communication technologies, such as the Internet) and political experience are intertwined, with the various implications for the permeability of borders separating the political from the non-political, the private and public spheres, the sometimes opposing and complementary channels and forms of political information. Communications in what has been labelled the 'global digital age' have given 'rise to unprecedented autonomy for communicative subjects to communicate at large' (Castells, 2011, p. 135). They have the power to narrow, as well as widen the political horizon of individuals (Bennett and Iyengar, 2008). According to this view, politics is not a 'distinct and self-contained part of public life', but, rather, 'largely a mediated experience' (Delli Carpini and Williams, 2001, p. 161).[1] Understanding how social actors/citizens experience and enact politics requires appreciating the significance of mediated political communication 'both in the governing process and in citizen perceptions of society and its problems' (Bennett and Entman, 2001, p. 1).

The psychology of political communication

Media and communication scholars are concerned with theorising the different ages of political communication (Blumler, 2001; Blumler and Kavannagh, 1999) and *how* political communications reach their targets through 'old' and 'new' mass media (Deacon and Wring, 2011; Stanyer, 2007). Critical discourse analysts are concerned with mediatised political discourse as a 'complex discourse practice involving the mixing of genres and discourses of politics, conversation and entertainment' (Fairclough, 2010, p. 156). Political psychologists and political scientists are mostly interested in the *conditions* under which political communications take place, are constructed, and are generally effective: their psychological antecedents and consequents (Crigler, 1996; Kinder, 2003).

This section critically reviews political psychological research that embraces the assumption that a deeper understanding of the link

---

[1] At the heart of politics as mediated experience lie three tensions: between diversity and commonality, between free information choice and necessary citizen education, and between treating people as consumer audiences or as active citizen publics (Bennett and Entman, 2001).

between communication and politics in the 'information age' neces-
sitates the careful description of underlying psychological mechanisms
and processes. The study of the effects of mass communication on publics or audiences has been a longstanding concern in social psychology
and political science (see, inter alia, Berelson *et al.*, 1954; Campbell *et al.*,
1960; Lazarsfeld *et al.*, 1944; Lippmann, 1922). It is usually thought
that mass communication could influence citizens in three ways: in
terms of how they 'make sense of politics', how they 'decide what is
important in politics', and how they 'evaluate the alternatives that politics puts before them' (Kinder, 2003, p. 358). In technical terms, these
aspects are usually referred to as *framing*, *agenda setting* and *priming* (for
an overview see Nisbet and Feldman, 2010; Scheufele and Tewksbury,
2007). These will be explored briefly in turn.

The notion of 'framing' relies on the idea that in order to make sense
of social information, social actors must rely on the presence, cooperation, information and interaction with others. Political psychologists
see social actors as continually involved in conversations over the meanings of events, people and circumstances. This is done through an
exchange of frames (Gamson, 1992).[2] It is commonly argued that most
of contemporary politics is carried out through the construction and
dissemination of frames (both those fashioned by political elites, as well
as those crafted by journalists and journalistic practices). This includes,
among other things, issues of frame building, frame setting, individual-
level framing processes, as well as feedback or relation between individual framing and media framing (cf. Scheufele, 1999; Scheufele and
Iyengar, in press).

The formation and dissemination of public opinion in the public
sphere is seen as a competition *of* and *for* frames, with the ones that
prevail having the greater prospect of influencing and shaping how the
public perceives the political process.[3] For instance, the way in which
a message is framed can have an effect on its meaning, and increase
or decrease the likelihood of its being accepted. One can, for example,
elicit more favourable orientations towards 'affirmative action' if this is
presented as 'equal opportunity' rather than 'reverse discrimination'
(Bosveld *et al.*, 1997). This is something that politicians and 'spin

---

[2] Frames are relatively stable cognitive/interpretative mechanisms that allow people to
navigate the social and political landscape, and organise/reorganise already existing
and new information. Frames act as guiding principles to making sense of events,
issues and people, in specific ways.
[3] According to Castells, 'the framing of the public mind is largely performed through
processes that take place in the media' (2011, p. 157). It is dominant political elites
that 'wield the greatest control over news frames' (pp.163–4).

doctors' are very much aware of. Most contemporary issues (managing 'support' for potentially illegitimate wars or seemingly unpopular governmental policies; justifying controversial circumstances of political failings and responsibility) rely on, but are not limited to, basic issues of framing and descriptive language of states of affairs (Kinder and Sanders, 1996).

For instance, Just et al. (1996; see also Gamson, 1992) demonstrate how people draw upon few frames in political discourse when offering an account of politically contentious issues. Using in-depth interviews on topics such as strategic defence initiatives, apartheid in South Africa, issues around drug abuse and AIDS, Just et al. (1996) identify a series of well-defined cognitive and affective frames or positions that participants employ: talking about the human side of events ('the human impact frame') together with using 'emotionally laden terms to evaluate the positive or negative impact of policies, events, people, and problems' (p. 137); talking about issues in 'economic terms, making judgments by citing costs of policies, by suggesting a profit motive' (p. 139) ('the economic frame'); relying on a common polarising frame ('us vs. them') and making reference to 'a sense of power or powerlessness with regard to an issue' (p. 142).

Frames are 'like recipes, advice from experts on how citizens should cook up their opinions' (Kinder, 2003, p. 360). Frames can cause large numbers of people to think differently about politics; they can lead to opinion change (Kinder and Sanders, 1996; Nelson et al., 1997) or political cynicism (Cappella and Jamieson, 1997).

'Agenda setting' studies (Iyengar and Kinder, 1987; McCombs and Shaw, 1972) are interested in the process by which members of the wider public come to consider some public/political issues as more important than others. From Lazarsfeld and Merton's (1948) early attempt to focus on the agenda setting power of the media (especially news media) to McCombs and Shaw's (1972) discovery of an almost perfect correlation between issues voters believed to be most serious and those issues given great coverage and importance in the news at the time, agenda setting effects have proved to be a robust and dominant phenomenon. Nonetheless, Kinder (2003) identifies problems with the pioneering studies on agenda setting (e.g. McCombs and Shaw, 1972). One of the major drawbacks that Kinder identifies is related to studies missing the 'real variation in agenda setting, which is temporal rather than spatial' (pp. 362–3). Experimental and survey research have shown that political issues become high priority issues for the public 'after they first become high priority for newspapers and networks' (p. 363; see also Miller and Krosnick, 2000). Priority and salience issues change over time, and agenda setting is 'dynamic – problems emerge, move for a while to the centre of the stage, and then gradually drift back to the wings' (2000, p. 363). As a consequence, these issues need to be investigated over time.

The issue of how social actors evaluate the alternatives that politics presents them with has been approached using the notion of 'priming'. The various alternatives with which social actors are presented are complex, and such complexity requires a certain level of cognitive organisation and appraisal in the shaping of evaluative dimensions. Through priming, evaluative dimensions are supplied by media and political mass communicators. Through media coverage some standards are made salient whereas others are relegated to the 'dustbin' of public issues: the more frequently some aspects are *primed* in the news media, the more people will make them part of their social and political evaluations. Priming has been seen as a pivotal mechanism at the heart of political campaigns (Jacobs and Shapiro, 2000) and a supportive lever on gathering and manufacturing support for the political agendas and issues of political parties. Priming through the news media allows some political issues to be seen as not only associated with, but also as 'owned' by, political parties. Priming has received strong experimental support (Iyengar and Kinder, 1987; Miller and Krosnick, 2000; Valentino, 1999; Valentino *et al.*, 2002). These studies have demonstrated that priming can be put to work under controlled experimental conditions. But what happens when you take (and research) priming outside the psychological laboratory? What is the dynamic and relative importance of priming in 'natural' situations where communications streams are not neatly kept under control, and are fluctuating, unstable? How is priming shaped when treated as a communicative phenomenon?

Priming in itself does not guarantee that the public news media agenda will alter political evaluations. Consider, for instance, the unfailing level of support for former US president Bill Clinton shortly after the Monika Lewinsky scandal (see Zaller, [1992] 2005), which went against the agenda setting and priming predictions. Both agenda setting and priming concerns seem to put forward a particular vision of politics and political evaluations. It is a vision where both the politics of the elites and the political evaluations of social actors are a matter of 'salience' or 'fit', rather than debate or dialogue. According to Iyengar, 'because public opinion is based on narrow and issue-specific considerations, changes in the salience of issues are likely to shift the distribution of preferences and, thereby, to alter political outcomes' (1993, p. 211). It is salience, form and frequency of presentation that count, rather than substance of political argument. Also, by suggesting that 'agenda-setting and priming are ... most prevalent among highly knowledgeable and trusting citizens' (Miller and Krosnick, 2000, p. 313), it is implied that not everyone is an integral member of the political process. It champions and furthers a view of politics where politics should be directed solely to those who are equipped to make sense of it.

Other approaches to political communication have seen it as a process of meaning-making (Crigler, 1996). According to Crigler (1996) 'all the participants in the communication process – media, officials, and the public – are viewed as engaged in constructing messages and meanings' (p. 7). What Crigler refers to as a 'constructionist' approach to political communication is concerned with issues of presentation and arrangement of political information, the messages and political images intended, and individual understanding of coverage. The focus is on the construction of political meaning as a 'dynamic' and 'interactive' process by which 'elites and individuals give meaning to political events' (p. 1) and where both the content and presentation of messages matter.[4] There is no doubt that political psychologists consider political communication as a process of meaning-making. Notwithstanding the sophisticated understanding that experimental paradigms can offer us, there is, nonetheless, a crucial element missing. Experimental research on framing, priming or agenda setting effects offers an individualistic and static view of political communication processes. According to this view, political communication is the outcome of cognitive processing. How much does that tell us about communications and politics itself?

Political communication and language

The language of politics allows for a multitude of interpretations and possibilities of expression by both elites and ordinary social actors (Edelman, 1988, 2001). Yet, for the majority of political psychologists, the language of politics and political action is said not to exist independently of cognitive and emotional information-processing mechanisms. The processing of political information *precedes* political action. Cognitive and affective structures 'constrain the complexity of interpretations that people produce' (Crigler, 1996, p. 9; see also Marcus

---

[4] Crigler's vision is grounded in (and complements) concerns with two-sided information flows, where 'dominant and countervalent messages, can have different effects in different segments of the population, depending on citizens' political awareness and ideological orientations and on the relative intensities of the two messages' (Zaller, [1992] 2005, p. 185).

et al., 2000). For instance, the study of 'political cognition' empha-
sises the active role of individuals in processing information based on
schemas and heuristics for various concepts, events, people and social
objects. The role of individual cognitive activity is to 'tame' (McGraw,
2003; Taber, 2003) the information flux. People use heuristic shortcuts
(Popkin, 1991) and schemas (Graber, 1988) to 'think' about politics.[5]

Even when the interaction between the participants in the communication process – media, officials and the public – is highlighted (cf.
Crigler, 1996), there is a still a sense that this is only part of the story.
It is argued that the promise of understanding and exploring this interaction lies entirely with the study of political cognitions and affect of
participants as part of the communication process. Discursive, communicative and cultural processes are seen as merely reflecting cognitive and affective frames (Neuman *et al.*, 2007) and individual-centred
and predisposition-based aspects (Becker *et al.*, 2010; Becker and
Scheufele, 2011). The idea that the organisation of political communication operates within the diverse discursive and cultural patterns of
public and private spheres, of global and local settings of production
and consumption of media discourses, is not given sufficient attention.

By proceeding in this way, the psychological study of political and
mediated communication risks seriously misjudging the social functions of language (cf. Edelman, 2001). Language is seen more as a
transparent medium of exchanging ideas and information and less as
fulfilling *constructive, constitutive* and *interpretive* functions. Most social
and political psychologists would agree that political (mediated) language 'is inevitably evocative of fears, hopes, reassurances or threats'
(Edelman, 2001, p. 98). Where some of them differ, though, is in how
they *treat* political (mediated) language. Cognitive analyses of mediated communication rely exclusively on a *representational* function of
language, where political sense making is mediated by frames, scripts
and cognitive processes such as priming, and the function of language
is to reflect, represent these issues and support rational conclusions and
decision-making processes. Political meanings are not only created by
cognitive processing or the salience of certain frames over others, but
also by the interpretive dynamic of impressions, interests, values, errors
and expectations of those who actively use language at different levels
of social and political organisation.

[5] More complex heuristics and schemas require more complex cognitive processing.
Accessibility and familiarity are two key aspects of processing information in general, and political information in particular (Iyengar, 1993; Neuman *et al.*, 1992).
The influence of television news, of newspapers, and other media outlets originates in
making (political) information accessible and familiar.

Language is a 'tool that creates worlds and versions of worlds' (Edelman, 2001, p. 82; cf. Billig, 1996; Wittgenstein, 1953). Mass-mediated politics is constitutive of an array of discourses, discursive genres, social practices and forms of life (take, e.g., the ritualistic language of the press, the representative language of politicians, the political common sense of ordinary social actors). Political communication systems, as well as the various roles of those who participate in them – politicians, professional political journalists, audience members, and so on – are diverse, flexible, unfinished projects, continually shifting between foreground and background, between elite and grass roots, between formal and informal communications, between regulated and unregulated institutional practices (Blumler, 2001). Elite structuration or framing (of messages, for instance), media processes of production and public interpretation and consumption depend on specific discursive and material (organisational/professional) configurations of repertoires of culture, market and political power.

Cognitive and rational choice analyses of mediated political communication seem to undermine and underplay the importance of paying attention to the plurivalence of language that would help the understanding of the multiple possibilities, perspectives and social worlds inherent in mediated/political communication situations. It is usually contended that a *theory of democracy and politics* accompanies (or should accompany) every effort at understanding the 'delivery, distribution, quality, and uses of information by citizens' (Entman and Bennett, 2001, p. 468). But one should not stop at this. One also needs a *theory of language* to complement theories of democracy and politics, and guide empirical enquiry (see also Chapters 1 and 2, and Chapters 7 and 8).

The point here is not that cognitive analyses of political communication do not offer a (social) commentary on politics, but that this commentary is limited to issues of information processing, psychological needs, rational decision-making, and not necessarily directed at the everyday discursive, actual communicative experience and enactment of politics. One needs to study mediated political communication differently, by focusing on politics itself and political discourse in particular as complex forms of human activities and practices realised in a variety of very specific cultural and institutional settings, in social interaction, through a variety of discursive forms and genres. Fairclough (2010, p. 421, emphasis in original) captures this point when he writes: 'in any communication people inevitably draw on, anticipate and respond to particular social and institutional practices (ways of doing things), both explicitly and implicitly. They are involved in an *interdiscursive* process of creatively drawing on the potential range of established discourses, genres and styles.' The strength, effectiveness and forms of political communications depend on their discursive and sociocultural features and the range of settings, activities and practices that they mediate. This suggests that discursive approaches to political communication may have a significant contribution to make to this area of political psychological research. As Chapters 7 and 8 have shown, discursive researchers have been mostly concerned with detailed rhetorical and discursive analyses of the language of politics, and critical linguistic analyses of political communication. The remainder of this chapter will address some of these concerns with examples drawn from the ethnography of politics, communicative styles of politicians, political advertising and political humour.

Political communication and politics 'as usual'

In political communication, politicians are both text producers and recipients (Schäffner, 2010). As Schäffner writes, 'processes of communication and mediation of politics occur within and across genres and discourse types' (p. 255). When one describes political discourse as a complex form and network of social activities, then one can start to see the importance of investigating how political discourse is actually produced, circulated and consumed. Certain activities and discursive practices are constructed and aimed by politicians at other politicians; other discursive practices are aimed and tailored for the general public. What Wodak (2011) refers to as 'politics as usual' is the outcome of a series of intricate discursive, social and institutional practices.

One example is the practice of translation, which increasingly plays an essential role in global political communication. European politics (and especially the politics of the EU) rely heavily on practices of translation to convey political messages. As Schäffner (2010) has demonstrated, 'textual profiles of translations' are not neutral containers for political messages to get across party and national interest lines but closely determined by 'the communicative aims and by the institutional policies and ideologies' (p. 273). By investigating how press conferences and political positions are reported in European newspapers, Schäffner has shown the extent to which European and international political communication is mediated by translation and how practices of translation can engender a struggle over both connotation and denotation of political meanings.

According to Wodak (2011) one should be able to describe 'politics as usual' ('real' politics) by considering the range of practices, activities and contexts in which and through which politics takes place. The increased 'fictionalisation' and dramatisation of politics has led to the alteration of the 'boundaries and border-crossings between "real" and "fictional" in politics and its media representation' (p. 155).[6] One way to address this is to engage in ethnographic-type analyses of actual networks of political practices. Following a member of the European parliament throughout his entire day, Wodak (2011) notes how politicians can effortlessly switch 'between different frames and contexts, each time selecting and employing the appropriate genre, politeness markers, professional jargon, salient *topoi* and argumentative moves' (p. 152). Political agendas leave (discursive) traces as politicians 'perform' in public meetings, press-conferences, or private conversations with their aides.

Different types of knowledge (on a continuum from 'technical' knowledge of political procedures to 'lay' knowledge and assumptions about politics) are adduced to support these performances. Discursive research on political communication has shown how political knowledge is mobilised via direct, unequivocal statements but also through presuppositions, implicatures, metaphors, as strategic ways of 'packaging' political information (cf. Chilton, 2004). Wodak (2011) shows, for example, how the politics of the EU is apprehended in metaphorical terms. She discusses the many metaphors embedded in the discourse of European Parliament members as 'conceptual frames and possible utopias of what the EU should achieve in the future and how it should be structured and organized' (p. 63). Wodak notes the frequent uses of 'container metaphors' ('the melting pot', 'the fortress', 'the heart of Europe', 'the unified European family'), 'war and sports metaphors' (e.g. depicting European integration as a 'fight/struggle'), 'organizational and economic metaphors' ('thresholds', 'benchmarks'). She points to how the 'patchwork' metaphor was flexibly used to 'represent the fragmentation of an enlarged Europe' (p. 106). The representation of the EU does not exist independently of (strategic) ways of packaging political information but is organised, *as* political knowledge, in a network of conceptual and metaphorical frames.

Political knowledge as a network of conceptual and metaphorical frames is usually complemented by political and personal knowledge

---

[6] The increased dramatisation of politics (see, e.g., the huge success of the US drama *The West Wing*, and the popularity of *The Thick of It* in the UK) can facilitate the formation and reproduction of a black and white vision of politics where the complexity of politics itself is reduced. As Wodak argues, when politics is fictionalised, 'heroes and villains are easily recognisable and good and bad values are clear-cut and dichotomous. No shades of grey become apparent and ideological dilemmas are quickly reconciled' (2011, p. 204).

organised in what Leudar and Nekvapil (2000, 2004; see also Nekvapil and Leudar, 2002) have called 'dialogical networks'. For example, Leudar *et al.* (2008) show how various 'hostility' themes 'are inscribed in the media reports of social events, and in local inhabitants' talk' (p. 191) in the context of accounting for being a refugee or asylum seeker in the UK.[7] For Leudar *et al.* (2008) media representations, community narratives and refugees' own stories do not exist independently but are linked in 'dialogical networks' of opinions. Leudar *et al.* illustrate how, while refugees orient towards the hostile representations in their constructions of themselves, the media and local community can sometimes fail to include or acknowledge the refugees' own stories as part of their accounts. Leudar *et al.* identify a discrepancy between, on the one hand, refugees' and asylum seekers' view of themselves and how they narrate their lives and, on the other hand, what is written about them in the media and how they are talked about in the localities where they live.

The varied ways in which politicians, the media and ordinary people position themselves in relation to each other point to the idea that it seems generally more sensible to consider media and individual opinions as relationally and communicatively constructed expressions, part and parcel of existing or newly created conceptual and dialogical networks, rather than pre-existing attributes of institutions and individuals, or cognitive systems.

Political communication, political style and political accountability

Through detailed attention to discursive and social practices, one can show the complexity of political communication, and how this is actually *accomplished* in particular political contexts. The micro-analysis (Bull, 2002, 2003) and discursive analysis (Fairclough, 2010) of politicians' rhetorical style (the case of former prime minister Tony Blair's New Labour rhetoric) have contributed to demonstrating how political communications are actually accomplished *in situ*. For instance, Bull (2000) describes the communicative skills of politicians in resolving communicative problems such as repeated questions, challenges to perceived equivocal responses or challenges to perceived contradictions in political policies.

---

[7] According to Leudar *et al.*, 2008, these themes vary in their generality and particularity, and can be used for various purposes such as stripping refugees and asylum seekers of their humanity or excluding their experiences from the reporting of events.

According to Bull (2000), in news interviews and other public encounters, politicians are driven by a desire to maintain positive face and 'to be approved of by others' (p. 5). Analysing a series of televised interviews broadcast at the time of the 1997 British general election, Bull considers the substance of Blair's equivocation in response to questions about the Labour Party policy between 1983 and 1997 (the rise of New Labour, movement to the centre ground of politics, etc.). The analysis highlights two of the most important features in Blair's discourse. First, in order to emphasise both political continuity and change, Blair makes extensive use of the ambiguous term 'modernisation' (p. 12); yet he never directly critiques 'old Labour'. Second, 'changes' to party policy are presented as principled, and 'change' in general is portrayed as a universal process of political life, and not peculiar to Labour. By constructing 'change' in this way, Blair is 'avoiding making highly face-damaging remarks both about himself and about the Labour party as a whole' (p. 13). In Bull's view, Blair's use of the ambiguous language of 'modernisation' can be seen as a strategy to manage face and present the best possible look for himself and his party.

In his analysis of New Labour's political language, Fairclough (2010) identifies some interesting features of Blair's political style. Fairclough sees Blair's success of capturing the 'popular mood' after Lady Diana's death in 1997 as partly the result of a 'mixed language' (p. 387):

I feel like everyone else in the country today – utterly devastated. Our thoughts and prayers are with Princess Diana's family – in particular her two sons, two boys – our hearts go out to them. We are today a nation, in Britain, in a state of shock, in mourning, in grief that is so deeply painful for us.

On the one hand, one can notice the established, conventional, sort of public language that elites use to communicate on behalf of the nation on official circumstances ('our thoughts and prayers', 'we are today a nation'). On the other hand, there is a moral personal language ('I feel like everyone else'). According to Fairclough (2010, p. 388), Blair uses 'a vernacular language of affect as well as a public one' (e.g. the references to 'utterly devastated' and 'state of shock').[8] The shift from 'sons' to 'boys' personalises the tone to a 'more intimate, family way'. The power of Blair's style lies in his 'ability to combine formality and informality, ceremony and feeling, publicness and privateness' and his 'capacity to ... "anchor" the public politician in the "normal person"' (p. 388). He is continually reasserting the political image of a normal, honest, affable, politician.

---

[8] On the role of emotion terms in discourse see Edwards (1997, 1999).

Blair is able to mix, with considerable success, a personal language with a more formal, representative language when he talks about the death of princess Diana[9]. Both Bull and Fairclough point to the idea that political personality and political style are not 'pre-given, they are carefully constructed' (Fairclough, 2010, p. 388). Different political contexts and settings require different political 'styles', different plays and organisations of political communication.

The complexity of political communications, and how these are *accomplished* in particular political and institutional contexts, can also be studied through a focus on questioning – for some, the new account-ability of mediated democratic politics. It is a commonplace of demo-cratic politics that politicians are accountable to journalists and other politicians in terms of answering questions (Clayman and Heritage, 2002; Housley and Fitzgerald, 2002; Hutchby, forthcoming; Tileagă, 2010). It is in political debates, 'talk shows' and political news inter-views that the 'liberal democratic role of broadcasting is found in its purest form, *mediating* between the public and its politicians, providing the former with access to raw political discourse, and providing the politicians with a channel of direct access to the people' (McNair, 2011, p. 76, emphasis in original).

The public management of political accountability in political news interviews can be seen as an 'opportunity to furnish the object of debate with various categorisations, predications and assessments' (Housley and Fitzgerald, 2002, p. 58). Tileagă (2010) is a typical investigation of the discursive dynamic of political accountability. The context is that of managing the representation of a socio-political event: the Romanian revolution of 1989. The extract shown below is from a political news interview featuring Ion Iliescu, a main protagonist of the December 1989 events and president of Romania at the time. Iliescu's emergence from the revolutionary fervour, first on public television, and later as the leader and founder of the National Salvation Front, are only some aspects that made him a controversial figure of the Romanian revo-lution. One of the most important critical positions levelled at Iliescu (coming from the liberal media and intellectuals) was the idea of a failure to establish transparent democratic accountability for the hor-rifying bloodshed and killing of innocent people in December 1989. Iliescu's defence was predominantly framed around producing and dis-seminating a dominant representation of the Romanian revolution as

---

[9] In other contexts, when talking about the war or terrorism, Blair was able to present a different discursive style, a combination of 'moral authority' and 'toughness' (see van Dijk, 2006, for an example).

'authentic' (as opposed to representations of the 'revolution' as the outcome of a coup d'état or external conspiracy), foundational and a turning point in the nation's history. Moreover, Iliescu has constantly and fiercely denied any suggestion of involvement, stake or (direct) responsibility in relation to the 1989 events.

The interview took place on public national television on the occasion of the fourteenth anniversary of the Romanian revolution. By virtue of being made publicly accessible to virtually anyone with a television set in those days (a revolution *en direct*), the events of December 1989 have come to be invested with a range of meanings, which have been the subject of negotiation, contestation and articulation within various ideological representations of the events. These representations include a range of ideas, going from that of the 'pure' revolution to that of the internal/external plot and coup d'état (see Cesereanu, 2004 for more details).

Extract 1

19	IR[10]	Don't you think that (.) the appearance of the confabulations on the subject
20		of the revolution, as you called them (.) is in some respect also facilitated by
21		the poverty of information regarding what happened then? (0.2)
22	IE	Not only the poverty of information, but first of all poverty (0.2) that causes a
23		feeling of disappointment in people, that after 14 years from (.) the revolution
24		(.) people's hope for the better is not (.) confirmed
25		for (.) the vast majority (.) otherwise (.) sure, there'll always be political
26		games (.) there was no revolution in (.) in the world which has not been
27		contested by (.) different (.) er (.) forces (.) in all the countries of the world (.)
28		and the French revolution (.) even today is still subject to debate (.) so,
29		>this is not< the (.) >essential< (.) problem (.)
30		as well, exploring the details (.) and contesting the essence of the problem
31		(.) this is the subject that should preoccupy us (.) otherwise, sure (.)
32		the preoccupation for exploring details too is a good thing (.) and it's the
33		business of historians (.) of people who can (.) help to (.)

The question at line 19 is directly addressed to the interviewee, Ion Iliescu. The interviewer displays an orientation 'to the constraint that they should maintain a neutralistic stance by producing utterances that are at least minimally recognisable as "questions"' (Greatbatch, 1998, p. 168). The question embodies 'very strong preferences for a "yes" answer' (Clayman and Heritage, 2002, p. 209). The question raises the

[10] IR is used to denote the interviewer; IE is used to refer to Ion Iliescu.

possibility that the position(s) of the critics treated by the interviewee as 'confabulations on the subject of the revolution' (lines 19–20) may not only have a politically motivated underpinning, but may be linked to a different dimension of accountability, that of not knowing what happened back then ('the poverty of information', line 21).

The 'poverty of information' is quickly acknowledged as a reasonable candidate answer, but followed immediately by a shift to an objective condition, that of a social fact: 'Poverty' itself is said to be the condition of most people whose 'hope for better is not confirmed' (line 24). Iliescu does not deny the legitimacy of the question and is apparently in agreement with the viewpoint contained in interviewer's challenge. Yet, the essence of the matter is said to lie elsewhere: the objective 'feeling of disappointment' (line 23) caused by poverty. The shift to 'poverty' foregrounds the issue of addressing the 'real issue' at stake. The shift is 'legitimate and properly motivated' (Clayman and Heritage, 2002, p. 264) by the self-justificatory perspective offered.

'Otherwise (.) sure, there'll always be political games', at lines 25–6, introduces a normalising and naturalising move for understanding (political) controversy and contestation. Note the use of the extreme case formulation 'always' and the metaphor 'political games' that are used to establish, uncontroversially, the perennial and natural/objective character of political controversy (see Jefferson, 1985; Edwards, 2000 on the use of extreme case formulations). The dimension of political accountability implied by the question is shifted/evaded by introducing an alternative dimension: pointing to what is seen as an essential feature of revolutions: their contestation (lines 26–7). A similar register of extreme case formulations is used: 'There was no revolution in (.) in the world which has not been contested', 'in all the countries of the world', thereby constructing the argument as factual. The implication of this account is that 'revolutions' should be understood in perspective, in *historical* (not linked to local contexts and events) and *categorical* terms (Tileagă, 2008). By virtue of acquiring membership in the social category 'revolution', the December 1989 events can be described as sharing the same essential feature: that of being (constantly and essentially) contested. Together with the earlier reference to the pervasiveness of 'political games', the constitution of contestation as an essential attribute of 'revolutions' represents the background for delegitimising (local) critical voices and sidestepping a public dimension of accountability around knowing the truth.

The account at lines 31–3 allows for overstepping the thrust of criticism that is linked to 'what happened then' and 'what is the truth' (and the connected question of 'how can one know the truth'). It subverts the terms in which one can even begin to understand and respond to those issues by projecting a dimension of knowledge that is role-bound: 'the preoccupation for exploring details too is a good thing (.) and it's the business of historians' (lines 32–3). This is presented as a concession (Antaki and Wetherell, 1999) whereby the attention to details is not directly dismissed; it is instead seen as *desirable*, but not an *actual* and *appropriate* concern for the present speakers (and, by implication, wider audience). A 'preferred' and ideological reading of a pivotal national event (the Romanian revolution) is firmly in place. But this is an ideological reading that downplays alternative dimensions of accountability and the idea that political categories and labels are 'often controversial both in their denotations and in their connotations' (Edelman, 2001, p. 79; see also Connolly, 1993).

Political advertising and political humour

Political communication consists not only of verbal or written statements, but also of 'visual means of signification such as dress, make-up, hairstyle, and logo design, i.e. all those elements of communication which might be said to constitute a political "image" or identity' (McNair, 2011, p. 4). Political advertising is the medium that creates and disseminates political images and identities (Kaid and Holtz-Bacha, 2006). Political advertising refers to various forms of political communication, from the traditional mass media political content (party political broadcasts) to billboards, leaflets, campaign websites, Twitter and YouTube streams, virtual/online posters, viral campaigns, and so forth.

Different forms of mediation work to '"theme" and "place" the political in very different ways ... within terms that include criticism and derision as well as affirmation' (Richardson *et al.*, 2011, p. 321). Online political advertising is a case in point, a special example of mediation where the 'political' is placed in a network of activities that opens multiple possibilities of interpreting political messages that are usually beyond the originator's control. Increasingly, the Internet has provided political campaigners with a 'new forum for the release of their campaign messages' (Burgess, 2011, p. 182). Following on from Barack Obama's creative use of new media in the 2008 general elections, in 2010, for the British general elections, British journalists rushed to welcome everyone to the first e-election (Harris, 2010).

With the advent of new technologies, especially social networking, virtually everyone can create content or subvert, modify, enrich existing content. This has opened a range of possibilities for online activists, (maverick) bloggers, or film/visual artists to produce and disseminate content that has the possibility to affect the manner in which people think about very specific political issues. The focus here is on the role of political humour to influence the manner in which people think about political issues. From political cartoons and caricatures in newspapers (Richardson *et al.*, 2011) mocking the ways, words and moods of politicians and political parties to the use of humour in presidential debates (Stewart, 2011), the creative and subversive capacities of verbal, visual and semiotic forms have no limits (see also Lockyer and Pickering, 2001; Speier, 1998). According to Richardson *et al.* (2011) election campaigns offer a 'particularly fruitful time for visual satirists'. Endless possibilities are opened to 'subvert, distort and exaggerate character traits to humorous effect' (p. 312; but see Kuipers, 2011 for the links between humour, scandal and outrage). As McNair (2011, p. 41) argues

politicians and parties now routinely use YouTube to post campaign messages and advertisements, but these are subverted by online users – 'mashed' up, re-edited, digitally retouched – in ways that satirise and mock the sender. Political communication on the internet is vulnerable to the interventions of digital content-generating users to a degree never true of 'old' media, centralised and top-down as they were.

The classic billboard poster or the online poster are seen as means of disseminating pre-packaged political information about the candidate's or party's political programme. As Burgess (2011) notes 'despite their ubiquity, posters have often been overlooked by those seeking to analyse and understand the electoral role of different media, notably television and more recently the internet' (p. 181). Posters are featured as illustrations of central political messages of political campaigns, static containers of political messages and images, but are rarely treated in their own right as part and parcel of the political communication process.

Online campaign posters are vulnerable to the interventions of online users. A case in point was the UK 2010 general election and the notoriety of mydavidcameron.com as the most prominent online election website. mydavidcameron.com presented visitors with the opportunity to spoof official Conservative election material by manipulating it, recomposing it, 'rewriting' it, with the help of printed or pictorial aspects (see Figures 9.1 and 9.2). February 2010 saw the launch of Conservative's second major billboard campaign ('I've never voted Tory before'), supposedly aimed at those who had not voted Conservative before. Each poster featured a different character: 'Julie from Llandundno', 'Ian

Figure 9.1 UK Conservative party original posters
Source: mydavidcameron.com (last accessed June 2012)

from Congleton' and 'Danielle from Brighton'. The same characters appeared in YouTube videos and television party election broadcasts.

Political jokes are directed against 'established institutions, policies, or publicly recognised values' (Speier, 1998, p. 1353) or publicly professed and endorsed values. The capacity of online users to subvert official campaign messages points towards a conception where political messages can be seen as artefacts, constructions that reflect the particular agenda and values of political parties. Political messages are shaped by processes of coding and encoding. Messages are encoded ideologically by politicians and political parties with a 'preferred' political meaning, but audiences and publics may decode (and even recode)

Figure 9.2 UK Conservative party spoof posters
Source: mydavidcameron.com (last accessed June 2012)

these messages with a certain liberty reflecting 'particular cultural [and political] codes which, in turn, related to their broader social circumstances' (Franklin, 2004, p. 215). Irony and ridicule permit audiences to discover for themselves, to spot 'the incongruity between claim and fact' (Billig, 2005, p. 77). The laughter is left to the audience.

The posters deal with (frame) the stakes and interests of the 'electorate'. The seriousness of the political message is transformed by ridicule, jocularity and careful wit. Notice the rhetorical use of 'absurdity' (Antaki, 2003) in the 'I'm 7' poster and the play on appearance versus reality in 'being made unemployed sounds fun' poster. The visual layout remains the same; it is the political message that is subverted. The spoofed words of the poster protagonists represent a reaction to the 'performance' and political assumptions contained in the original posters. As Billig writes, humour is to be seen as rhetorical, 'for rhetoric is part of social communication' (2005, p. 195). Using humour rhetorically, speakers and writers can do various things: critique or praise, support or negate, resist or further certain practices. Politics is encountered not only through the seriousness of the party political message, but also through the subversive sense of parody. Only then does political language (and political communication itself) become a key *political* issue. It is perhaps too often assumed that political communications take place in a fairly predictable, 'clear and efficient way' and in a stable environment, and that there is no disagreement about the very terms of the debate. Political humour engenders a dynamic political language that creates and reflects alternative social and political worlds (Edelman, 2001). In order to understand how political humour works in these circumstances and others, one needs to understand the social and political purposes of humour and ridicule (Billig, 2005). Ridicule is critical for the maintenance of reasonable political common sense. For the spoofers on mydavidcameron.com the defence of an alternative political common sense is paramount and reflected in their posters. Puns, irony and other manifestations of everyday humour can flout established conventions of political communication. Political irony and ridicule can break the rules of the dominant manifestations and expressions of politics. What is sometimes considered 'online mockery' (Burgess, 2011, p. 185) or 'vandalism' are merely attempts by people to produce (their) politics actively in their own terms; attempts to move from *consumers* of politics to active *producers* of it. The spoof posters reflect that acceptable politics is not only party politics; it is politics created by citizens as active users, creators and transformers of politics.

Towards a discursive approach to political communication

As argued in the previous chapter, political psychologists display a tendency to treat language as an independent variable or as expressing the working of inner cognitive processes. In the study of mediated politics and political communications, language is largely stripped of its constructive and constitutive properties. Political communication and the public *use* of language is seen as a property and emergence of cognitive processes (heuristics, framing, priming) and not an intrinsic feature of social practices/activities and social interaction between people. Discursive analyses can help us better understand the discursive and cultural patterning of political communications. Political psychologists can learn more about the intricacies of political communications by looking at the various ways in which political communications are publicly accomplished and displayed. It is crucial to be more explicit about the discursive (and ideological) underpinnings of political communication (and its mediation); that is, to analyse social and political reasoning, political commitments and positions, issues of stake and accountability, made relevant by people themselves in talk, texts or through visual means, and to treat these as the outcome of contingent, *situated* and *practical* accomplishments, and an integral part of *what goes on* in a variety of political practices and settings. As Chapters 7 and 8 have shown, this move entails treating politics as a domain of social practice and a complex web of social activities.

By broadening its theoretical and empirical sweep, it is hoped that political psychology would be able to understand better the social and political structuring and restructuring of various manifestations of political communications that constitute 'the nature of politics in a fundamental sense' (Fairclough, 2010, p. 158). This includes the formation and dissemination of political beliefs, political knowledge, practices and representations of the political, social and political identities, the framing and interconnectedness of political relations. Political psychologists can borrow and learn from media/communication and discursive theorists interested in the complexity of political communication. Political psychologists have historically lacked the theoretical basis of seeing communication and discourse as an element of the social and political, and the methodological resources to produce detailed analyses of communication and discourse that go beyond the listing of thematic repertoires and discursive 'frames'. Discursive perspectives to political communication can fill this gap and create the much-needed dialogue between discourse and media/communication studies and psychological approaches to political communication.

One could argue that there are two kinds of determinism when attempting to understand mediated political communications: a *technological determinism* (that posits a necessary and essential link between political communications and the nature of new technologies) and *psychological/cognitive determinism* (that posits a necessary and essential link between political communications and information-processing paradigms of cognitive science). Both can narrow rather than broaden the political horizon of individuals and researchers alike. Both can be complemented by a vision of mediated politics that treats political communications as a carefully produced discourse, an *interactive* and *social interactional* process of political meaning making. As Kinder aptly argues, political psychologists have the responsibility 'to integrate communication results into the larger story of politics ... a truly successful science of mass communications cannot be just a wing of cognitive psychology, as important as psychology has been to the development of the field' (2003, p. 379). A serious move away from cognition and a genuine reorientation towards language and active communication processes can give political psychologists a broader foundation from which to address the complexity and the continually transforming nature of political communication and political discourse.

Epilogue

As the preceding pages have shown, one can gain a deeper understanding of political behaviour and the strength and utility of political psychology by emphasising its diversity of perspectives. Of course, the global world of political psychology extends beyond the boundaries of Europe and North America. Issues, topics, innovations in political psychology are not limited to what European academics and their North American colleagues choose to study. Nor are they limited to psychological issues. Around the world, new and creative ways of understanding the different manifestations of political behaviour are being developed: some are simply borrowing the models and the tools of their more prestigious American colleagues; others proceed independently, developing critiques, finding new gaps and imagining new research tools and hypotheses more suited to researching local social and political contexts. One of the major challenges of political psychology rests with how best to promote alternative ways of doing political psychology.

In its search for integrated and integrative perspectives, contemporary political psychology (especially in North America) is preoccupied with devising new technologies of research that can potentially change or transform the field. There is nothing wrong with this approach. The conceptual tools of cognitive science, evolutionary science, genetics, or the tools of neuroscience are pushing political psychology in new exciting directions. But problems can arise when this approach is used to predict and prescribe the future of political psychology. There is a lot of truth in Helen Haste's statement: 'predicting the future is hazardous; prescribing the future is a doomed exercise' (2012, p. 1). It remains to be seen whether the future of political psychology lies with a dialogue with cognitive science, evolutionary science, or the neurosciences, especially when these approaches are drawn upon uncritically. This dialogue can potentially turn political psychology into a system governed by the problems and priorities of other fields. What we can be sure of, nonetheless, is that, as political psychologists, we can always turn to the lives of 'concrete' human beings, to describing and interpreting their social practices, social interactions, motivations, representations, as they appear to them in their full contingency.

There is a tendency in political psychology to assume that individuals, groups, and communities, are engaged in a *total* search for meaning in the form of values, political knowledge, social identities, and so on. The alternative to this is to argue that this search for meaning is, for all practical purposes, *fragmentary*, *unfinished* and *relative* to the contexts in which it is performed. As this book has shown, a more careful and systematic focus on sociocultural aspects of political ideologies, social representations and social identities, language and social action, can guide social and political psychologists to offer more comprehensive and insightful analyses and commentaries on socio-cognitive, cultural and discursive aspects of politics and political behaviour. Perspectives described in this book can constitute the foundation for a less reductionist and more insightful interpretation of a variety of individual and group political behaviours and manifestations of politics.

Political psychologists should perhaps more deliberately call overt attention to their own methods, assumptions and processes of production of results, and more explicitly indicate the *constructed* rather than the *found* nature of their concepts, tools and effects. Political psychology is, arguably, entrenched in the idea that positive knowledge (knowledge that originates in researcher-controlled research methodologies) can be used to solve social problems (Mutz, 2009). The only problem is that this type of approach can sometimes neglect the diversity of political logics embedded in political world views of different groups, communities, individuals, as well as their contradictions, ambiguities, dilemmas. Psychology and politics, as provinces of human activity and the human condition, serve to foreground situated, particularistic and contingent images of human nature, personhood, communication and collective action.

Contemporary political psychologists draw upon (and have devised) methods and forms of knowledge that are more far-reaching and wide-ranging than those available to their forerunners. In 1967, Ring could write of social psychology: 'we are a field of many frontiersmen, but few settlers' (p. 120). Today, we can say that social and political psychology is a field of many settlers, but few frontiersmen or frontierswomen. Some researchers think of this as a critical gain; others see it as an illusory advantage. In order to understand the future direction of social and political psychology, the contemporary political psychologist must look to the past, and to the classical writers of its discipline. The problems raised by the early social psychologies of Halbwachs, Lippmann, Bartlett or Tarde have all dealt with the 'most immediate and down-to-earth events of daily life, physical and symbolic exchanges between individuals' (Moscovici, 1988, p. 213), the events and problems that their own societies posed to them. By turning its attention to the very latest developments in cognitive or evolutionary science, political psychology is perhaps turning its back on its ability to promote an intellectual milieu open to wider perspectives dedicated more to the exploration of meaningful life worlds than to the pursuit of data.

Bibliography

Abell, J., Condor, S., and Stevenson, C. (2006). 'We are an island': geographical imagery in accounts of citizenship, civil society and national identity in Scotland and in England. *Political Psychology*, **27**, 191–217.

Adorno, T. W., Frenkel-Brunswick, E., Levinson, D. J., and Sanford, R. N. ([1950] 1982). *The authoritarian personality*. New York: Harper.

Allport, G. W. (1954). *The nature of prejudice*. Reading, MA: Addison-Wesley.

(1962). The general and the unique in psychological science. *Journal of Personality*, **30**, 405–22.

Allyn, J., and Festinger, L. (1961). The effectiveness of unanticipated persuasive communications. *Journal of Abnormal and Social Psychology*, **62**, 35–40.

Altemeyer, B. (1981). *Right-wing authoritarianism*. Winnipeg: University of Manitoba Press.

(1996). *The authoritarian specter*. Cambridge, MA: Harvard University Press.

Anderson, L., and McGuire, W. (1965). Prior reassurance of group consensus as a factor in producing resistance to persuasion. *Sociometry*, **28**, 44–56.

Andrews, M. (2007). *Shaping history: narratives of political change*. Cambridge University Press.

Ansolabehere, S., Rodden, J., and Snyder, J. (2008). The strength of issues: using multiple measures to gauge preference stability, ideological constraint, and issue voting. *American Political Science Review*, **102**, 215–32.

Antaki, C. (2003). The uses of absurdity. In H. van den Berg, M. Wetherell and H. Houtkoop Steenstra (eds.) *Analyzing race talk: multidisciplinary perspectives on the research interview* (pp. 85–102). Cambridge University Press.

(2006). Producing a 'cognition'. *Discourse Studies*, **8**, 9–15.

Antaki, C., and Leudar, I. (2001). Recruiting the record: using opponents' exact words in Parliamentary argumentation. *Text*, **21**, 467–88.

Antaki, C., and Wetherell, M. (1999). Show concessions. *Discourse Studies*, **1**, 7–27.

Antaki, C., Condor, S., and Levine, M. (1996). Social identities in talk: speakers' own orientations. *British Journal of Social Psychology*, **35**, 473–92.

Arendt, H. (1958). *The human condition*. Chicago, IL: University of Chicago Press.

Aristotle. (1909). *Rhetorica*. Cambridge University Press.

Assmann, A. (2008). Transformations between history and memory. *Social Research*, **75**, 49–72.

Atkinson, J. M. (1984). *Our masters' voices*. London: Methuen.

Atkinson, P., and Silverman, D. (1997). Kundera's immortality: the interview society and the invention of the self. *Qualitative Inquiry*, 3, 304–25.

Augoustinos, M., and Every, D. (2010). Accusations and denials of racism: managing moral accountability in public discourse. *Discourse & Society*, 21, 251–56.

Augoustinos, M., and Reynolds, J. K. (2001). Prejudice, racism and social psychology. In M. Augoustinos and J. K. Reynolds (eds.) *Understanding prejudice, racism and social conflict* (pp. 1–23). London: Sage.

Augoustinos, M., Hastie, B., and Wright, M. (2011). Apologizing for historical injustice: emotion, truth and identity in political discourse. *Discourse & Society*, 22, 507–31.

Augoustinos, M., and Tileagă, C. (2012). Twenty five years of discursive psychology. *British Journal of Social Psychology*, 51, 405–12.

Augoustinos, M., Tuffin, K., and Rapley, M. (1999). Genocide or failure to gel? Racism, history and nationalism in Australian talk. *Discourse & Society*, 10, 351–78.

Augoustinos, M., Tuffin, K., and Every, D. (2005). New racism, meritocracy and individualism: constraining affirmative action in education. *Discourse & Society*, 16, 315–39.

Austin, J. L. (1962). *How to do things with words*. Oxford: Clarendon Press.

Azzi, A. E., Chryssochoou, X., Klandermans, B., and Simon, B. (eds.) (2011). *Identity and participation in culturally diverse societies*. Oxford: Wiley-Blackwell.

Backes, U. (2009). *Political extremes: a conceptual history from antiquity to the present*. London: Routledge.

Backes, U., and Moreau, P. (2011). *The extreme right in Europe: current trends and perspectives*. Göttingen: Vandenhoeck & Ruprecht.

Baker-Brown, G., Ballard, E., Bluck, S., deVries, B., Suedfeld, P., and Tetlock, P. (1986). *Scoring manual for integrative and conceptual complexity*. Vancouver: University of British Columbia.

Bartels, L. (2003). Democracy with attitudes. In M. MacKuen and G. Rabinowitz (eds.) *Electoral democracy* (pp. 48–82). Ann Arbor: University of Michigan Press.

Barthes, R. ([1957] 1993). *Mythologies*. London: Vintage.

(1977). *Image-music-text*. London: Fontana.

Bartlett, F. C. ([1932] 1995). *Remembering: a study in experimental and social psychology*. Cambridge University Press.

Bastian, B., and Haslam, N. (2011). Experiencing dehumanization: cognitive and emotional effects of everyday dehumanization. *Basic and Applied Social Psychology*, 33, 295–303.

Bauer, M. W., and Gaskell, G. (1999). Towards a paradigm for research on social representations. *Journal for the Theory of Social Behaviour*, 29, 163–86.

(2008). Social representations theory: a progressive research programme for social psychology. *Journal for the Theory of Social Behaviour*, 38, 335–53.

Baumeister, R., and Hastings, S. (1997). Distortions of collective memory: how groups flatter and deceive themselves. In J. Pennebaker, D. Paez and B. Rimé (eds.) *Collective memory of political events: social psychological perspectives* (pp. 277–94). Mahwah, NJ: Lawrence Erlbaum.

Baumeister, R., Vohs, K., and Funder, D. (2007). Psychology as the science of self-reports and finger movements: whatever happened to actual behavior? *Perspectives in Psychological Science*, 2, 396–403.

Becker, A. B., and Scheufele, D. A. (2011). New voters, new outlook? Predispositions, social networks, and the changing politics of gay civil rights. *Social Science Quarterly*, 92, 324–45.

Becker, A. B., Dalrymple, K. E., Brossard, D., Scheufele, D. A., and Gunther, A. (2010). Getting citizens involved: how controversial policy debates stimulate issue participation during a political campaign. *International Journal of Public Opinion Research*, 22, 181–203.

Beissinger, M. R. (2009). Debating the color revolutions: an interrelated wave. *Journal of Democracy*, 20, 74–7.

Bennett, W. L., and Entman, R. M. (eds.) (2001). *Mediated politics: communication in the future of democracy*. New York: Cambridge University Press.

Bennett, W. L., and Iyengar, S. (2008). A new era of minimal effects? The changing foundations of political communication. *Journal of Communication*, 58, 707–31.

Benwell, B., and Stokoe, E. (2006). *Discourse and identity*. Edinburgh University Press.

Berelson, B. (1952). Democratic theory and public opinion. *Public Opinion Quarterly*, 16, 313–30.

Berelson, B., Lazarsfeld, P., and McPhee, W. (1954). *Voting: a study of opinion formation in a presidential election*. Chicago, IL: Chicago University Press.

Berinsky, A. (ed.) (2012). *New directions in public opinion*. New York: Routledge.

Billig, M. (1976). *Social psychology and intergroup relations*. London: Academic Press.

(1978). *Fascists: a social psychological view of the National Front*. London: Academic Press.

(1985). Prejudice, categorisation and particularisation: from a perceptual to a rhetorical approach. *European Journal of Social Psychology*, 15, 79–103.

(1987). *Arguing and thinking: a rhetorical approach to social psychology*. Cambridge University Press.

(1988). The notion of 'prejudice': Some rhetorical and ideological aspects. *Text*, 8, 91–111.

(1991). *Ideology and opinions*. London: Sage.

(1993). Studying the thinking society: social representations, rhetoric and attitudes. In G. Breakwell and D. Canter (eds.) *Empirical approaches to social representations*. Oxford University Press.

(1995). *Banal nationalism*. London: Sage.

(1996). *Arguing and thinking: a rhetorical approach to social psychology* (2nd edn). Cambridge University Press.

(1997). Discursive, rhetorical and ideological messages. In C. McGarty and S. A. Haslam (eds.) *The message of social psychology*. Oxford: Blackwell.

(1998). *Talking of the Royal family* (2nd edn). London: Routledge.

(1999). *Freudian repression*. Cambridge University Press.

(2002). Henri Tajfel's 'Cognitive aspects of prejudice' and the psychology of bigotry. *British Journal of Social Psychology*, 41, 171–88.

(2003). Political rhetoric. In D. O. Sears, L. Huddy, and R. Jervis (eds.) *Oxford handbook of political psychology* (pp. 222–52). New York: Oxford University Press.

(2005). *Laughter and ridicule: towards a social critique of humour.* London: Sage.

(2008). *The hidden roots of critical psychology: understanding the impact of Locke, Shaftesbury and Reid.* London: Sage.

(2012). Undisciplined beginnings, academic success, and discursive psychology. *British Journal of Social Psychology,* 51, 413–24.

Billig, M., and MacMillan, K. (2005). Metaphor, idiom and ideology: the search for 'no smoking guns' across time. *Discourse & Society,* 16, 459–80.

Billig, M., Condor, S., Edwards, D., Gane, M., Middleton, D., and Radley, A. (1988). *Ideological dilemmas: a social psychology of everyday thinking.* London: Sage.

Blumer, H. (1948). Public opinion and public opinion polling. *American Sociological Review,* 13, 542–54.

Blumler, J. G. (2001). The third age of political communication. *Journal of Public Affairs,* 1, 201–9.

Blumler, J. G., and Kavannagh, D. (1999). The Third Age of political communication: influences and features. *Political Communication,* 16, 209–30.

Bosveld, W., Koomen, W., and Vogelaar, R. (1997). Construing a social issue: effects on attitudes and the false consensus effect. *British Journal of Social Psychology,* 36, 263–72.

Bourdieu, P. (1979). Public opinion does not exist. In A. Mattelart and S. Siegelaub (eds.) *Communication and class struggle* (vol. I) (pp. 124–130). New York: International General/ Intl Mass Media Research Centre.

(2012). *Sur l'État: Cours au Collège de France (1989–1992).* Paris: Seuil.

Bourhis, R. Y., and Giles, H. (1977). The language of intergroup distinctiveness. In H. Giles (ed.) *Language, ethnicity and intergroup relations.* London: Academic Press.

Braithwaite, V. (1994). Beyond Rokeach's equality-freedom model: two-dimensional values in a one-dimensional world. *Journal of Social Issues,* 50, 67–94.

(2009a). The value balance model and democratic governance. *Psychological Inquiry,* 20, 87–97.

(2009b). Security and harmony value orientations and their roles in attitude formation and change. *Psychological Inquiry,* 20, 162–7.

Breakwell, G. (1978). Some effects of marginal social identity. In H. Tajfel (ed.) *Differentiation between social groups.* London: Academic Press.

Brewer, M. B. (2010). Social identity complexity and acceptance of diversity. In R. J. Crisp (ed.) *The psychology of social and cultural diversity* (pp. 11–33). Oxford: Wiley-Blackwell.

Brewer, M. B., and Campbell, D. T. (1976). *Ethnocentrism and intergroup attitudes: East African evidence.* New York: Sage.

Brockmeier, J. (2002). Remembering and forgetting: narrative as cultural memory. *Culture and Psychology,* 8, 15–43.

(2010). After the archive: remapping memory. *Culture & Psychology,* 16, 5–35.

Brown, R. (1965). *Social psychology.* London: Collier-Macmillan.

Brown, R. J. (1995). *Prejudice: its social psychology*. Oxford: Blackwell.

Brown, R., and Gilman, A. F. (1960). *The pronouns of power and solidarity*. Indianapolis, IN: Bobbs-Merrill.

Brown, S. D. (2008). The quotation marks have a certain importance: prospects for a 'memory studies'. *Memory Studies*, 1, 261–71.

Bruner, J. S. (1957). On perceptual readiness. *Psychological Review*, 64, 123–152.

(1986). *Actual minds, possible worlds*. Cambridge, MA: Harvard University Press.

(2001). Self-making and world-making. In J. Brockmeier and D. Carbaugh (eds.) *Narrative and identity: studies in autobiography, self, and culture* (pp. 25–38). Amsterdam: John Benjamins.

Bucur, M. (2009). *Heroes and victims: remembering war in twentieth-century Romania*. Bloomington: Indiana University Press.

Bull, P. (2000). Equivocation and the rhetoric of modernisation: an analysis of televised interviews with Tony Blair in the 1997 British General Election. *Journal of Language and Social Psychology*, 19, 222–47.

(2002). *Communication under the microscope: the theory and practice of microanalysis*. London: Psychology Press.

(2003). *The microanalysis of political communication: claptrap and ambiguity*. London: Routledge.

Bunce, V. J., and Wolchik, S. (2009). Debating the color revolutions: getting real about 'real causes'. *Journal of Democracy*, 20, 69–73.

Burgess, C. (2011). 'This election will be won by people not posters'... In D. Wring, R. Mortimore and S. Atkinson (eds.) *Political communication in Britain* (pp. 181–97). London: Palgrave-Macmillan.

Burgess, M., Ferguson, N, and Hollywood, I. (2007). Rebels' perspectives of the legacy of past violence and of the current peace in post-agreement Northern Ireland: an interpretative phenomenological analysis. *Political Psychology*, 28, 69–88.

Cameron, L., and Turner, R. (2010). The application of diversity-based interventions to policy and practice. In R. J. Crisp (ed.) *The psychology of social and cultural diversity* (pp. 322–52). Oxford: Wiley-Blackwell.

Campbell, A., Converse, P., Miller, W., and Stokes, D. (1960). *The American voter*. New York: Wiley.

Campbell, D. T. (1956). Enhancement of contrast as a composite habit. *Journal of Abnormal and Social Psychology*, 53, 350–355.

Campbell, S. (2008). The second voice. *Memory Studies*, 1, 41–8.

Cantril, H. (1942). Public opinion in flux. *Annals of the American Academy of Political and Social Science*, 22, 136–52.

Cappella, J. N., and Jamieson, K. H. (1997). *Spiral of cynicism: the press and the public good*. New York: Oxford University Press.

Caprara, G. V., Schwartz, S., Capanna, C., Vecchione, M., and Barbaranelli, C. (2006). Personality and politics: values, traits, and political choice. *Political Psychology*, 27, 1–28.

Castells, M. (2011). *Communication power*. Oxford University Press.

Cesereanu, R. (2004). *Decembrie '89. Deconstrucţia unei revoluţii*. Iaşi: Polirom.

(2008). The Final Report on the Holocaust and the Final Report on the Communist Dictatorship in Romania. *East European Politics and Societies*, 22, 270–81.

Charteris-Black, J. (2005). *Politicians and rhetoric: the persuasive power of metaphor*. Basingstoke and New York: Palgrave Macmillan.

Chilton, P. (1996). *Security metaphors: Cold War discourse from containment to common European home*. Berne and New York: Peter Lang.

(2004). *Analysing political discourse: theory and practice*. London: Routledge.

Chilton, P., and Ilyin, M. (1993). Metaphor in political discourse. *Discourse & Society*, 4, 7–31.

Chilton, P., and Schäffner, C. (1997). Discourse and politics. In T. van Dijk (ed.) *Discourse as social interaction* (vol. II) (pp. 206–31). London: Sage.

Chouliaraki, L., and Fairclough, N. (1999). *Discourse in late modernity: rethinking critical discourse analysis*. Edinburgh University Press.

Christie, R., and Jahoda, M. (eds.) (1954). *Studies in the scope and method of 'The Authoritarian Personality'*. New York: Free Press.

Ciobanu, M. (2009). Criminalising the past and reconstructing collective memory: the Romanian Truth Commission. *Europe-Asia Studies*, 61, 313–36.

Clayman, S., and Heritage, J. (2002). *The news interview: journalists and public figures on the air*. Cambridge University Press.

Clémence, A., Doise, W., de Rosa, A. S., and Gonzalez, L. (1995). La représentation sociale des droits de l'homme: une recherche internationale sur l'étendue et les limites de l'universalité. *International Journal of Psychology*, 30, 181–212.

Cohrs, J. C., and Stelzl, M. (2010). How ideological attitudes predict host society members' attitudes toward immigrants: exploring cross-national differences. *Journal of Social Issues*, 66, 673–94.

Condor, S. (2000). Pride and prejudice: identity management in English people's talk about 'this country'. *Discourse & Society*, 11, 163–93.

(2006). Temporality and collectivity: diversity, history and the rhetorical construction of national entitativity. *British Journal of Social Psychology*, 45, 657–82.

(2010). Devolution and national identity: the rules of English dis/engagement. *Nations & Nationalism*, 16, 525–43.

(2011). Sense and sensibility: the conversational etiquette of English national self-identification. In A. Aughey and C. Berberich (eds.) *These Englands: a conversation on national identity*. Manchester University Press.

Condor, S., and Figgou, L. (2012). Rethinking the prejudice problematic: a collaborative cognition approach. In J. Dixon and M. Levine (eds.) *Beyond prejudice: extending the social psychology of conflict, inequality and social change* (pp. 200–22). Cambridge University Press.

Condor, S., and Gibson, S. (2007). 'Everybody's entitled to their own opinion': ideological dilemmas of liberal individualism and active citizenship. *Journal of Community and Applied Social Psychology*, 6, 178–99.

Condor, S., Abell, J., Figgou, L., Gibson, S., and Stevenson, C. (2006). 'They're not racist … ': Prejudice denial, mitigation and suppression in dialogue, *British Journal of Social Psychology*, 45, 441–462.

Condor, S., Tileagă, C., and Billig, M. (in press). Political rhetoric. In L. Huddy, D. O. Sears and J. Levy (eds.) *Oxford handbook of political psychology* (2nd edn). New York: Oxford University Press.

Connerton, P. (1989). *How societies remember.* Cambridge University Press.

Connolly, W. (1993). *The terms of political discourse* (3rd edn). Oxford: Wiley-Blackwell.

Converse, P. E. (1962). Information flow and the stability of partisan attitudes. *Public Opinion Quarterly,* **26,** 578–99.

(1964). The nature of belief systems in mass publics. In D. Apter (ed.) *Ideology and discontent* (pp. 206–61). New York: Free Press.

(1987). Changing conceptions of public opinion in the political process. *Public Opinion Quarterly* (Supplement: 50th Anniversary Issue), **51,** S12–S24.

(2006a). The nature of belief systems in mass publics. *Critical Review: A Journal of Politics and Society,* **18,** 1–74.

(2006b). Democratic theory and electoral reality. *Critical Review: A Journal of Politics and Society,* **18,** 297–329.

(2009). Perspectives on mass belief systems and communication. In R. J. Dalton and H.-D. Klingemann (eds.) *The Oxford handbook of political behavior* (pp. 144–60). New York: Oxford University Press.

Conway, M. (1997). The inventory of experience: memory and identity. In J. Pennebaker, D. Paez and B. Rimé (eds.) *Collective memory of political events: social psychological perspectives* (pp. 21–46). Mahwah, NJ: Lawrence Erlbaum.

Coulter, J. (2001). Human practices and the observability of the 'macro-social'. In T. R. Schatzki, K. K. Cetina and E. Savigny (eds.) *The practice turn in contemporary theory* (pp. 29–41). London: Routledge.

Crigler, A. N. (1996). Making sense of politics: constructing political messages and meanings. In A. N. Crigler (ed.) *The psychology of political communication* (pp. 1–10). Ann Arbor: University of Michigan Press.

Crisp, R., and Hewstone, M. (eds.) (2000). Crossed categorization and intergroup bias: the moderating role of intergroup and affective context. *Journal of Experimental Social Psychology,* **36,** 357–83.

(2006). *Multiple social categorization: processes, models and applications.* Hove, Sussex: Psychology Press.

(2007). Multiple social categorization. In M. P. Zanna (ed.) *Advances in experimental social psychology* (vol. XXXIX, pp. 163–254). Orlando, FL: Academic Press.

Crisp, R., Hewstone, M., and Rubin, M. (2001). Does multiple categorization reduce intergroup bias? *Personality and Social Psychology Bulletin,* **27,** 76–89.

Dalton, R. J. (2008). *Citizen politics: public opinion and political parties in advanced industrial democracies* (5th edn). Washington, DC: CQ Press.

Dalton, R. J., and Klingemann, H.-D. (2009). Citizens and political behavior. In R. J. Dalton and H.-D. Klingemann (eds.) *The Oxford handbook of political behavior* (pp. 3–28). New York: Oxford University Press.

D'Anieri, P. (2006). Explaining the success and failure of post-communist revolutions. *Communist and Post-Communist Studies,* **39,** 331–50.

Danziger, K. (2008). *Marking the mind: a history of memory*. Cambridge University Press.

Deacon, D., and Wring, D. (2011). Reporting the 2010 General election: old media, new media – old politics, new politics. In D. Wring, R. Mortimore and S. Atkinson (eds.) *Political communication in Britain*. London: Palgrave.

de Brito, A. B., Enriquez, C. G., and Aguilar, P. (2001). *The politics of memory: transitional justice in democratizing societies*. New York: Oxford University Press.

Delli Carpini, M. X., and Keeter, S. (1996). *What Americans know about politics and why it matters*. New Haven, CT: Yale University Press.

Delli Carpini, M. X., and Williams, B. (2001). Let us entertain you: politics in the new media environment. In L. Bennett and R. Entman (eds.) *Mediated politics: communication in the future of democracy* (pp. 160–91). New York: Cambridge University Press.

De Weerd, M., and Klandermans M. (1999). Group identification and social protest: farmer's protest in the Netherlands. *European Journal of Social Psychology*, **29**, 1,073–95.

Dewey, J. ([1927] 1954). *The public and its problems*. New York: Holt, Rinehart & Winston.

Diab, L. N. (1959). Authoritarianism and prejudice in near-Eastern students attending American universities. *Journal of Social Psychology*, **50**, 175–87.

Dimitrov, M. (2009). Debating the color revolutions: popular autocrats. *Journal of Democracy*, **20**, 78–81.

Dixon, J., and Levine, M. (eds.) (2012). *Beyond prejudice: extending the social psychology of conflict, inequality and social change*. Cambridge University Press.

Doise, W. (2002). *Human rights as social representations*. London: Routledge.

Doise, W., and Staerklé, C. (2002). From social to political psychology: the societal approach. In K. Monroe (ed.) *Political psychology* (pp. 151–72). Hillsdale, NJ: Lawrence Erlbaum.

Doise, W., Deschamps, J.-C., and Meyer, G. (1978). The accentuation of intracategory similarities. In H. Tajfel (ed.) *Differentiation between social groups*. London: Academic Press.

Doise, W., Clémence, A., and Lorenzi-Cioldi, F. (1993). *The quantitative analysis of social representations*. Hemel Hempstead: Harvester Wheatsheaf.

Doise, W., Spini, D., and Clémence, A. (1999). Human rights studied as social representations in a cross-national context. *European Journal of Social Psychology*, **29**, 1–29.

Doise, W., Staerklé, C., Clémence, A. and Savory, F. (1998). Human rights and Genevan youth: a developmental study of social representations. *Swiss Journal of Psychology*, **57**, 86–100.

Doosje, B., Van den Bos, K., and Loseman, A. (in press). Radicalization process of Islamic youth in the Netherlands: the role of uncertainty, perceived injustice and perceived group threat. *Journal of Social Issues*.

Dovidio, J. F., Gaertner, S., and Saguy, T. (2007). Another view of 'we': majority and minority group perspectives on a common ingroup identity. *European Review of Social Psychology*, **18**, 296–330.

(2009). Commonality and the complexity of 'we': social attitudes and social change. *Personality and Social Psychology Review*, **13**, 3–20.

Drury, J., and Reicher, S. (2000). Collective action and psychological change: the emergence of new social identities. *British Journal of Social Psychology*, **39**, 579–604.

(2009). Collective psychological empowerment as a model of social change: researching crowds and power. *Journal of Social Issues*, **65**, 707–25.

Duckitt, J. (1988). Normative conformity and racial prejudice in South Africa. *Genetic, Social, and General Psychology Monographs*, **114**, 413–37.

(2003). Prejudice and intergroup hostility. In D. Sears, L. Huddy and R. Jervis (eds.) *Oxford handbook of political psychology* (pp. 559–600). Oxford University Press.

Duckitt, J., Bizumic, B. and Heled, E. (2010). A tripartite approach to right-wing authoritarianism: the Authoritarianism-Conservatism-Traditionalism model. *Political Psychology*, **31**, 685–715.

Duveen, G. (2001). Representations, identities, resistance. In K. Deaux and G. Philogene (eds.) *Social representations: introductions and explorations*. Oxford: Blackwell.

Dzihic, V., and Segert, D. (2012). Lessons from 'post-Yugoslav' democratization: functional problems of stateness and the limits of democracy. *East European Politics and Societies*, **26**, 239–53.

Edelman, M. (1967). *The symbolic uses of politics*. Urbana, IL: University of Illinois Press.

(1988). *Constructing the political spectacle*. Chicago, IL: Chicago University Press.

(1977). *Political language: words that succeed and policies that fail*. New York: Academic Press.

(2001). *The politics of misinformation*. Cambridge University Press.

Edley, N., and Wetherell, M. (1997). Jockeying for position: the construction of masculine identities. *Discourse & Society*, **8**, 203–17.

(1999). Imagined futures: young men's talk about fatherhood and domestic life. *British Journal of Social Psychology*, **38**, 181–94.

Edwards, D. (1997). *Discourse and cognition*. London: Sage.

(1999). Emotion discourse. *Culture & Psychology*, **5**, 271–91.

(2000). Extreme case formulations: softeners, investment and doing nonliteral. *Research on Language and Social Interaction*, **23**, 347–73.

(2003). Analysing racial discourse: a view from discursive psychology. In H. van den Berg, H. Houtkoop-Steenstra and M. Wetherell (eds.) *Analyzing interviews on racial issues: multidisciplinary approaches to interview discourse* (pp. 31–48).

(2006). Facts, norms and dispositions: practical uses of the modal *would* in police interrogations. *Discourse Studies*, **8**, 475–501.

(2007). Managing subjectivity in talk. In A. Hepburn and S. Wiggins (eds.) *Discursive research in practice: new approaches to psychology and interaction* (pp. 31–49). Cambridge University Press.

(2012). Discursive and scientific psychology. *British Journal of Social Psychology*, **51**, 425–35.

Edwards, D., and Potter, J. (1992a). *Discursive Psychology*. London: Sage.

(1992b). The Chancellor's memory: rhetoric and truth in discursive remembering. *Applied Cognitive Psychology*, 6, 187–215.

(1993). Language and causation: a discursive action model of description and attribution. *Psychological Review*, 100, 23–41.

(2001). Discursive psychology. In A. McHoul and M. Rapley (eds.) *How to analyse talk in institutional settings* (pp. 12–24). New York: Continuum.

Edwards, D., Ashmore, M., and Potter, J. (1995). Death and furniture: the rhetoric, politics and theology of bottom line arguments against relativism. *History of the Human Sciences*, 8, 25–49.

Eiser, J. R. (1971). Enhancement of contrast in the absolute judgment of attitude statements. *Journal of Personality and Social Psychology*, 17, 1–10.

Ekman, J., and Linde, J. (2005). Communist nostalgia and the consolidation of democracy in Central and Eastern Europe. *Journal of Communist Studies and Transition Politics*, 21, 354–74.

Elcheroth, G., Doise, W., and Reicher, S. (2011). On the knowledge of politics and the politics of knowledge: how a social representations approach helps us rethink the subject of political psychology. *Political Psychology*, 32, 729–58.

Ellemers, N., and Barreto, M. (2009). Collective action in modern times: how modern expressions of prejudice prevent collective action. *Journal of Social Issues*, 65, 749–68.

Ensink, T. (1996). The footing of a Royal address: an analysis of representativeness in political speech, exemplified in Queen Beatrix' address to the Knesset on March 28, 1995. *Current Issues in Language and Society*, 3, 205–32.

Entmann, R., and Bennett, L. (2001) Communication in the future of democracy: a conclusion. In L. Bennett and R. Entman (eds.) *Mediated politics: communication in the future of democracy* (pp. 468–480). New York: Cambridge University Press.

Erjavec, K., and Volcic, Z. (2007). 'War on terrorism' as a discursive battleground: Serbian recontextualization of G.W. Bush's discourse. *Discourse and Society*, 18, 123–37.

Eysenck, H. J. (1954). *The psychology of politics*. London: Routledge & Kegan Paul.

Fairclough, N. (1992). *Discourse and social change*. Cambridge: Polity Press.

(1995a). *Critical discourse analysis*. London: Longman.

(1995b). *Media discourse*. London: Edward Arnold.

(2000). *New Labour, new language*. London: Routledge.

(2010). *Critical discourse analysis: the critical study of language*. London: Longman.

Fairclough, I., and Fairclough, N. (2011). Practical reasoning in political discourse: the UK government's response to the economic crisis in the 2008 Pre-Budget Report. *Discourse and Society*, 22, 243–68.

Fairclough, N., and Wodak, R. (1997). Critical discourse analysis. In T. A. van Dijk (ed.) *Discourse as social interaction* (vol. II). London: Sage.

Farnen, R. F. and Meloen, J. (2000). *Democracy, authoritarianism and education: a cross-national empirical survey*. Houndmills, Hants: Macmillan.

Feldman, S. (2003). Values, ideology and the structure of political attitudes. In D. O. Sears, L. Huddy and R. Jervis (eds.) *Oxford handbook of political psychology* (pp. 477–510). New York: Oxford University Press.

Ferguson, N., Burgess, M., and Hollywood, I. (2008). Crossing the Rubicon: deciding to become a paramilitary in Northern Ireland. *International Journal of Conflict and Violence*, 2, 130–137.

(2010). Who are the victims? Victimhood experiences in postagreement Northern Ireland. *Political Psychology*, 31, 857–86.

Finkenauer, C., Gisle, L., and Luminet, O. (1997). When individual memories are socially shaped: flashbulb memories of sociopolitical events. In J. Pennebaker, D. Paez and B. Rime (eds.) *Collective memory of political events: social psychological perspectives* (pp. 191–208). Mahwah, NJ: Lawrence Erlbaum.

Finlayson, A. (2004). Political science, political ideas and rhetoric. *Economy and Society*, 33, 528–49.

Finlayson. A. (2007). From beliefs to arguments: interpretative methodology and rhetorical political analysis. *British Journal of Politics and International Relations*, 9, 545–63.

Fitzgerald, R., and Housley, W. (2002). Identity, categorization and sequential organization: the sequential and categorial flow of identity in a radio phone-in. *Discourse and Society*, 13, 579–602.

Fivush, R. (2008). Remembering and reminiscing: how individual lives are constructed in family narratives. *Memory Studies*, 1, 49–58.

Fleischmann, F., Phalet, K., and Klein, O. (2011). Religious identification and politicization in the face of discrimination: support for political Islam and political action among the Turkish and Moroccan second generation in Europe. *British Journal of Social Psychology*, 50, 628–48.

Fowler, R. (1991). *Language in the news: discourse and ideology in the press.* London: Routledge.

Fowler, R., Hodge, R., Kress, G., and Trew, T. (1979). *Language and control.* London: Routledge & Kegan Paul.

Franklin, B. (2004). *Packaging politics: political communications in Britain's media democracy.* London: Bloomsbury Academic.

Frijda, N. (1997). Commemorating. In J. Pennebaker, D. Paez and B. Rime (eds.) *Collective memory of political events: social psychological perspectives* (pp. 103–30). Mahwah, NJ: Lawrence Erlbaum.

Fromm, E. (1942). *Fear of freedom.* London: Routledge & Kegan Paul.

Gaertner, S. L., and Dovidio, J. F. (2000). *Reducing intergroup bias: the common ingroup identity model.* Philadelphia, PA: Psychology Press.

Galasińska, A., and Galasiński, D. (eds.) (2010). *The post-communist condition: public and private discourses of transformation.* Amsterdam/Philadelphia, PA: John Benjamins.

Gallie, W. B. (1956). Essentially contested concepts. *Proceedings of the Aristotelian Society*, 56, 167–98.

Gallinat, A. (2006). Difficult stories: public discourse and narrative identity in Eastern Germany. *Ethnos*, 71, 343–66.

(2009). Intense paradoxes of memory: researching moral questions about remembering the socialist past. *History and Anthropology*, 20, 183–99.

Gallup, G., and Rae, S. F. (1940). *The pulse of democracy: the public opinion poll and how it works.* Oxford: Simon & Schuster.

Gamson, W. A. (1992). *Talking politics.* Cambridge University Press.

Garton Ash, T. (1990). *We the people: the revolution of '89*. Cambridge: Penguin.

Gély, R., and Sanchez-Mazas, M. (2006). The philosophical implications of research on the social representations of human rights. *Social Science Information*, 45, 387–410.

Gergen, K. (1973). Social psychology as history. *Journal of Personality and Social Psychology*, 26, 309–320.

(1994). *Realities and relationships: soundings in social construction*. Cambridge, MA: Harvard University Press.

(2005). Narrative, moral identity and historical consciousness: a social constructionist account. In J. Straub (ed.) *Narration, identity and historical consciousness* (pp. 99–119). New York: Berghahn Books.

Gillespie, A. (2008). Social representations, alternative representations and semantic barriers. *Journal for the Theory of Social Behaviour*, 38, 375–91.

Gillespie, A., Cornish, F., Aveling, E. L., and Zittoun, T. (2008). Conflicting community commitments: a dialogical analysis of a British woman's World War II diaries. *Journal of Community Psychology*, 36, 35–52.

Gordon, C. (2004). 'Al Gore's our guy': linguistically constructing a family political identity. *Discourse & Society*, 15, 607–31.

Graber, D. A. (1988). *Processing the news: how people tame the information tide* (2nd edn). Lanham, MD: University Press of America.

Graumann, C. F. (1998). Verbal discrimination: a neglected chapter in the social psychology of aggression. *Journal for the Theory of Social Behaviour*, 28, 41–61.

Greatbatch, D. (1998). Conversation analysis: neutralism in British news interviews. In A. Bell and P. Garrett (eds.) *Approaches to media discourse* (pp. 163–185). Oxford: Blackwell.

Halbwachs, M. ([1952] 1992). *On collective memory*. Chicago, IL: Chicago University Press.

Hall, N. R., and Crisp, R. J. (2005). Considering multiple criteria for social categorization can reduce intergroup bias. *Personality and Social Psychology Bulletin*, 31, 1,435–44.

Hamilton, D., and Trolier, T. (1986). Stereotypes and stereotyping: an overview of the cognitive approach. In J. F. Dovidio and S. L. Gaertner (eds.) *Prejudice, discrimination and racism*. Orlando, FL: Academic Press.

Hammack, P. L., and Pilecki, A. (2012). Narrative as a root metaphor for political psychology. *Political Psychology*, 33, 75–103.

Hardt, H., and Splichal, S. (eds.) (2000). *Ferdinand Tönnies on public opinion: selections and analyses*. New York: Rowman & Littlefield.

Harré, R., and Gillett, G. (1994). *The discursive mind*. London: Sage.

Harré, R., and Secord, P. F. (1972). *The explanation of social behaviour*. Oxford: Blackwell.

Harris, J. (2010). Welcome to the first e-election. *Guardian*, 17 March. Available online at www.guardian.co.uk/politics/2010/mar/17/labour-conservatives-general-election-online (last accessed January 2011).

Haslam, N., and Loughnan, S. (2012). Prejudice and dehumanization. In J. Dixon and M. Levine (eds.) *Beyond prejudice: extending the social psychology of conflict, inequality and social change* (pp. 89–104). Cambridge University Press.

Haslam, S. A., and Wilson, A. (2000). In what sense are prejudiced beliefs personal? The importance of ingroup shared stereotypes. *British Journal of Social Psychology*, **39**, 45–63.

Haste, H. (2012). Where do we go from here in political psychology. *Political Psychology*, **33**, 1–9.

Hastie. R., and Dawes, R. (2010). *Rational choice in an uncertain world: the psychology of judgment and decision making* (2nd edn). Thousand Oaks, CA: Sage.

Heath, A., Fisher, S., and Smith, S. (2005). The globalization of public opinion research. *Annual Review of Political Science*, **8**, 297–333.

Heaven, P. (2001). Prejudice and personality: the case of the authoritarian and social dominator. In M. Augoustinos and K. Reynolds (eds.) *Understanding prejudice, racism and social conflict* (pp. 89–104). London: Sage.

Henry, P. J., Sidanius, J., Levin, S., and Pratto, F. (2005). Social dominance orientation, authoritarianism, and support for intergroup violence between the Middle East and America. *Political Psychology*, **26**, 569–84.

Hepburn, A., and Wiggins, S. (eds.) (2007). *Discursive research in practice: new approaches to psychology and interaction*. Cambridge University Press.

Herbst, S. (1995). *Numbered voices: how opinion polling has shaped American politics*. Chicago, IL: University of Chicago Press.

(1998). *Reading public opinion: How political actors view the democratic process*. Chicago, IL: University of Chicago Press.

(2012). The history and meaning of public opinion. In A. J. Berinsky (ed.) *New directions in public opinion* (pp. 19–31). New York: Routledge.

Heritage, J. (1984). *Garfinkel and ethnomethodology*. Cambridge: Polity Press.

Heritage, J., and Clayman, S. (2010). *Talk in action: interaction, identities and institutions*. Chichester: Wiley-Blackwell.

Heritage, J., and Greatbatch, D. (1986). Generating applause: a study of rhetoric and response at party political conferences. *American Journal of Sociology*, **92**, 110–57.

Herrmann, R. (2003). Image theory and strategic interaction in international relations. In D. O. Sears, L. Huddy and R. Jervis (eds.) *Oxford handbook of political psychology* (pp. 285–314). New York: Oxford University Press.

Herzlich, C. (1973). *Health and illness: a social psychological analysis*. New York: Academic Press.

Hill, J. (2008). *The everyday language of White racism*. Chichester: Wiley-Blackwell.

Hobsbawm, E., and Ranger, T. (1992). *The invention of tradition*. Cambridge University Press.

Hodges, A. (2008). The politics of recontextualization: discursive competition over claims of Iranian involvement in Iraq. *Discourse* and *Society*, **19**, 483–505.

Hodgkin, K., and Radstone, S. (eds.) (2003). *Contested pasts: the politics of memory*. London: Routledge.

Hofstede, G. (2001). *Culture's consequences: comparing values, behaviors, institutions, and organizations across nations* (2nd edn). Thousand Oaks, CA: Sage.

Hofstede, G., and McCrae, R. (2004). Personality and culture revisited: linking traits and dimensions of culture. *Cross-Cultural Research*, **38**, 52–88.

Hogea, A. (2010). Coming to terms with the communist past in Romania: an analysis of the political and media discourse concerning the Tismăneanu Report. *Studies of Transition States and Societies*, **2**, 16–30.

Hogg, M. A., and Abrams, D. (1988). *Social identification: a social psychology of intergroup relations and group processes*. London: Routledge.

Hogg. M. A., and Blaylock, D. (2012). *Extremism and the psychology of uncertainty*. Chichester: Wiley-Blackwell.

Holtz, P., and Wagner, W. (2009). Essentialism and attribution of monstrosity in racist discourse: right-wing Internet postings about Africans and Jews. *Journal of Community and Applied Social Psychology*, **19**, 411–25.

Hopkins, N. (2011). Dual identities and their recognition: minority group members' perspectives. *Political Psychology*, **32**, 251–70.

Hopkins, N., and Kahani-Hopkins, V. (2004). Identity construction and political activity: beyond rational actor theory. *British Journal of Social Psychology*, **43**, 339–56.

(2006). Minority group members' theories of intergroup contact: a case study of British Muslims' conceptualizations of 'Islamophobia' and social change. *British Journal of Social Psychology*, **45**, 245–64.

(2009). Reconceptualizing 'extremism' and 'moderation': from categories of analysis to categories of practice in the construction of collective identity. *British Journal of Social Psychology*, **48**, 99–113.

Hopkins, N., Reicher, S., Harrison, K., Cassidy, C., Bull, R., and Levine, M. (2007). Helping to improve the group stereotype: On the strategic dimension of prosocial behavior. *Personality and Social Psychology Bulletin*, **33**, 776–88.

Housley, W., and Fitzgerald, R. (2002). Categorization, national identity and debate. In S. Hester and W. Housley (eds.) *Language, interaction and national identity* (pp. 38–59). Aldershot: Ashgate.

(2003). Moral discrepancy and political discourse: accountability and the allocation of blame in a political news interview. *Sociological Research Online*, **8**(2), www.socresonline.org.uk/8/2/housley.html (last accessed February 2012).

Hovland, C., and Weiss, W. (1952). The influence of source credibility in communication effectiveness. *Public Opinion Quarterly*, **15**, 635–50.

Hovland, C., Janis, I., and Kelley, H. (1953). *Communication and persuasion: psychological studies of opinion change*. New Haven, CT: Yale University Press.

Howarth, C. (2002). Identity in whose eyes? The role of representations in identity construction. *Journal for the Theory of Social Behaviour*, **32**, 145–62.

(2004). Re-presentation and resistance in the context of school exclusion: reasons to be critical. *Journal of Community and Applied Social Psychology*, **14**, 356–77.

(2006). A social representation is not a quiet thing: exploring the critical potential of social representations theory. *British Journal of Social Psychology*, **45**, 65–86.

(2010). Social representations theory, communication and identity. In D. Hook, B. Franks and M. Bauer (eds.) *Communication, culture and social change: the social psychological perspective.* London: Palgrave Macmillan.

Huckfeldt, R. (2009). Information, persuasion, and political communication networks. In R. J. Dalton and H.-D. Klingemann (eds.) *The Oxford handbook of political behavior* (pp. 100–22). New York: Oxford University Press.

Huckfeldt, P., Johnson, E., and Sprague, J. (2002). Political environments, political dynamics, and the survival of disagreement. *Journal of Politics*, **64**, 1–21.

(2004). *Political disagreement: the survival of diverse opinions within communication networks.* New York: Cambridge University Press.

Huddy, L. (2001). From social to political identity: a critical examination of social identity theory. *Political Psychology*, **22**, 127–56.

(2003). Group identity and political cohesion. In D. O. Sears, L. Huddy and R. Jervis (eds.) *Oxford handbook of political psychology* (pp. 511–58). New York: Oxford University Press.

(2004). Contrasting theoretical approaches to intergroup relations. *Political Psychology*, **25**, 947–67.

Huddy, L., Francis N., and Marilyn, L. (2000). The polls–trends: support for the Women's Movement. *Public Opinion Quarterly*, **64**, 309–50.

Huddy, L., Khatib, N., and Capelos, T. (2002). The polls-trends: reactions to the terrorist attacks of September 11, 2001. *Public Opinion Quarterly*, **66**, 418–50.

Hutchby, I. (2006). *Media talk: conversation analysis and the study of broadcasting.* Maidenhead: Open University Press.

(forthcoming). *The televised interview: political news as social interaction.* Cambridge: Polity Press.

Huyssen, A. (2003). *Present pasts: urban palimpsests and the politics of memory.* Stanford, CA: Stanford University Press.

Iacob, B. C. (2010). Avem nevoie de o pedagogie a memoriei colective a trecutului comunist. Available at www.evz.ro/detalii/stiri/bogdan-cristian-iacob-avem-nevoie-de-o-pedagogie-a-memoriei-colective-a-trecutului-comunist-90689.html (last accessed January 2011).

Igartua, J., and Paez, D. (1997). Art and remembering traumatic events: the case of the Spanish Civil War. In J. Pennebaker, D. Paez and B. Rimé (eds.) *Collective memory of political events: social psychological perspectives* (pp. 79–102). Mahwah, NJ: Lawrence Erlbaum.

Igo, S. (2007). *The averaged American: Surveys, citizens, and the making of a mass public.* Cambridge, MA: Harvard University Press.

Inglehart, R. (1977). *The silent revolution.* Princeton, NJ: Princeton University Press.

(1990). *Culture shift in advanced industrial societies.* Princeton, NJ: Princeton University Press.

(2003). How solid is mass support for democracy – and how do we measure it? *PS: Political Science and Politics*, **36**, 51–7.

(2009). Postmaterialist values and the shift from survival to self-expression values. In R. J. Dalton and H.-D. Klingemann (eds.). *The Oxford handbook of political behavior* (pp. 223–39). New York: Oxford University Press.

Inglehart, R., and Abramson, P. (1999). Measuring postmaterialism. *American Political Science Review*, **93**, 665–677.

Inglehart, R., and Baker, W.E. (2000). Modernization, cultural change, and the persistence of traditional values. *American Sociological Review*, **65**, 19–51.

Inglehart, R., and Welzel, C. (2005). *Modernization, cultural change, and democracy: the human development sequence*. Cambridge University Press.

Iniguez, L., Valencia, J., and Vazquez, F. (1997). The construction of remembering and forgetfulness: memories and histories of the Spanish Civil War. In J. Pennebaker, D. Paez and B. Rimé (eds.) *Collective memory of political events: social psychological perspectives* (pp. 237–52). Mahwah, NJ: Lawrence Erlbaum.

Israel, J., and Tajfel, H. (eds.) (1972). *The context of social psychology: a critical assessment*. London: Academic Press.

Iyengar, S. (1993). Agenda-setting and beyond: television news and the strength of political issues. In W. Riker (ed.) *Agenda formation* (pp. 1–27). Ann Arbor: University of Michigan Press.

Iyengar, S., and Kinder, D. R. (1987). *News that matters: television and American opinion*. Chicago, IL: Chicago University Press.

Jacobs, L. R., and Shapiro, R. (2000). *Politicians don't pander: political manipulation and the loss of democratic responsiveness*. Chicago, IL: University of Chicago Press.

Jahoda, G. (1988). Critical notes and reflections on 'social representations'. *European Journal of Social Psychology*, **18**, 195–209.

Jamieson, K. H. (1988). *Eloquence in an electronic age*. New York: Oxford University Press.

Janis, I. (1954). Personality correlates of susceptibility to persuasion. *Journal of Personality*, **22**, 504–18.

Janis, I., and Feshbach, S. (1953). Effects of fear-arousing communications. *The Journal of Abnormal and Social Psychology*, **48**, 78–92.

Jaspal, R., and Cinnirella, M. (2010). Coping with potentially incompatible identities: accounts of religious, ethnic, and sexual identities from British Pakistani men who identify as Muslim and gay. *British Journal of Social Psychology*, **49**, 849–70.

Jefferson, G. (1985). An exercise in the transcription and analysis of laughter. In T. A. van Dijk (ed.) *Handbook of discourse analysis* (vol. III) (pp. 25–34). London: Academic Press.

(2004). Glossary of transcript symbols with an Introduction. In G. H. Lerner (ed.) *Conversation analysis: Studies from the first generation* (pp. 13–23). Philadelphia, PA: John Benjamins.

Jervis, R. (2004). The implications of prospect theory for human nature and values. *Political Psychology*, **25**, 163–76.

Jodelet, D. ([1989] 1991). *Madness and social representations*. Hemel Hempstead: Harvester Wheatsheaf.

(2008). Social representations: the beautiful invention. *Journal for the Theory of Social Behaviour*, **38**, 411–30.

Joffe, H. (2002). Social representations and health psychology. *Social Science Information*, **41**, 559–80.

(2003). Risk: from perception to social representation. *British Journal of Social Psychology*, **42**, 55–73.

Johnson-Laird, P. N. (1983). *Mental models: towards a cognitive science of language, inference, and consciousness*. Cambridge, MA: Harvard University Press.

Jost, J. T., and Banaji, M. (1994). The role of stereotyping in system-justification and the production of false consciousness. *British Journal of Social Psychology*, **33**, 1–27.

Jost, J. T., and Thompson, E. P. (2000). Group-based dominance and opposition to equality as independent predictors of self-esteem, ethnocentrism, and social policy attitudes among African Americans and European Americans. *Journal of Experimental Social Psychology*, **36**, 209–32.

Jost, J. T., Banaji, M., and Nosek, B. (2004). A decade of system justification theory: accumulated evidence of conscious and unconscious bolstering of the status quo. *Political Psychology*, **25**, 881–919.

Jost, J. T., Federico, C. M., and Napier, J. L. (2009). Political ideology: its structure, functions, and elective affinities. *Annual Review of Psychology*, **60**, 307–33.

Jovchelovitch, S. (2007). *Knowledge in context: representations, community and culture*. London: Routledge.

(2008). The rehabilitation of common sense: social representations, science and cognitive polyphasia. *Journal for the Theory of Social Behaviour*, **38**, 431–48.

(2010). From social cognition to the cognition of the social. *Papers on Social Representations*, **19**, 3.1–3.10.

Just, M. R., Crigler, A. N., and Neuman, W. R. (1996). Cognitive and affective dimensions of political conceptualization. In A. N. Crigler (ed.) *The psychology of political communication* (pp. 133–48). Ann Arbor: Michigan University Press.

Kaid, L., and Holtz-Bacha, C. (2006). *The Sage handbook of political advertising*. London: Sage.

Kaltwasser, C. (2012). The ambivalence of populism: threat and corrective for democracy. *Democratization*, **19**, 184–208.

Kansteiner, W. (2002). Finding meaning in memory: a methodological critique of collective memory studies. *History & Theory*, **41**, 179–97.

Kiesler, C., and Kiesler, S. (1969). *Conformity*. Reading, MA: Addison-Wesley.

Kinder, D. R. (2003). Communication and politics in the age of information. In D. O. Sears, L. Huddy and R. Jervis (eds.) *Oxford handbook of political psychology* (pp. 357–93). New York: Oxford University Press.

(2006). Belief systems today. *Critical Review: A Journal of Politics and Society*, **18**, 197–216.

Kinder, D. R., and Kam, C. D. (2009). *Us against them: ethnocentric foundations of American opinion*. Chicago, IL : Chicago University Press.

Kinder, D. R., and Sanders, L. (1996). *Divided by color*. Chicago, IL: Chicago University Press.

King, C. (2007). Remembering Romanian communism. *Slavic Review*, **66**, 718–23.

Klandermans, B. (1997). *The social psychology of protest*. Oxford: Blackwell.

(2003). Collective political action. In D. O. Sears, L. Huddy and R. Jervis (eds.) *Oxford handbook of political psychology* (pp. 670–709). New York: Oxford University Press.

Klandermans, B., and Mayer, N. (2006). *Extreme right activists in Europe: through the magnifying glass.* London: Routledge.

Klandermans, B., Sabucedo, J. M., and Rodriguez, M. (2002). Politicization of collective identity: farmer's identity and farmer's protest in the Netherlands and Spain. *Political Psychology*, **23**, 235–51.

Klandermans, B., van der Toorn, J., and van Stekelenburg, J. (2008). Embeddedness and identity: how immigrants turn grievances into action. *American Sociological Review*, **73**, 992–1,012.

Korosteleva, E. (2003). Is Belarus a demagogical democracy? *Cambridge Review of International Affairs*, **16**, 525–33.

(2009). The limits of EU governance: Belarus's response to the European Neighbourhood Policy. *Contemporary Politics*, **15**, 229–45.

(2012). Questioning democracy promotion: Belarus' response to the 'colour revolutions'. *Democratization*, **19**, 37–59.

Kuipers, G. (2011). The politics of humour in the public sphere: cartoons, power and modernity in the first transnational humour scandal. *European Journal of Cultural Studies*, **14**, 63–80.

Kuklinski, J., and Peyton, B. (2009). Belief systems and political decision making. In R. J. Dalton and H.-D. Klingemann (eds.) *The Oxford handbook of political behavior* (pp. 45–64). New York: Oxford University Press.

LaCapra, D. (1994). *Representing the Holocaust: history, theory, trauma.* Ithaca, NY: Cornell University Press.

Laclau, E. (1993). The signifiers of democracy. In J. H. Carens (ed.) *Democracy and possessive individualism* (pp. 221–34). Albany: State University of New York Press.

Lakoff, G. (2002). *Moral politics: what conservatives know that liberals don't.* Chicago, IL: University of Chicago Press.

(2010). *The political mind.* London: Viking.

Lakoff, G., and Johnson, M. (1980). *Metaphors we live by.* Chicago, IL: Chicago University Press.

Lane, R. (1962). *Political ideology: why the common man believes what he does.* New York: Free Press.

Lasswell, H. D. (1930). *Psychopathology and politics.* Chicago, IL: Chicago University Press.

Lasswell, H. D., Leites, N., and associates (1949) *Language of politics: Studies in quantitative semantics.* New York: George W. Stuart.

Lau, R., and Redlawsk, D. (2001). An experimental study of information search, memory and decision making during a political campaign. In J. Kuklinski (ed.) *Political psychology and public opinion* (pp. 136–59). New York: Cambridge University Press.

(2006). *How voters decide: information processing during election campaigns.* New York: Cambridge University Press.

Lavine, H. (2002). On-line versus memory-based process models. In K. R. Monroe (ed.) *Political psychology* (pp. 225–48). Mahwah, NJ: Lawrence Erlbaum.

(2010). *Political psychology*, vol. I: *Theoretical approaches.* New York: Sage.

Lazarsfeld, P. F., and Merton, R. K. (1948). Mass communication, popular taste and organized social action. In L. Bryson (ed.) *The communication of ideas* (pp. 95–118). New York: Harper.

Lazarsfeld, P. F., Berelson, B., and Gaudet, H. (1944). *The people's choice*. New York: Duell, Sloan and Pearce.

LeCouteur, A., Rapley, M., and Augoustinos, M. (2001). 'This very difficult debate about Wik': stake, voice and the management of category memberships in race politics. *British Journal of Social Psychology*, 40, 35–57.

Lee, I., Pratto, F., and Johnson, T. B. (2011). Intergroup consensus/disagreement in support of group-based hierarchy: an examination of socio-structural and psycho-cultural factors. *Psychological Bulletin*, 137, 1,029–64.

Lemaine, J. (1966). Inegalité, comparaison et incomparabilité: esquisse d'une théorie de l'originalité sociale. *Bulletin de Psychologie*, 20, 1–9.

Leudar, I., and Nekvapil, J. (2000). Presentations of Romanies in the Czech media: on category work in television debates. *Discourse & Society*, 11, 487–513.

(2004). Media dialogical networks and political argumentation. *Journal of Language and Politics*, 3, 247–66.

Leudar, I., Hayes, J., Nekvapil, J., and Turner Baker, J. (2008). Hostility themes in media, community and refugee narratives. *Discourse and Society*, 19, 187–221.

Leventhal, H., Singer, R., and Jones, S. (1965). Effects of fear and specificity of recommendation upon attitudes and behavior. *Journal of Personality and Social Psychology*, 2, 20–9.

Leventhal, H., Watts, J., and Pagano, F. (1967). Effects of fear and instructions on how to cope with danger. *Journal of Personality and Social Psychology*, 6, 313–21.

Levin, S., Federico, C. M., Sidanius, J., and Rabinowitz, J. (2002). Social dominance orientation and intergroup bias: the legitimation of favoritism for high-status groups. *Personality and Social Psychology Bulletin*, 28, 144–57.

Levine, M., and Thompson, K. (2004). Identity, place, and bystander intervention: social categories and helping after natural disasters. *The Journal of Social Psychology*, 144, 229–45.

Levine, M., Cassidy, C., and Brazier, G. (2002). Self-categorization and bystander non-intervention: two experimental studies. *Journal of Applied Social Psychology*, 32, 1,452–63.

Levine, M., Prosser, A., Evans, D., and Reicher, S. (2005). Identity and emergency intervention: how social group membership and inclusiveness of group boundaries shape helping behavior. *Personality and Social Psychology Bulletin*, 31, 443–53.

Levitsky, S., and Way, L. (2002). Elections without democracy: the rise of competitive authoritarianism. *Journal of Democracy*, 13, 51–65.

(2010). *Competitive authoritarianism: hybrid regimes after the Cold War*. Cambridge University Press.

Leyens, J.-P., Cortes, B., Demoulin, S., Dovidio, J., Fiske, S., Gaunt, R., Paladino, M.-P., Rodriguez-Perez, A., Rodriguez-Torres, R., and Vaes, J. (2003). Emotional prejudice, essentialism, and nationalism. The 2002 Tajfel Lecture. *European Journal of Social Psychology*, 33, 703–17.

Linden, A., and Klandermans, B. (2007). Revolutionaries, wanderers, converts, and compliants: life histories of extreme right activists. *Journal of Contemporary Ethnography*, 36, 184–201.

Lippmann, W. (1922). *Public opinion*. London: Allen & Unwin.

([1927] 2009). *The phantom public*. New Jersey: Transaction Publishers.

Lockyer, S., and Pickering, M. (2001). Dear shit-shovellers: humour, censure and the discourse of complaint, *Discourse & Society*, 12, 633–51.

Lowenthal, D. (1989). Nostalgia tells it like it wasn't. In M. Chase and C. Shaw (eds.) *The imagined past: history and nostalgia* (pp. 18–32). Manchester and New York: Manchester University Press.

Lukes, S. (1973). *Individualism*. Oxford: Basil Blackwell.

Lynn, N., and Lea, S. (2003). 'A phantom menace and the New Apartheid': the social construction of asylum-seekers in the United Kingdom. *Discourse & Society*, 14, 425–52.

Marcus, G., Neuman, W., and MacKuen, M. (2000). *Affective intelligence and political judgement*. Chicago, IL: University of Chicago Press.

Marcus, G., Sullivan, J., Theiss-Morse, E., and Wood, S. (1995). *With malice toward some: how people make civil liberties judgements*. New York: Cambridge University Press.

Mark, J. (2010). *The unfinished revolution: making sense of the communist past in Central and Central-Eastern Europe*. New Haven, CT: Yale University Press.

Marková, I. (2000). Amédée or how to get rid of it: social representations from a dialogical perspective. *Culture & Psychology*, 6, 419–60.

(2001). Dialogical perspectives of democracy as social representation. *Critical Studies*, 16, 125–39.

(2004). *Trust and democratic transition in post-communist Europe*. Oxford University Press.

(2006). On 'the inner alter' in dialogue. *International Journal for Dialogical Science*, 1, 125–48.

(2008). The epistemological significance of the theory of social representations. *Journal for the Theory of Social Behavior*, 38, 461–87.

(2012). 'Americanization' of European social psychology. *History of the Human Sciences*, 25, 108–16.

Martin, J. L. (2001). The authoritarian personality, 50 years later: what questions are there for political psychology? *Political Psychology*, 22, 1–26.

Matsuda, M., Lawrence, C., Delgado, R., and Crenshaw, K. (1993). *Words that wound: critical race theory, assaultive speech, and the first amendment*. Boulder, CO: Westview Press.

McClosky, H. (1964). Consensus and ideology in American politics. *American Political Science Review*, 58, 361–82.

McCombs, M., and Shaw, D. (1972). The agenda-setting function of mass media. *Public Opinion Quarterly*, 36, 176–87.

McGarty, C., and Penny, R. E. (1988). Categorization, accentuation and social judgement. *British Journal of Social Psychology*, 27, 147–57.

McGee, M. C. (1980). The 'ideograph': a link between rhetoric and ideology. *Quarterly Journal of Speech*, 66, 1–16.

McGraw, K. M. (2001). Political accounts and attribution processes. In J. H. Kuklinski (ed.) *Citizens and politics: perspectives from political psychology* (pp. 160–97). New York: Cambridge University Press.

(2003). Political impressions: formation and management. In D. O. Sears, L. Huddy and R. Jervis (eds.) *Oxford handbook of political psychology* (pp. 394–432). New York: Oxford University Press.

McGuire, W. J. (1964). Inducing resistance to persuasion: some contemporary approaches. In L. Berkowitz (ed.) *Advances in experimental social psychology* (vol. I) (pp. 191–229). San Diego, CA: Academic Press.

(1993). The poly-psy relationship: three phases of a long affair. In S. Iyengar and W. J. McGuire (eds.) *Explorations in political psychology* (pp. 9–35). Durham, NC: Duke University Press.

McGuire, W., and Papageorgis, D. (1961). The relative efficacy of various types of prior belief-defense in producing immunity against persuasion. *Public Opinion Quarterly*, **26**, 24–34.

McKinlay, A., and McVittie, C. (2008). *Social psychology and discourse*. Oxford: Wiley-Blackwell.

McNair, B. (2011). *An introduction to political communication* (5th edn). London: Routledge.

McSweeney, B. (2002). Hofstede's model of national cultural differences and their consequences: a triumph of faith – a failure of analysis. *Human Relations*, **55**, 89–118.

Merino, M. E., and Tileagă, C. (2011). The construction of ethnic minority identity: a discursive psychological approach to ethnic self-definition in action. *Discourse and Society*, **22**, 86–101.

Merriam, C. E. (1924). The significance of psychology for the study of politics. *The American Political Science Review*, **18**, 469–88.

Middleton, D., and Brown, S. D. (2005). *The social psychology of experience: studies in remembering and forgetting*. London: Sage.

(2007). Issues in the socio-cultural study of memory: making memory matter. In J. Valsiner and A. Rosa (eds.) *The Cambridge handbook of socio-cultural psychology* (pp. 661–77). Cambridge University Press.

Middleton, D., and Edwards, D. (eds.) (1990). *Collective remembering*. London: Sage.

Mill, J. S. (2008). *On liberty and other essays* (ed. with an Introduction and Notes by John Gray). Oxford University Press.

Miller, B. (1999). *Narratives of guilt and compliance in unified Germany: Stasi informers and their impact on society*. London: Routledge.

(2003). Portrayals of past and present selves in the life stories of former Stasi informers. In R. Humphrey, R. Miller and E. Zdravomyslova (eds.) *Biographical research in Eastern Europe: altered lives and broken biographies* (pp. 101–14). Aldershot: Ashgate.

Miller, J. M., and Krosnick, J. A. (2000). News media impact on the ingredients of presidential evaluations: politically knowledgeable citizens are guided by a trusted source. *American Journal of Political Science*, **44**, 301–15.

Misztal, B. (2003). *Theories of social remembering*. Milton Keynes: Open University Press.

(2005). Memory and democracy. *American Behavioral Scientist*, **48**, 1,320–38.

Moghaddam, F. (2008). The psychological citizen and the two concepts of social contract: a preliminary analysis. *Political Psychology*, **29**, 881–901.

Mondak, J. (2010). *Personality and the foundations of political behavior.* New York: Cambridge University Press.

Mondak, J., and Gearing, A. (2003). Civic engagement in a post-communist state. In G. Bădescu and E. M. Uslaner (eds.) *Social capital and the transition to democracy* (pp. 140–64). London: Routledge.

Mondak, J., and Halperin, K. D. (2008). A framework for the study of personality and political behavior. *British Journal of Political Science*, **38**, 335–62.

Mondak, J., and Hibbing, M. (2012). Personality and public opinion. In A. Berinsky (ed.) *New directions in public opinion* (pp. 217–38). New York: Routledge.

Mondak, J., Hibbing, M., Canache, D., Seligson, M., and Anderson, M. (2010). Personality and civic engagement: an integrative framework for the study of trait effects on political behavior. *American Political Science Review*, **104**, 85–110.

Monroe, K. R., Hankin, J., and van Vechten, R. B. (2000). The psychological foundations of identity politics. *Annual Review of Political Science*, **3**, 419–47.

Montgomery, M. (2008). The discourse of the broadcast news interview: a typology. *Journalism Studies*, **9**, 260–77.

Moscovici, S. (1961). *La Psychanalyse, son image et son public.* Paris: Presses Universitaires de France.

(1972). Society and theory in social psychology. In J. Israel and H. Tajfel (eds.) *The context of social psychology: a critical assessment* (pp. 17–68). London: Academic Press.

(1981). On social representations. In J. P. Forgas (ed.) *Social cognition* (pp. 181–209). New York: Academic Press.

(1984). The phenomenon of social representations. In R. Farr and S. Moscovici (eds.) *Social representations* (pp. 3–70). Cambridge University Press.

(1988). Notes towards a description of social representations. *European Journal of Social Psychology*, **18**, 211–50.

(1989). Les thèmes d'une psychologie politique. *Hermès*, **5–6**, 13–20.

(1998). The history and actuality of social representations. In U. Flick (ed.) *The Psychology of the Social* (pp. 209–247). Cambridge University Press.

(2008). *Psychoanalysis: its image and its public.* Cambridge: Polity Press.

(2011). An essay on social representations and ethnic minorities. *Social Science Information*, **50**, 442–61.

Moscovici, S., and Marková, I. (2006). *The making of modern social psychology: the hidden story of how an international social science was created.* Cambridge: Polity Press.

Moscovici, S., and Pérez, J. (1997). Representations of society and prejudice. *Papers on Social Representations*, **6**, 27–36.

(2005). Discrimination vs. ontologization of the Gypsies. In D. Abrams, M. A. Hogg and J. M. Marques (eds.) *The social psychology of inclusion and exclusion.* New York: Psychology Press.

Musolff, A. (2004). *Metaphor and political discourse: analogical reasoning in debates about Europe.* London: Palgrave Macmillan.

(2010). *Metaphor, nation and the Holocaust: the concept of the body politic.* London: Routledge.

Mutz, D. (2009). Political psychology and choice. In R. J. Dalton and H.-D. Klingemann (eds.) *The Oxford handbook of political behavior* (pp. 80–99). New York: Oxford University Press.

Myers, G. (1998). Displaying opinions: topics and disagreement in focus groups. *Language in Society,* 27, 85–111.

Negrine, R. (2008). *The transformation of political communication: continuities and changes in media and politics.* Houndmills and New York: Palgrave Macmillan.

Nekvapil, J., and Leudar, I. (2002). On dialogical networks: arguments about the migration law in Czech mass media in 1993. In S. Hester and W. Housley (eds.) *Language, interaction and national identity: studies in the social organization of national identity in talk-in-interaction.* London: Ashgate.

Nelson, T. E., Clawson, R. A., and Oxley, Z. M. (1997). Media framing of a civil liberties conflict and its effect on tolerance. *American Political Science Review,* 91, 567–83.

Nesbitt-Larking, P., and Kinnvall, C. (2012). The discursive frames of political psychology. *Political Psychology,* 33, 45–59.

Neuman, R., Just, M. R., and Crigler, A. N. (1992). *Common knowledge. News and the construction of political meaning.* Chicago, IL: Chicago University Press.

Neuman, R., Marcus, G., Crigler, A., and Mackuen, M. (eds.) (2007) *The affect effect: dynamics of emotion in political thinking and behavior.* Chicago, IL: University of Chicago Press.

Nisbet, M. C., and Feldman, L. (2010). The social psychology of political communication. In D. Hook, B. Franks and M. Bauer (eds.) *The social psychology of communication* (pp. 284–99). London: Palgrave Macmillan.

Noelle-Neumann, E. (1993). *The spiral of silence: public opinion – our social skin.* Chicago, IL: Chicago University Press.

Nora, P. (1998). The era of commemoration. In P. Nora (ed.) *Realms of memory: the construction of the French past* (pp. 609–37). New York: Columbia University Press.

O'Doherty, K., and Augoustinos, M. (2008). Protecting the nation: nationalist rhetoric on asylum seekers and the Tampa. *Journal of Community and Applied Social Psychology,* 18, 576–92.

Olick, J. (1999). Collective memory: the two cultures. *Sociological Theory,* 17, 333–48.

(2003). What does it mean to normalize the past? Official memory in German politics since 1989. In J. K. Olick (ed.) *States of memory: continuities, conflicts, and transformations in national retrospection* (pp. 259–88). Durham, NC: Duke University Press.

(2007). *The politics of regret: on collective memory and historical responsibility.* London: Routledge.

Olick, J., and Robbins, J. (1998). Social memory studies: from 'collective memory' to the historical sociology of mnemonic practices. *Annual Review of Sociology,* 24, 105–40.

Onorato, R. S., and Turner, J. C. (2004). Fluidity in the self-concept: the shift from personal to social identity. *European Journal of Social Psychology*, 34, 257–78.

Opotow, S. (1990). Moral exclusion and injustice: an introduction. *Journal of Social Issues*, 46, 1–20.

Osborne, T., and Rose, N. (1999). Do the social sciences create phenomena?: the case of public opinion research. *British Journal of Sociology*, 50, 367–96.

Osgood, C. E. (1978). Conservative words and radical sentences in the semantics of international politics. *Studies in the Linguistic Sciences*, 8, 43–61.

Paez, D., Basabe, N., and Gonzalez, J. L. (1997). Social processes and collective memory: a cross-cultural approach to remembering political events. In J. Pennebaker, D. Paez and B. Rimé (eds.) *Collective memory of political events: social psychological perspectives* (pp. 147–74). Mahwah, NJ: Lawrence Erlbaum.

Pehrson, S., and Leach, C. W. (2012). Beyond 'old' and 'new': for a social psychology of racism. In J. Dixon and M. Levine (eds.) *Beyond prejudice: extending the social psychology of conflict, inequality and social change* (pp. 120–38). Cambridge University Press.

Pennebaker, J., and Banasik, B. (1997). On the creation and maintenance of collective memories: history as social psychology. In J. Pennebaker, D. Paez and B. Rime (eds.) *Collective memory of political events: social psychological perspectives* (pp. 3–20). Mahwah, NJ: Lawrence Erlbaum.

Pennebaker, J., Paez, D., and Rimé, B. (eds.) (1997). *Collective memory of political events: social psychological perspectives.* Mahwah, NJ: Lawrence Erlbaum.

Perreault, S., and Bourhis, R. Y. (1999). Ethnocentrism, social identification and discrimination. *Personality and Social Psychology Bulletin*, 25, 92–103.

Pettigrew, T. F. (1958). Personality and socio-cultural factors in inter-group attitudes: a cross-national comparison. *Journal of Conflict Resolution*, 2, 29–42.

Petty, R. E., and Cacioppo, J. T. (1981). *Attitudes and persuasion.* Iowa City, IA: Brown.

  (1984). The effects of involvement on responses to argument quantity and quality: central and peripheral routes to persuasion. *Journal of Personality and Social Psychology*, 46, 69–81.

  (1986). *Communication and persuasion: central and peripheral routes to attitude change.* New York: Springer-Verlag.

Pickering, M., and Keightley, E. (2006). The modalities of nostalgia. *Current Sociology*, 54, 919–41.

Polkinghorne, D. E. (1988). *Narrative knowing and the human sciences.* Albany, NY: State of New York University Press.

Poole, R. (2008). Memory, history and the claims of the past. *Memory Studies*, 1, 149–66.

Popkin, S. (1991). *The reasoning voter.* Chicago, IL: Chicago University Press.

Potter, J. (1996). *Representing reality: Discourse, rhetoric and social construction.* London: Sage.

  (1998). Discursive social psychology: from attitudes to evaluative practices. *European Review of Social Psychology*, 9, 233–66.

214   Bibliography

(2012). Re-reading *Discourse and Social Psychology*: transforming social psychology. *British Journal of Social Psychology*, **51**, 436–55.

Potter, J., and Edwards, D. (1999). Social representations and discursive psychology: from cognition to action. *Culture & Psychology*, **5**, 447–58.

(2001). Discursive social psychology. In W. Robinson and H. Giles (eds.) *The new handbook of language and social psychology* (pp. 103–18). Chichester, Sussex: Wiley.

Potter, J., and Wetherell, M. (1987). *Discourse and social psychology: beyond attitudes and behaviour*. London: Sage.

Potter, J., and Wetherell, M. (1988). Accomplishing attitudes: fact and evaluation in racist discourse. *Text*, **8**, 51–68.

Pratto, F., Sidanius, J., and Levin, S. (2006). Social dominance theory and the dynamics of intergroup relations: taking stock and looking forward. *European Review of Social Psychology*, **17**, 271–320.

Pratto, F., Sidanius, J., Stallworth, L. M., and Malle, B. F. (1994). Social dominance orientation: a personality variable predicting social and political attitudes. *Journal of Personality & Social Psychology*, **67**, 741–63.

Pridham, G. (2000). Confining conditions and breaking with the past: historical legacies and political learning in transitions to democracy. *Democratization*, **7**, 36–64.

Puchta, C., and Potter, J. (2002). Manufacturing individual opinions: market research focus groups and the discursive psychology of evaluation. *British Journal of Social Psychology*, **41**, 345–63.

(2004). *Focus group practice*. London: Sage.

Radstone, S. (2010). Nostalgia: home-comings and departures. *Memory Studies*, **3**, 187–91.

Rancière, J. (2007). *On the shores of politics*. London: Verso.

Rapley, M. (1998). Just an ordinary Australian: self-categorisation and the discursive construction of facticity in 'racist' political rhetoric. *British Journal of Social Psychology*, **37**, 325–44.

(2001). "How to do X without doing Y': accomplishing discrimination without 'being racist' – 'doing equity'. In M. Augoustinos and K. J. Reynolds (eds.) *Understanding prejudice, racism and social conflict* (pp. 231–50). London: Sage.

Reicher, S. (2001). Studying psychology, studying racism. In M. Augoustinos and J. K. Reynolds (eds.) *Understanding prejudice, racism and social conflict* (pp. 273–98). London: Sage.

(2004). The context of social identity: domination, resistance, and change. *Political Psychology*, **25**, 921–45.

(2011). Promoting a culture of innovation: BJSP and the emergence of new paradigms in social psychology. *British Journal of Social Psychology*, **50**, 391–98.

Reicher, S., and Hopkins, N. (1996a). Seeking influence through characterizing self-categories: an analysis of anti-abortionist rhetoric. *British Journal of Social Psychology*, **35**, 297–11.

(1996b). Self-category constructions in political rhetoric: an analysis of Thatcher's and Kinnock's speeches concerning the British Miners Strike (1984–1985). *European Journal of Social Psychology*, **26**, 353–71.

(2001). *Self and nation*. London: Sage.

Reicher, S., Cassidy, C., Wolpert, I., Hopkins, N., and Levine, M. (2006). Saving Bulgaria's Jews: an analysis of social identity and the mobilisation of social solidarity. *European Journal of Social Psychology*, **36**, 49–72.

Reicher, S., Spears, R., and Haslam, A. (2010). The social identity approach in social psychology. In M. Wetherell and C. T. Mohanty (eds.) *The Sage handbook of identities* (pp. 45–62). London: Sage.

Reisigl, M., and Wodak, R. (2001). *Discourse and discrimination: rhetorics of racism and antisemitism*. London: Routledge.

(eds.) (2000). *The semiotics of racism*. Vienna: Passagen Verlag.

Reynolds, K. J., and Turner, J. C. (2001). Prejudice as a group process: the role of social identity. In M. Augoustinos and K. Reynolds (eds.) *Understanding prejudice, racism and social conflict* (pp. 159–79). London: Sage.

Reynolds, K. J., Turner, J. C., Haslam, S. A., Ryan, M. K., Bizumic, B., and Subasic, E. (2007). Does personality explain ingroup identification and discrimination? Evidence from the minimal group paradigm. *British Journal of Social Psychology*, **46**, 517–39.

Richardson, K., Parry, K., and Corner, J. (2011). Genre and the mediation of election politics. In D. Wring, R. Mortimore and S. Atkinson (eds.) *Political communication in Britain* (pp. 304–24). London: Palgrave Macmillan.

Riesman, D. (1954). *Individualism reconsidered*. New York: Free Press.

Rigney, A. (2008). Divided pasts: a premature memorial and the dynamics of collective remembrance. *Memory Studies*, **1**, 89–97.

Rijswijk, W., Hopkins, N., and Johnston, H. (2009). The role of social categorization and identity threat in the perception of migrants. *Journal of Community and Applied Social Psychology*, **19**, 515–20.

Ring, K. (1967). Experimental social psychology: some sober questions about some frivolous values. *Journal of Experimental Social Psychology*, **3**, 113–23.

Riots Communities and Victims Panel (2011). *5 Days in August*. http://webarchive.nationalarchives.gov.uk/20121003195935/http:/riotspanel. independent.gov.uk/wp-content/uploads/2012/04/Interim-report-5-Days-in-August.pdf (last accessed July 2012).

Roccas, S., and Brewer, M. (2002). Social identity complexity. *Personality and Social Psychology Review*, **6**, 88–106.

Roccas, S., Schwartz, S., and Amit, A. (2010). Personal value priorities and national identification. *Political Psychology*, **31**, 393–419.

Roiser, M., and Willig, C. (2002). The strange death of the authoritarian personality: 50 years of psychological and political debate. *History of the Human Sciences*, **15**, 71–96.

Rokeach, M. (1956). Political and religious dogmatism: an alternate to the authoritarian personality. *Psychological Monographs*, **70**, 18.

(1960). *The open and closed mind*. New York: Basic Books.

(1968). *Beliefs, attitudes, and values*. New York: Free Press.

(1973). *The nature of human values*. New York: Free Press.

(1979). *Understanding human values: individual and societal*. New York: Free Press.

Rommetveit, R. (1968). *Words, meanings, and messages: theory and experiments in psycholinguistics*. New York: Academic Press.

Rorty, R. (1989). *Contingency, irony and solidarity.* Cambridge University Press.

Rose, R. (2009). Perspectives on political behavior in time and space. In R. J. Dalton and H.-D. Klingemann (eds.) *The Oxford handbook of political behavior* (pp. 283–304). New York: Oxford University Press.

Rowe, S., Wertsch, J. V., and Kosyaeva, T. Y. (2002). Linking little narratives to big ones: narrative and public memory in history museums. *Culture & Psychology*, **8**, 97–113.

Salvatore, S., and Valsiner, J. (2010). Between the general and the unique: overcoming the nomothetic versus idiographic opposition. *Theory & Psychology*, **20**, 817–833.

Santa Ana, O. (1999). 'Like an animal I was treated': anti-immigrant metaphor is US public discourse. *Discourse & Society*, **10**, 191–224.

Sapiro, V. (2004). Not your parents' political socialization: introduction for a new generation. *Annual Review of Political Science*, **7**, 1–23.

Satter, D. (2012). *It was a long time ago, and it never happened anyway: Russia and the communist past.* New Haven, CT: Yale University Press.

Schäffner, C. (2010). Political communication mediated by translation. In U. Okulska and P. Cap (eds.) *Perspectives in politics and discourse* (pp. 255–78). Amsterdam: John Benjamins.

Schatz, R., and Lavine, H. (2007). Waving the flag: national symbolism, social identity, and political engagement. *Political Psychology*, **28**, 329–55.

Schatz, R., Staub, E., and Lavine, H. (1999). On the varieties of national attachment: blind versus constructive patriotism. *Political Psychology*, **20**, 151–74.

Scheufele, D. (1999). Framing as a theory of media effects. *Journal of Communication*, **49**, 103–22.

Scheufele, D., and Tewksbury, D. (2007). Framing, agenda setting, and priming: the evolution of three media effects models. *Journal of Communication*, **57**, 9–20.

Scheufele, D., and Iyengar, S. (in press). The state of framing research: a call for new directions. In K. Kenski and K. H. Jamieson (eds.) *The Oxford handbook of political communication theories.* New York: Oxford University Press.

Schiffrin, D., Tannen, D., and Hamilton, H. (eds.) (2003). *The handbook of discourse analysis.* Oxford: Blackwell.

Schmid, K., and Hewstone, M. (2010). Combined effects of intergroup contact and multiple categorization: consequences for intergroup attitudes in diverse social contexts. In R. Crisp (ed.) *The psychology of social and cultural diversity* (pp. 299–321). Oxford: Wiley-Blackwell.

Schmid, K., Hewstone, M., Tausch, N., Jenkins, R., Hughes, J, and Cairns, E. (2010). Identities, groups and communities: the case of Northern Ireland. In M. Wetherell and C. T. Mohany (eds.) *The Sage handbook of identities.* (pp. 455–75). London: Sage.

Schmitt, M., Branscombe, N., and Kappen, D. (2003). Attitudes toward group-based inequality: social dominance or social identity? *British Journal of Social Psychology*, **42**, 161–86.

Schütz, A. (1973). *Collected papers I. The problem of social reality* (ed. M.A. Natanson and H. L. van Breda). Dordrecht, The Netherlands: Martinus Nijhoff.

(1976). *Collected papers II. Studies in social theory* (ed. and with an introduction by A. Brodersen). Dordrecht, The Netherlands: Martinus Nijhoff.

Schwartz, S. H. (1992). Universals in the content and structure of values: theoretical advances and empirical tests in 20 countries. In M. Zanna (ed.) *Advances in social psychology* (vol. XXV) (pp. 1–65). New York: Academic Press.

(2006). Basic human values: theory, measurement, and applications. *Revue Française de Sociologie*, 47, 249–88.

(2009). Basic values: how they motivate and inhibit prosocial behavior. In M. Mikulincer and P. Shaver (eds.) *Prosocial motives, emotions, and behavior: the better angels of our nature* (pp. 221–41). Washington, DC: American Psychological Association Press.

Schwartz, S. H., and Bardi, A. (2001). Value hierarchies across cultures: taking a similarities perspective. *Journal of Cross Cultural Psychology*, 32, 268–90.

Schwartz, S. H., and Bilsky, W. (1987). Toward a universal psychological structure of human values. *Journal of Personality and Social Psychology*, 53, 550–62.

Schwartz, S., Caprara, G. V., and Vecchione, M. (2010). Basic personal values, core political values, and voting: a longitudinal analysis. *Political Psychology*, 31, 421–52.

Sears, D., Huddy, L., and Jervis, R. (2003). The psychologies underlying political psychology. In D. O. Sears, L. Huddy and R. Jervis (eds.) *Oxford handbook of political psychology* (pp. 3–16). New York: Oxford University Press.

Shin, D. (2009). Democratization: perspectives from global citizenries. In R. J. Dalton and H.-D. Klingemann (eds.) *The Oxford handbook of political behavior* (pp. 259–82). New York: Oxford University Press.

Shin, D., and Wells, J. (2005). Is democracy the only game in town? *Journal of Democracy*, 16, 88–101.

Sibley, C. G., and Duckitt, J. (2010). The ideological legitimation of the status quo: longitudinal tests for a social dominance model. *Political Psychology*, 31, 109–37.

Sibley, C. G., and Liu, J.H. (2010). Social dominance orientation: testing a global individual difference perspective. *Political Psychology*, 31, 175–207.

Sidanius, J. (1993). The psychology of group conflict and the dynamics of oppression: a social dominance perspective. In S. Iyengar and W. McGuire (eds.) *Explorations in political psychology* (pp. 183–219). Durham, NC: Duke University Press.

Sidanius, J., and Kurzban, R. (2003). Evolutionary approaches to political psychology. In D. O. Sears, L. Huddy and R. Jervis (eds.) *Oxford handbook of political psychology* (pp. 146–81). New York: Oxford University Press.

Sidanius, J., and Pratto, F. (1999). *Social dominance: an intergroup theory of social hierarchy and oppression*. New York: Cambridge University Press.

(2003). Social dominance theory and the dynamics of inequality: a reply to Schmitt, Branscombe, & Kappen and Wilson & Liu. *British Journal of Social Psychology*, 42, 207–13.

Sidanius, J., Feshbach, S., Levin, S., and Pratto, F. (1997). The interface between ethnic and national attachment: ethnic pluralism or ethnic dominance. *Public Opinion Quarterly*, 61, 102–33.

Sidanius, J., Pratto, F., van Laar, C., and Levin, S. (2004). Social dominance theory: its agenda and method. *Political Psychology*, **25**, 845–80.

Siegman, A. W. (1961). A cross-cultural investigation of the relationship between ethnic prejudice, authoritarian ideology and personality. *Journal of Abnormal and Social Psychology*, **63**, 654–55.

Shotter, J. (1977). *Images of man in psychological research*. London: Methuen.

Simon, B., and Grabow, O. (2010). The politicization of migrants: further evidence that politicized collective identity is a dual identity. *Political Psychology*, **31**, 717–38.

Simon, B., and Klandermans, B. (2001). Politicized collective identity: a social psychological analysis. *American Psychologist*, **56**, 319–31.

Simon, B., Loewy, M., Stürmer, S., Weber, U., Freytag, P., Habig, C., Kampmeier, C., and Spahlinger, P. (1998). Collective identification and social movement participation. *Journal of Personality and Social Psychology*, **74**, 646–58.

Skinner, D., and Squillacote, R. (2010). New bodies: beyond illness, dirt, vermin and other metaphors of terror. In U. Okulska and P. Cap (eds.) *Perspectives in politics and discourse* (pp. 43–60). Amsterdam: John Benjamins.

Skultans, V. (1998). *The testimony of lives: narrative and memory in post-Soviet Latvia*. London: Routledge.

 (2001). Arguing with the KGB Archives: archival and narrative memory in post-soviet Latvia. *Ethnos*, **66**, 320 –43.

Smith, D. (1974). The social construction of documentary reality. *Sociological Inquiry*, **44**, 257–68.

 (1978). 'K is mentally ill': the anatomy of a factual account. *Sociology*, **12**, 23–53.

 (2005). *Institutional ethnography: a sociology for people*. Cambridge, MA.: AltaMira Press.

Speer, S., and Potter, J. (2000). The management of heterosexist talk: conversational resources and prejudiced claims. *Discourse and Society*, **11**, 543–72.

Speier, H. (1998). Wit and politics: an essay on laughter and power. *American Journal of Sociology*, **103**, 1,352–401.

Staerklé, C., Sidanius, J., Green, E. G. T., and Molina, L. E. (2010). Ethnic minority-majority asymmetry in national attitudes around the world: a multilevel analysis. *Political Psychology*, **31**, 491–519.

Stan, L. (2006). The vanishing truth: politics and memory in post-communist Europe. *East European Quarterly*, **40**, 383–408.

 (2007). Comisia Tismăneanu: repere internaţionale. *Sfera Politicii*, **126–7**, 7–13.

 (2012). Witch-hunt or moral rebirth? Romanian Parliamentary debates on lustration. *East European Politics and Societies*, **26**, 274–95.

Stanyer, J. (2007). *Modern political communication*. Cambridge: Polity Press.

Stein, J. G. (2002). Political learning and political psychology: a question of norms. In K. Monroe (ed.) *Political psychology* (pp. 107–20). Hillsdale, NJ: Lawrence Erlbaum.

Stelzl, M., and Seligman, C. (2009). Multiplicity across cultures: multiple national identities and multiple value systems. *Organization Studies*, **30**, 959–73.

Stenner, K. (2005). *The authoritarian dynamic.* Cambridge University Press.

Stewart, P. (2011). The influence of self- and other-deprecatory humor on presidential candidate evaluation during the 2008 US election. *Social Science Information,* 50, 201–22.

Stokoe, E. (2009). Doing actions with identity categories: complaints and denials in neighbour disputes. *Text & Talk,* 29, 75–97.

Stokoe, E., and Edwards, D. (2007). 'Black this, black that': racial insults and reported speech in neighbor complaints and police interrogations. *Discourse & Society,* 18, 337–72.

Stott, C. J., and Drury, J. (2000). Crowds, context and identity: dynamic categorization processes in the 'poll tax riot'. *Human Relations,* 53, 247–73.

Stott, C. J., Hutchison, P., and Drury, J. (2001). 'Hooligans' abroad? Intergroup dynamics, social identity and participation in collective 'disorder' at the 1998 World Cup Finals. *British Journal of Social Psychology,* 40, 359–84.

Stürmer, S., and Simon, B. (2009). Pathways to collective protest: calculation, identification, or emotion? A critical analysis of the role of group-based anger in social movement participation. *Journal of Social Issues,* 65, 681–705.

Subasic, E., Reynolds, K. J., and Turner, J. C. (2008). The political solidarity model of social change: dynamics of self-categorization in intergroup power relations. *Personality and Social Psychology Review,* 12, 330–52.

Subasic, E., Schmitt, M. T., and Reynolds, K. J. (2011). Are we all in this together? Co-victimization, inclusive social identity and collective action in solidarity with the disadvantaged. *British Journal of Social Psychology,* 50, 707–25.

Suedfeld, P. (1994). President Clinton's policy dilemmas: a cognitive analysis. *Political Psychology,* 15, 337–49.

Suedfeld, P., Conway, L. G., and Eichhorn, D. (2001). Studying Canadian leaders at a distance. In O. Feldman and L. O. Valenty (eds.) *Profiling political leaders: cross-cultural studies of personality and political behavior* (pp. 3–19). Westport, CT: Praeger.

Suedfeld, P., Tetlock, P. E., and Ramirez, C. (1977). War, peace, and integrative complexity: UN speeches on the Middle East problem, 1947–1976. *Journal of Conflict Resolution,* 21, 427–42.

Suedfeld, P., Tetlock, P. E., and Streufert, S. (1992). Conceptual/integrative complexity. In C. P. Smith, J. W. Atkinson, D. C. McClelland and J. Veroff (eds.), *Motivation and personality: handbook of thematic content analysis* (pp. 393–400). New York: Cambridge University Press.

Suedfeld, P., Wallace, M. D., and Thachuk, K. L. (1993). Changes in integrative complexity among Middle East leaders during the Persian Gulf crisis. *Journal of Social Issues,* 49, 183–199.

Sykes, M. (1985). Discrimination in discourse. In T. A. van Dijk (ed.) *Handbook of discourse analysis* (vol. IV). London: Academic Press.

Sztompka, P. (1994). *The sociology of social change.* Chichester: John Wiley & Sons.

(2000). Cultural trauma: the other face of social change. *European Journal of Social Theory,* 3, 449–66.

(2004). The trauma of social change: a case of postcommunist societies. In J. C. Alexander, R. Eyerman, B. Giesen, N. J. Smelser and P. Sztompka (eds.) *Cultural trauma and collective identity* (pp. 155–95). Berkeley, CA: University of California Press.

Taber, C. (2003). Information processing and public opinion. In D. O. Sears, L. Huddy and R. Jervis (eds.) *Oxford handbook of political psychology* (pp. 433–76). New York: Oxford University Press.

Taber, C., and Lodge, M. (2006). Motivated skepticism in the evaluation of political beliefs. *American Journal of Political Science*, **50**, 755–69.

Tajfel, H. (1969). Cognitive aspects of prejudice. *Journal of Social Issues*, **25**, 79–97.

(1972). Experiments in a vacuum. In J. Israel and H. Tajfel (eds.) *The context of social psychology: a critical assessment*. London: Academic Press.

(1978). *Differentiation between social groups: studies in the social psychology of intergroup relations*. London: Academic Press.

(1981a). Cognitive aspects of prejudice. In H. Tajfel, *Human groups and social categories* (pp. 127–42). Cambridge University Press.

(1981b). Social stereotypes and social groups. In J. C. Turner and H. Giles (eds.) *Intergroup behaviour* (pp. 144–67). Oxford: Blackwell.

Tajfel, H., and Turner, J. (1979). An integrative theory of intergroup conflict. In W. G. Austin and S. Worchel (eds.) *The social psychology of intergroup relations*. Monterey, CA: Brooks-Cole.

Tajfel, H., and Turner, J. (1986). The social identity theory of intergroup behaviour. In S. Worchel and W. G. Austin (eds.) *Psychology of intergroup relations* (pp. 7–24). Chicago, IL: Nelson Hall.

Tajfel, H., and Wilkes, A. L. (1963). Classification and quantitative judgment. *British Journal of Psychology*, **54**, 101–14.

Tajfel, H., Flament, C., Billig, M., and Bundy, R. P. (1971). Social categorization and intergroup behaviour. *European Journal of Social Psychology*, **1**, 149–78.

Tănăsoiu, C. (2007). The Tismăneanu report: Romania revisits its past. *Problems of Post-Communism*, **54**, July/August.

Tarde, G. ([1969] 2010). *On communication and social influence: selected papers* (ed. and with an introduction by Terry N. Clark). Chicago, IL: Chicago University Press.

Taylor, C. (2004). *Modern social imaginaries*. Durham, NC: Duke University Press.

te Molder, H., and Potter, J. (eds.) (2005). *Conversation and cognition*. Cambridge University Press.

Tetlock, P. E. (1981a). Personality and isolationism: content analysis of senatorial speeches. *Journal of Personality and Social Psychology*, **41**, 737–43.

(1981b). Pre- to postelection shifts in presidential rhetoric: impression management or cognitive adjustment? *Journal of Personality and Social Psychology*, **41**, 207–12.

(1983). Cognitive style and political ideology. *Journal of Personality and Social Psychology*, **45**, 118–26.

(1984). Cognitive style and political belief systems in the British House of Commons. *Journal of Personality and Social Psychology*, **46**, 365–75.

(1985). Integrative complexity of American and Soviet foreign policy rhetoric: a time-series analysis. *Journal of Personality and Social Psychology*, **49**, 565–85.

(1988). Monitoring the integrative complexity of American and Soviet policy rhetoric: what can be learned? *Journal of Social Issues*, **44**, 101–31.

(2003). Thinking the unthinkable: sacred values and taboo cognitions. *Trends in cognitive science*, **7**, 320–4.

(2005). *Expert political judgment: how good is it and how can we know?* Princeton University Press.

Tetlock, P. E., and Boettger, R. (1989). Accountability: a social magnifier of the dilution effect. *Journal of Personality & Social Psychology*, **57**, 388–98.

Tetlock, P. E., Hannum, K. A., and Micheletti, P. M. (1984). Stability and change in the complexity of senatorial debate: testing the cognitive versus rhetorical style hypotheses. *Journal of Personality and Social Psychology*, **46**, 979–90.

Thoemmes, F., and Conway, L. (2007). Integrative complexity of 41 US presidents. *Political Psychology*, **28**, 193–226.

Thompson, J. (2009). Apology, historical obligations and the ethics of memory. *Memory Studies*, **2**, 195–210.

Tileagă, C. (2005). Accounting for extreme prejudice and legitimating blame in talk about the Romanies. *Discourse & Society*, **16**, 603–24.

(2006). Representing the 'other': a discursive analysis of prejudice and moral exclusion in talk about Romanies. *Journal of Community and Applied Social Psychology*, **16**, 19–41.

(2007). Ideologies of moral exclusion: a critical discursive reframing of depersonalization, delegitimization and dehumanization. *British Journal of Social Psychology*, **46**, 717–37.

(2008). What is a revolution? National commemoration, collective memory and managing authenticity in the representation of a political event. *Discourse & Society*, **19**, 359–82.

(2009a). The social organization of representations of history: the textual accomplishment of coming to terms with the past. *British Journal of Social Psychology*, **48**, 337–55.

(2009b). 'Mea culpa': the social production of public disclosure and reconciliation with the past. In A. Galasinska and M. Krzyzanowski (eds.) *Discourse and transformation in Central and Eastern Europe* (pp. 173–87). London: Palgrave.

(2010). Cautious morality: public accountability: moral order and accounting for a conflict of interest. *Discourse Studies*, **12**, 223–39.

(2011a). (Re)writing biography: memory, identity, and textually mediated reality in coming to terms with the past. *Culture & Psychology*, **17**, 197–215.

(2011b). Context, mental models and discourse analysis. *Journal of Sociolinguistics*, **15**, 124–34.

(2012). The right measure of guilt: moral reasoning, transgression and the social construction of moral meanings. *Discourse & Communication*, 6, 203–22.

Tilly, C. (2002). *Stories, identities and political change*. Lanham: Rowman & Littlefield.

Tilly, C., and Tarrow, S. (2006). *Contentious politics*. Boulder, Colo.: Paradigm.

Tismăneanu, V. (2007). Confronting Romania's past: a response to Charles King. *Slavic Review*, 66, Winter.

(2008). Democracy and memory: Romania confronts its Communist past. *The Annals of the American Academy of Political and Social Science*, 617, 166–80.

(2010a). Despre nostalgia comunismului, peronism şi spaima de libertate. Available at http://tismaneanu.wordpress.com/2010/12/15/desprenostalgia comunismului-peronism-si-spaima-de-libertate/ (last accessed January 2011).

(2010b). Plâng românii după comunism? Amintirea dictaturii şi anxietătile prezentului. Available at http://tismaneanu.wordpress.com/2010/09/23/amintireacomunismului-si-anxietatile-prezentului/ (last accessed January 2011).

Todorova, M., and Gille, S. (eds.) (2010). *Post-communist nostalgia*. Oxford: Berghahn Books.

Tsirogianni, S., and Gaskell, G. (2011). The role of plurality and context in social values. *Journal for the Theory of Social Behaviour*, 41, 441–65.

Turner, J. (1999a). The prejudiced personality and social change: a self-categorization perspective. The Tajfel Lecture at the European Association of Experimental Social Psychology. Oxford, 7–11 July.

(1999b). Some current themes in research on social identity and self-categorization theories. In N. Ellemers, R. Spears and B. Doosje (eds.) *Social identity: context, commitment, content* (pp. 6–34). Oxford: Blackwell.

Turner, J., and Reynolds, K. (2003). Why social dominance theory has been falsified. *British Journal of Social Psychology*, 42, 199–206.

Turner, J., Hogg, M. A., Oakes, P. J., Reicher, S., and Wetherell, M. (1987). *Rediscovering the social group: a self-categorization theory*. Oxford and New York: Basil Blackwell.

Valentine, G., and Sporton, D. (2009). The subjectivities of young Somalis: the impact of processes of disidentification and disavowal. In M. Wetherell (ed.) *Identity in the 21st century: new trends in changing times* (pp. 157–74). London: Palgrave.

Valentino, N. (1999). Crime and the priming of racial attitudes during evaluations of the President. *Public Opinion Quarterly*, 63, 293–320.

Valentino, N., Hutchings, V., and White, I. (2002). Cues that matter: how political ads prime racial attitudes during campaigns. *American Political Science Review*, 96, 75–90.

Valsiner, J. (2007). *Culture in minds and societies: foundations of cultural psychology*. London: Sage.

Valsiner, J., and van der Veer, R. (2000). *The social mind: the construction of an idea.* Cambridge University Press.

van der Eijk, C., and Franklin, M. (2009). *Elections and voters.* London: Palgrave.

van der Noll, J., Poppe, E., and Verkuyten, M. (2010). Political tolerance and prejudice: differential reactions towards Muslims in the Netherlands. *Basic and Applied Social Psychology,* **32**, 46–56.

van der Valk, I. (2003). Right-wing parliamentary discourse on immigration in France. *Discourse & Society,* **14**, 309–48.

van Dijk, T. A. (1984). *Prejudice and discourse.* Amsterdam: Benjamins.

(1987). *Communicating racism: ethnic prejudice in thought and talk.* London: Sage.

(1988). *News as discourse.* Hillsdale, NJ: Lawrence Erlbaum.

(1989). Mediating racism: the role of media in the reproduction of racism. In R. Wodak (ed.) *Language, power and ideology.* Amsterdam: Benjamins.

(1991). *Racism and the Press.* London: Routledge.

(1992). Discourse and the denial of racism. *Discourse & Society,* **3**, 87–118.

(1993a). *Elite discourse and racism.* Newbury Park, CA: Sage.

(1993b). Principles of critical discourse analysis. *Discourse & Society,* **4**, 249–83.

(1997). Political discourse and racism: describing others in western parliaments. In S. H. Riggins (ed.) *The language and politics of exclusion.* London: Sage.

(2001). Critical discourse analysis. In D. Schiffrin, D. Tannen and H. E. Hamilton (eds.) *The handbook of discourse analysis* (pp. 352–71). Oxford: Blackwell.

(2006). Discourse and manipulation. *Discourse & Society,* **17**, 359–83.

(2008). *Discourse and context: a sociocognitive approach.* New York: Cambridge University Press.

(2009). *Society and discourse: how social contexts influence text and talk.* New York: Cambridge University Press.

van Dijk, T. A., and Kintsch, W. (1983). *Strategies of discourse comprehension.* London: Academic Press.

van Dijk, T. A., Ting-Toomey, S., Smitherman, G., and Troutman, D. (1997). Discourse, ethnicity, culture and racism. In T. A. van Dijk (ed.) *Discourse as social interaction* (Discourse studies: a multidisciplinary introduction, vol. II) (pp. 144–80). London: Sage.

van Leeuwen, T. (1995). Representing social action. *Discourse & Society,* **6**, 81–106.

(2000). Visual racism. In M. Reisigl and R. Wodak (eds.) *The semiotics of racism* (pp. 333–50). Vienna: Passagen Verlag.

van Leeuwen, T., and Wodak, R. (1999). Legitimising immigration control: a discourse-historical approach. *Discourse Studies,* **1**, 83–118.

van Stekelenburg, J., and Klandermans, B. (2010). Individuals in movements: a social psychology of contention. In B. Klandermans and C. Roggeband (eds.) *Handbook of social movements across disciplines* (pp. 157–204). New York: Springer.

van Stekelenburg, J., Klandermans, B., and van Dijk, W. W. (2009). Context matters: explaining how and why mobilizing context influences motivational dynamics. *Journal of Social Issues*, 65, 815–38.

van Zomeren, M., and Iyer, A. (2009). Introduction to the social and psychological dynamics of collective action. *Journal of Social Issues*, 65, 645–60.

van Zomeren, M., and Klandermans, B. (2011). Towards innovation in theory and research on collective action and social change. *British Journal of Social Psychology*, 50, 573–4.

van Zomeren, M., and Spears, R. (2009). Metaphors of protest: a classification of motivations for collective action. *Journal of Social Issues*, 65, 661–79.

Vecchione, M., and Caprara, G. V. (2009). Personality determinants of political participation: the contribution of traits and self-efficacy beliefs. *Personality and Individual Differences*, 46, 487–92.

Velikonja, M. (2009). Lost in transition: nostalgia for socialism in post-socialist countries. *East European Politics and Societies*, 23, 535–1.

Verhulst, B., Eaves, L., and Hatemi, P. (2012). Correlation not causation: the relationship between personality traits and political ideologies. *American Journal of Political Science*, 56, 34–51.

Verkuyten, M. (1997). Discourses of ethnic minority identity. *British Journal of Social Psychology*, 36, 565–86.

(2001). 'Abnormalization' of ethnic minorities in conversation. *British Journal of Social Psychology*, 40, 257–78.

(2003). Discourses about ethnic group (de-)essentialism: oppressive and progressive aspects. *British Journal of Social Psychology*, 42, 371–91.

(2004). *The social psychology of ethnic identity*. Hove and New York: Psychology Press.

(2005). Immigration discourses and their impact on multiculturalism: a discursive and experimental study. *British Journal of Social Psychology*, 44, 223–41.

(2010). Multiculturalism and tolerance: an intergroup perspective. In R. Crisps (ed.) *The psychology of social and cultural diversity* (pp. 147–70). Oxford: Blackwell.

Verkuyten, M., and de Wolf, A. (2002). Being, feeling and doing: discourses and ethnic self-definitions among minority group members. *Culture & Psychology*, 8, 371–99.

Verkuyten, M., and Hagendoorn, L. (1998). Prejudice and self-categorisation: the variable role of authoritarianism and in-group stereotypes. *Personality and Social Psychology Bulletin*, 24, 99–110.

Wallace, C., Pichler, F., and Haerpfer, C. (2012). Changing patterns of civil society in Europe and America 1995–2005. Is Eastern Europe different? *East European Politics and Societies*, 26, 3–19.

Wallace, M., Suedfeld, P., and Thachuk, K. A. (1996). Failed leader or successful peacemaker? Crisis, behavior, and cognitive processes of Mikhail Sergeyevitch Gorbachev. *Political Psychology*, 17, 453–71.

Wallwork, J., and Dixon, J. (2004). Foxes, green fields and Britishness: on the rhetorical construction of place and national identity. *British Journal of Social Psychology*, 43, 21–39.

Walster, E., and Festinger, L. (1962). The effectiveness of 'overheard' persuasive communications. *Journal of Abnormal and Social Psychology*, **65**, 395–402.

Waśkiewicz, A. (2010). The Polish home army and the politics of memory. *East European Politics and Society*, **24**, 44–58.

Watson, R. (2009). *Analyzing practical and professional texts: a naturalistic approach*. Aldershot: Ashgate.

Way, L. (2008). The real causes of the color revolutions. *Journal of Democracy*, **19**, 55–69.

Welzel, C. (2009). Individual modernity. In R. J. Dalton and H.-D. Klingemann (eds.) *The Oxford handbook of political behavior* (pp. 185–205). New York: Oxford University Press.

Welzel, C., and Deutsch, F. (2011). Emancipative values and non-violent protest: the importance of 'ecological' effects. *British Journal of Political Science*, **42**, 465–79.

Wertsch, J. (2002). *Voices of collective remembering*. Cambridge University Press.

(2007). Collective memory. In J. Valsiner and A. Rosa (eds.) *The Cambridge handbook of sociocultural psychology* (pp. 645–60). Cambridge University Press.

(2008). Collective memory and narrative templates. *Social Research*, **75**, 133–56.

(2011). Beyond the archival model of memory and the affordances and constraints of narratives. *Culture & Psychology*, **17**, 21–9.

Wertsch, J., and Karumidze, Z. (2009). Spinning the past: Russian and Georgian accounts of the War of August 2008. *Memory Studies*, **2**, 377–91.

Wetherell, M. (1998). Positioning and interpretative repertoires: conversation analysis and post-structuralism in dialogue. *Discourse & Society*, **9**, 387–412.

(2003). Racism and the analysis of cultural resources in interviews. In H. van den Berg, H. Houtkoop-Steenstra and M. Wetherell (eds.) *Analyzing race talk: multidisciplinary perspectives on the research interview* (pp. 11–30). Cambridge University Press.

(ed.) (2009a). *Theorizing identities and social action*. London: Palgrave.

(ed.) (2009b). *Identity in the 21st century: new trends in changing times*. London: Palgrave.

Wetherell, M., and Potter, J. (1986). Discourse analysis and the social psychology of racism. *British Psychological Society Social Psychology Section Newsletter*, **15**, 24–9.

(1992). *Mapping the language of racism: discourse and the legitimation of exploitation*. Hemel Hempstead: Harvester Wheatsheaf.

White, H. (1992). Historical emplotment and the problem of truth. In S. Friedlander (ed.) *Probing the limits of representation: Nazism and the Final Solution* (pp. 37–53). Cambridge, MA: Harvard University Press.

White, J. (2011a). Left and Right as political resources. *Journal of Political Ideologies*, **16**, 123–44.

(2011b). Community, transnationalism, and the Left-Right metaphor, *European Journal of Social Theory*, **15**, 197–219.

Widdicombe, S., and Wooffitt, R. (1995). *The language of youth subcultures: social identity in action*. Hemel Hempstead: Harvester Wheatsheaf.

Wiggins, S., and Potter, J. (2003). Attitudes and evaluative practices: category vs. item and subjective vs. objective constructions in everyday food assessments. *British Journal of Social Psychology*, **42**, 513–31.

(2008). Discursive psychology. In C. Willig and W. Stainton Rogers (eds.) *The Sage handbook of qualitative research in psychology* (pp. 72–89). London: Sage.

Willinger, I. (ed.) (2007). *N/Osztalgia – ways of revisiting the socialist past*. Budapest, Hungary: Anthropolis.

Wills, J. (2009). Identity making for action: the example of London citizens. In Wetherell, M. (ed.) *Theorizing identities and social action* (pp. 157–76). London: Palgrave.

Wilson, J. (1990). *Politically speaking: the pragmatic analysis of political language*. Oxford: Blackwell.

(2001). Political discourse. In D. Schiffrin, D. Tannen and H. E. Hamilton (eds.) *The handbook of discourse analysis* (pp. 398–415). Oxford: Blackwell.

Winter, D. G. (2003). Personality and political behavior. In D. O. Sears, L. Huddy and R. Jervis (eds.) *Oxford handbook of political psychology* (pp. 110–45). New York: Oxford University Press.

(2006). Authoritarianism: with or without threat? *International Studies Review*, **8**, 524–27.

(2011). Philosopher-king or polarizing politician? A personality profile of Barack Obama. *Political Psychology*, **32**, 1,059–81.

Wittgenstein, L. (1953). *Philosophical investigations*. Oxford: Blackwell.

Wodak, R. (1990). The Waldheim affair and antisemitic prejudice in Austrian public discourse. *Patterns of Prejudice*, **24**, 18–33.

(1991). Turning the tables: antisemitic discourse in post-war Austria. *Discourse and Society*, **2**, 65–83.

(1996). The genesis of racist discourse in Austria since 1989. In C. Caldas-Coulthard and M. Coulthard (eds.) *Texts and practices: readings in critical discourse analysis* (pp. 107–28). London: Routledge.

(1997a). Das ausland and anti-semitic discourse: the discursive construction of the Other. In S. H. Riggins (ed.) *The language and politics of exclusion* (pp. 65–87). London: Sage.

(1997b). Others in discourse: racism and anti-semitism in present day Austria. *Research on Democracy and Society*, **3**, 275–96.

(2002). Friend or foe: the defamation or legitimate and necessary criticism? Reflections on recent political discourse in Austria. *Language & Communication*, **22**, 495–517.

(2011). *The discourse of politics in action: politics as usual*. London: Palgrave.

(ed.) (1989). *Language, power and ideology: studies in political discourse*. Amsterdam: Benjamins.

Wodak, R., and Matouschek, B. (1993). 'We are dealing with people whose origins one can clearly tell just by looking': critical discourse analysis and the study of neo-racism in contemporary Austria. *Discourse & Society*, **4**, 225–48.

Wodak, R., and Meyer, M. (eds.) (2002). *Methods of critical discourse analysis*. London: Sage.

Wodak, R., and van Dijk, T. A. (eds.) (2000). *Racism at the top. Parliamentary discourses on ethnic issues in six European states.* Klagenfurt, Austria: Drava.

Wodak, R., de Cillia, R., Reisgl, M., and Liebhart, K. (1999). *The discursive construction of national identity.* Edinburgh University Press.

Wolfe, A. (1998). *One nation, after all.* New York: Penguin.

Yumul, A., and Özkirimli, U. (2000). Reproducing the nation: 'banal nationalism' in the Turkish press. *Media, Culture & Society,* 22, 787–804.

Zaller, J. ([1992] 2005). *The nature and origins of mass opinion.* New York: Cambridge University Press.

Zaller, J., and Feldman, S. (1992). A simple theory of the survey response: answering questions versus revealing preferences. *American Journal of Political Science,* 36, 579–616.

Zerubavel, E. (2004). *Time maps: collective memory and the social shape of the past.* Chicago, IL: University of Chicago Press.

Index

Printed in Great Britain
by Amazon